VATICAN II AND PHENOMENOLOGY

STUDIES IN PHILOSOPHY AND RELIGION

1. FREUND, E.R. *Franz Rosenzweig's Philosophy of Existence: An Analysis of* The Star of Redemption. 1979. ISBN 90 247 2091 5.

2. OLSON, A.M. *Transcendence and Hermeneutics: An Interpretation of the Philosophy of Karl Jaspers.* 1979. ISBN 90 247 2092 3.

3. VERDU, A. *The Philosophy of Buddhism.* 1981. ISBN 90 247 2224 1.

4. OLIVER, H.H. *A Relational Metaphysic.* 1981. ISBN 90 247 2457 0.

5. ARAPURA, J.G. *Gnosis and the Question of Thought in Vedānta.* 1985. ISBN 90 247 3061 9.

6. HOROSZ, W. and CLEMENTS, T. *Religion and Human Purpose.* 1985. ISBN 90 247 3000 7.

7. SIA, S. *God in Process Thought.* 1985. ISBN 90 247 3103 8.

8. KOBLER, J.F. *Vatican II and Phenomenology.* 1985. ISBN 90 247 3193 3.

VATICAN II AND PHENOMENOLOGY
Reflections on the Life-World of the Church

JOHN F. KOBLER

1985 **MARTINUS NIJHOFF PUBLISHERS**
a member of the KLUWER ACADEMIC PUBLISHERS GROUP
DORDRECHT / BOSTON / LANCASTER

Distributors

for the United States and Canada: Kluwer Academic Publishers, 190 Old Derby Street, Hingham, MA 02043, USA
for the UK and Ireland: Kluwer Academic Publishers, MTP Press Limited, Falcon House, Queen Square, Lancaster LA1 1RN, UK
for all other countries: Kluwer Academic Publishers Group, Distribution Center, P.O. Box 322, 3300 AH Dordrecht, The Netherlands

Library of Congress Cataloging in Publication Data

Library of Congress Cataloging-in-Publication Data

Kobler, John F.
  Vatican II and phenomenology.

  (Studies in philosophy and religion ; v. 8)
  Bibliography: p.
  1. Vatican Council (2nd : 1962-1965) 2. Phenomenol-
ogy. 3. Chruch and the world. 4. Catholic Church--
Doctrines. I. Title. II. Series: Studies in philosophy
and religion (Martinus Nijhoff Publishers) ; v. 8.
BX830 1962.K55 1985   262'.02'01   85-13607
ISBN 90-247-3193-3
ISBN 90-247-3194-1 (pbk.)

ISBN 90-247-3193-3 (Hardback)
ISBN 90-247-2346-9 (series)

Copyright

PRINTED IN THE NETHERLANDS

MY MOTHER AND FATHER

TABLE OF CONTENTS

PREFACE

The thesis of this essay may be stated quite briefly: Vatican II is a demonstration-model of the phenomenological method employed on an international scale. It exemplifies the final developmental stage, postulated by Husserl, of an inter-subjective phenomenology which would take its point of departure, not from individual subjectivity, but from transcendental intersubjectivity. Vatican II, accordingly, offers a unique application of a universal transcendental philosophy in the field of religious reflection for the practical purposes of moral and socio-cultural renewal.

Phenomenology, as a distinctively European development, is relatively un-known in America — at least in its pure form. Our contact with this style of intuitive reflection is usually filtered through psychology or sociology.[1] How-ever, Edmund Husserl, The Father of Phenomenology, was originally trained in mathematics, and he entered the field of philosophy because he recognized that the *theoretical* foundations of modern science were disintegrating.[2] He foresaw that, unless this situation were rectified, modern men would eventually slip into an attitude of absolute scepticism, relativism, and pragmatism. After the First World War he saw this theoretical problem mirrored more and more in the social turbulence of Europe, and his thoughts turned to the need for a renewal at all levels of life.[3] In 1937 when Nazism was triumphant in Germany, and Europe on the brink of World War II, he wrote his last major work, *The Crisis of European Sciences and Transcendental Philosophy.*[4] In a sombre context reminiscent of Spengler's *The Decline of the West* Husserl argued for phenomenology as the last scientific hope for Europe's intellectual and cultural renewal.

Although the last few years of Husserl's life were dedicated to such a practical problem, his view of it always remained that of a *theoretician.* In his quest for philosophy as a rigorous science his level of reflection was comparable to that of Kant and Hegel at their most speculative. This fact is important in the light of Husserl's confrontation with empiricism.[5] He was convinced that the fragmen-tation of the sciences was due to an overly-narrow view of empiricism prejudiced in favor of particular data. Science needed a *new empiricism* capable of attaining universals, or general essences, on the basis of their intuitive givenness. Out of this new empiricism would develop a radically *new experience* and a fresh *new attitude* towards reality. Such new experiences and attitudes were needed to reground philosophy and science in their authentic Greek heritage and the true spirit of the Renaissance. It was in such an intellectual context that Husserl developed his notions of intentionality, the transcendental reduction, historicity, and the teleological nature of consciousness. All of these themes are comparable in complexity to any metaphysical concepts, and if they derive from "experience," it is a type of conceptually refined experience known only to highly trained theorists and not the average person.

In the postconciliar period relatively little has been written about this phenomenological dimension of the Council. Yet, if one takes the trouble to "demythologize" some of the religious terminology employed there, the phenomenological core of the Council begins to shine through. The best index, as a matter of fact, for appreciating the enormous impact on Vatican II by the bishops and theologians of Northern Europe is simply to read the conciliar documents in the light of the classical phenomenology developed by Husserl and which has been so influential in European circles, in one form or another, since the end of World War II.

The use of phenomenology at the Council has not touched the substance of Catholic doctrine, but it has given it a whole new tonality. The effect has been much like transposing a piece of music from C-major to C-minor. Or, to use an even more apt analogy, like the intellectual adjustment necessary to move from an industrialized society into an age of electronics. This psychological "gravity shift" is essentially to a radically new *modality*, particularly in the domain of *theoretical* conceptualization. In the book I employ a term popularly received in America to describe such a phenomenon: i.e., a "shift of the visual gestalt." The immediate question which arises from such considerations is, "Why?" What purpose did such complex reconceptualization processes serve? As our essay hopes to indicate, this theological adaptation was meant to serve the practical, pastoral renewal of the Church and, ultimately, of contemporary mankind.

Inasmuch as phenomenology is a very complex and, as yet, not fully systematized style of philosophical reflection, I have tried to return to the originary thought-pattern pioneered by Husserl himself. As an example of metaphenomenology, this book is something of a study in the archaeology of human consciousness. Difficult as this task may have been, I have found it an imperative one. In the American Church today the dominant theoretical mindset of theological professionals has been shaped more by Heidegger than by Husserl. Understandable as such a development may be, the spirit of *aggiornamento* would not allow me to rest content with it. Hence, my "return to the sources" in Husserl to achieve an in-depth renewal, both philosophical and religious. For the historical framework of the phenomenological movement as a whole, I have relied heavily, but not exclusively, on the careful work of Herbert Spiegelberg.[6] One book, however, deserves special mention since it focuses on a central problem related to my research into the Council: David Carr's *Phenomenology and the Problem of History*.[7] Lastly, for an introduction to the Council based on phenomenology the best book is Karol Wojtyla's *Sources of Renewal: The Implementation of Vatican II*.[8] Unfortunately, this beautiful and profound study is a "closed book" unless one has some reasonable acquaintance with phenomenological theory and method.

Vatican II and Phenomenology is an interdisciplinary study written with two audiences in mind: the educated public and professional scholars. The *educated public*, particularly in America, must be informed of the new horizons opened by a phenomenological interpretation of the Council since Vatican II is involved in a quite practical global enterprise involving all of mankind. The main text of this book is, accordingly, simply an extended essay meant to acquaint the educated public with the meaning and thrust of Vatican II in a concise way. These matters (i.e., Chapters 1–4 and 8–10) are handled in an essentially chronological way. However, the midsection of the book (i.e., Chapters 5–7) deals with some technical details and problems confronting the Church as it shifts from an objectivist (scholastic) style of reflection to a subjectivist (phenomenological) one. The book is finally rounded off by an Epilogue which tries to draw out some of the more startling historical and global implications of Vatican II.

Inasmuch as I have developed this book in a chronological way, *professional scholars* will find it has some of the maddening qualities associated with reading Husserl's works in their chronological order: ideas are occasionally repeated but with a slight shift in the thetic descriptive view. Since this book is an interdisciplinary study, the footnotes (which are unforgivably extensive) contain the really technical and developmental substance of the book. In order to lighten the scholarly task, however, I have placed the more extensive discussions at the end of the book under the rubric of some numbered "Excursus." A brief footnote reference will call attention to each "Excursus" as its technical topic arises in the course of the book's development.

In such a short book as this, which only intends to provide the fundamentals of a methodology and basic working insights, there is no need to comment on every document of the Council, particularly its prudential, practical directives.[9] Using techniques provided by phenomenology in correlation with well-known scholastic concepts, I shall concentrate my investigation on two major conciliar documents with more obvious pastoral implications: i.e., *Lumen Gentium* and *Gaudium et Spes*, both of which overtly deal with the Church but at diverse levels of conceptualization.[10] The practical end-product of these reflections will be a comprehensive socio-religious paradigm interpreting the pastoral renewal program of the Council. This paradigm, by reason of its grounding in phenomenology, communicates at both the notional and subliminal levels.

The subtitle of this book is: *Reflections on the Life-World of the Church.* Vatican II's analysis of the Church's experience of her own religious life-world may be its most creative contribution to the field of applied phenomenology. Although the idea of the life-world was introduced by Husserl in the *Crisis*, it has been left to other scholars such as Alfred Schutz and Thomas Luckmann to develop it, particularly for sociological purposes. Just as Schutz and Luckmann formulated their description of the structures of the natural life-world on the assumption of the essential validity and utility of Husserl's previous theoretical work, so the theologians of Vatican II worked on a comparable assumption regarding the legitimacy of the phenomenological method when they analysed the religious life-world of the Church. (This is not to imply, however, that such scholars had a univocal understanding of this methodology.) Illuminating this massive and complex project is one of the topics of this book. It should come as no surprise, then, that there is a certain parallelism, and even overlapping, of Vatican II's renewal goals and those of Husserl as expressed in the *Crisis*.

Inasmuch as the Constitution on Divine Revelation (*Dei verbum*)[11] is the theoretical companionpiece to *Lumen Gentium* (the document on the Church), this constitution will be treated in Chapter Ten of this book. This final chapter, which should be read in relationship with the whole discussion on *Lumen Gentium*, makes it clear that the Council is presenting a *phenomenology of religion*. This, of course, precipitates us into the whole area of the History of Religions (*Allgemeine Religionswissenschaft*). The reader, however, should be prepared to find in the phenomenology of religion provided by Vatican II something more innovative than that found in such theorists as Mircea Eliade and Henry Duméry. As the educated public may be expected to be more interested in the practical, pastoral correlation between *Lumen Gentium* and *Gaudium et Spes*, the professional scholar may be more interested in the phenomenology of religion provided by the correlation of *Dei verbum* and *Lumen Gentium*, both of which are dogmatic constitutions.

In conclusion I must emphasize that the *esthetic* dimension of the Council's finalized hermeneutics of Catholic religious beliefs is an important component of the themes developed by this essay. Beauty, of course, is not the decisive factor in accepting any scientific theory. But when beauty, a field theory of consciousness, and a uniquely new communication process are welded together to serve the global needs of mankind at a turning point of history, then the cumulative argument is not to be ignored. In this sense, consequently, Vatican II may be viewed as carrying out — and possibly surpassing — the humanistic goals of Husserl's *Crisis* and portending that a chapter has yet to be written in the intellectual and cultural history of the West.

ACKNOWLEDGMENTS

I would like to acknowledge the assistance which I received from many quarters. For a sabbatical to research and write this book: V. Rev. Roger Mercurio, CP, and V. Rev. Sebastian MacDonald, CP. For their technical help or criticism: V. Rev. Sebastian MacDonald, CP (theology), Professor Bernard Boelen, Fr. Theodore Vitali, CP, and Fr. Frederick Sucher, CP (philosophy), Fr. Enrico Cantore, SJ (science), Fr. Bernard Weber, CP (mathematics), and Fr. Kyran O'Connor, CP (German). For procuring research materials: Fr. Kenneth O'Malley, CP, Fr. Myron Gohmann, CP, Fr. Robert Ehrne, CP, and Mr. Ben Williams. For their pastoral reflections on current Church developments: Fr. Conleth Overman, CP, Fr. John Render, CP, Fr. Raphael Domzall, CP, and Fr. Michael Higgins, CP. For preparing the index: Fr. Kenneth O'Malley, CP. For long hours of patient typing: Mrs. Rose Siciliano. For their fraternal support while I did research at their locations: the Passionist Monastic Communities of Louisville, KY, Sierra Madre, CA, Detroit, MI, and Chicago, IL. These and many others too numerous to mention have advised and encouraged me in the course of my work, and I remember such help with gratitude. However, the final responsibility for any opinions expressed in this book rests with myself alone.

NOTES

Throughout this book note references are given by author and copyright (or publication) date in brackets according to the way such books or articles are listed in the bibliography.

Only minimal reference has been made to Tymieniecka [1971–1983], a work of advanced phenomenological research and learning. The reason for this is simple: my essay, a study in applied phenomenology, is geared primarily toward the educated public and, for pedagogical reasons, relies on source-materials more accessible to such a readership.

1. For psychology see Spiegelberg [1972]. For sociology see Bottomore and Nisbet [1978], pp. 499–556. Berger and Luckmann [1966] provides an easily available example of applied phenomenology in the field of sociology.
2. For anyone needing a quick introduction to the work of Husserl see Spiegelberg [1982], pp. 69–165. For a thematic introduction to Husserl see Natanson [1973a]. For an introduction to Husserl by a phenomenologist with a Christian background see Ricoeur [1967]. Or, easiest is: Stewart and Mickunas [1974].
3. See J. Allen, "Introduction to Husserl's 'Renewal: Its Problem and Method,'" in McCormick and Elliston [1981], pp. 324–331.

4. See Husserl [1970].

5. The inspiration for this confrontation with empiricism goes back to Husserl's teacher, F. Brentano. See Spiegelberg [1982], pp. 33–36. For Husserl's differences with empiricism and positivism see Spiegelberg [1982], p. 115. Ultimately the new experience (virtually the equivalent of a religious conversion) may be traced to the phenomenological (transcendental) reduction. See Spiegelberg [1982], p. 121. These ideas had an entrance into Catholic thought largely through the writings of G. Marcel. See Spiegelberg [1982], pp. 452–453.

6. See Spiegelberg [1972], [1975], [1981], [1982]. Perhaps the finest thematic introduction to the problems considered by this book would be Landgrebe [1966].

7. See Carr [1974].

8. See Wojtyla [1980]. Perhaps an easier introduction to the Council and its global context would be Frossard [1984]. For an average American's acerbic reaction to John Paul II's style of reflection see Wigginton [1983], pp. 266–270.

9. Such detailed pastoral guidelines and directives may, of course, reflect an important doctrinal sense. As Wojtyla [1980], p. 17 remarks: ". . . doctrinal acts of the magisterium have a pastoral sense, while on the other [hand] pastoral acts have a doctrinal significance, deeply rooted as they are in faith and morals." Inasmuch as Vatican II is a pastoral council in its totality, my purpose is to focus on its *quasi-theoretical* pastoral statements (i.e., its doctrinal constitutions) in order to distil their doctrinal (and humanistic) significance. If this is done properly, the doctrinal insights should provide a comprehensive hermeneutical sense or thrust to the Council's practical directives.

10. The actual texts of any Vatican II promulgated documents may be found in Latin Texts [1966]. The English translation of *Lumen Gentium* and *Gaudium et Spes* may be found in Abbott [1966], pp. 14–96 and pp. 199–331 respectively. I have used this English edition of the Council's documents throughout this book. All such quotations are reprinted with permission of America Press, Inc., 106 West 56 St., New York, NY 10019; © 1966 All Rights Reserved. The reader, however, may also want to consult Flannery [1975], [1982], or Gonzalez [1966].

11. See Abbott [1966], pp. 111–128.

PART I

THE HISTORICAL CONTEXT

CHAPTER 1

FROM PHENOMENOLOGY TO POPE JOHN XXIII

Some introductory remarks on phenomenology

The historical origins of philosophical phenomenology are quite well known today. Like most new movements it began with a problem and what seemed to be a promising key to the problem's solution. The *problem* was the "crisis in the sciences," which Husserl approached as a theoretical mathematician and logician. He diagnosed the problem as being rooted in the split between Galileo's objectivism and Cartesian subjectivism, the two dominant influences forming the modern scientific mind.[1] In the twentieth century this split had further fragmented into scientific reductionism, absolute historicism, and psychologism.[2] As a result, anything resembling the philosophical certainties of the past seemed irretrievably lost. The *promising key* to all these problems seemed to be the notion of intentionality developed by Franz Brentano.[3] As might be expected, when the deductive mindset of a theoretical mathematician appropriates an idea shaped by the inductive mindset of an empirical psychologist, that idea will take on a whole new course of development. Grounded as his conceptual *a priori* may have been in empirical data, Husserl began to see and experience reality in startlingly new ways. In this context of absolutely new beginnings he formulated both his slogan and "principle of principles:" *Back to the things themselves!*[4]

Not unexpectedly, this approach to the problems of scientific theory is — especially in its early history — reminiscent of Post-Kantian Idealism, and its exclusive reliance on what appears to be mere introspection without further verification procedures recalls the exaggerated reality-value attributed to psychological phenomena around the turn of the century. Phenomenology, as a distinctively European product, is not readily comprehended on this side of the ocean unless viewed within a social history markedly different from the American experience. Our intellectual attitude is still so shaped by the positivistic form of empricism that in most discussions of science we would favor some form of Operationalism.[5] In the area where philosophy and science tend to merge the work of men like A.N. Whitehead and M. Polanyi finds a readier audience in this country.[6] It would be no exaggeration to say that our current renewed interest in the finer workings of the human mind is sparked by the fact that we have invented *machines* which mimic these processes![7]

Phenomenology in Europe after World War II

Husserl did not, of course, solve the "crisis of the sciences." The ontological problem, or the question of being, also posed baffling difficulties for the most well-known phenomenologists. Husserl, it seems, was satisfied to reduce the ontological problem to a merely epistemological one.[8] Heidegger seems to have abandoned the quest entirely in later life, and Merleau-Ponty shortly before his death had likewise decided to rethink all his previous reflections on the problem.[9] In spite of such major difficulties phenomenology by midcentury had become the prevalent mindstyle among European intellectuals. Writing from France in 1950 the then-Head of the Division for International Cultural Cooperation (UNESCO), Herbert W. Schneider, summed up the matter thus:

> The influence of Husserl has revolutionized continental philosophies not because his philosophy has become dominant, but because any philosophy now seeks to accommodate itself to, and express itself in, phenomenological method. It is the *sine qua non* of critical respectibility. In America, on the contrary, phenomenology is in its infancy.[10]

I am not interested in tracing this new lease on life which phenomenology acquired in French existentialism.[11] The whole episode is significant as marking a definitive break with the *theoretical* problem of the "crisis in the sciences" in favor of the more *practical* and personally more overwhelming problem of the "crisis in human beings." This latter crisis had been under development since the end of World War I when most of Europe's values deriving from the Enlightenment collapsed.[12] In the popular mind, at least, all preoccupation with a philosophy of science gave way before the new quest for a philosophical anthropology.[13] The new emphasis found in existentialism was quite foreign to Husserl's original concern for philosophy as a rigorous science.[14] Furthermore, in relation to the reigning objectivism in French science, existentialism came through as very "anti-scientific."[15] This development is, in many respects, reminiscent of German Romanticism's backlash to the Enlightenment. Herder used the tool of history; Sartre used the tool of phenomenology. Heidegger and Jaspers, each in his own way a proponent of a new *Existenz-philosophie*, disavowed the trends developing in the French version of phenomenology labeled as "existentialism."[16] But in 1944, when this new coalition of reason and unreason surfaced, it so seemed to embody the spirit of the times that its diagnostic tool, phenomenology, in quite eclectic ways proliferated into fields totally unrelated to Husserl's original purposes.[17]

Catholic intellectuals and phenomenology

What is of more pertinent interest, however, is the following passage from Spiegelberg:

> One of the most important events for the introduction of phenomenology into the French-speaking world was the study session of the Société Thomiste on Thomism and German contemporary phenomenology at Juvisy in September 1932. Jacques Maritain and Msgr. Noël presided. Father Daniel Fueling of the University of Salzburg gave an informed report on Husserl and Heidegger, and Father René Kremer of the University of Louvain compared the Thomist with the phenomenological position. In the momentous discussion not only Msgr. Noël and Étienne Gilson but also old phenomenologists like Alexandre Koyré and Edith Stein took a leading part, trying to play down the idealist character of phenomenology and to stress the differences between Husserl and Heidegger. The spirit of the discussion suggested the possibility of an assimilation of the phenomenological approach by Catholic philosophers without commitment to Husserl's or Heidegger's conclusions.[18]

The period from approximately 1930–1950 in France was an important one from the religious, intellectual point of view. Monumental changes which occurred then are intelligible today only if seen in relationship to the social cataclysms of the times. The depression had destroyed confidence in Capitalism.[19] The Cartesian tradition of the sciences seemed impotent in the face of such social problems. Fascism and Marxism were elbowing their way forward with politically radical answers. It was in the midst of such tumult that in 1931 Pope Pius XI issued his encyclical, *Quadragesimo Anno*.[20] This papal letter tried to sketch a broad blueprint for the reconstruction of the social order. Perhaps the most well-thought-out Catholic response to French problems was the Christian Personalist Movement of Emmanuel Mounier.[21] While this movement took its intellectual inspiration from a Christian understanding of the *person*, its inherent purpose was to offer a social and political alternative to Capitalism, Fascism, and Marxism.

What the Catholic academic community was searching for during this period was a way to genuinely *communicate* and *dialogue* with a largely pluralistic, secularized and socially disrupted community. (As we shall see later, this *local* problem has now become the *global* problem faced by Vatican II.) The aftermath of World War I had brought with it a popular negative reaction to the Cartesian tradition of the sciences. With the lucidity peculiar to the Cartesian

style of thinking French intellectuals embarked on a course decidedly subjectivistic and, with time, even non-cognitive.[22] Reality became more dialectic,
either in the Hegelian sense, or more especially that of Marx. With the writings
of Bergson reality began to be viewed in terms of a vitalistic evolution. In this
increasingly amorphous, not to say dangerous, intellectual environment Catholic
thinkers engaged in at least four major efforts at communication and dialogue:
(1) M. Blondel's reflections on *L'Action*; (2) J. Marechal's effort to develop a
transcendental Thomism related to the Kantian problematique; (3) de Chardin's
attempted correlation of Christianity and evolution; and (4) the 1932 opening
to phenomenology, which G. Marcel constructively employed in his religious
reflections. All of these creative, even heroic, efforts came to naught with the
advent of World War II. The scenario we are running here could easily be that
of Vatican II and the prospect of World War III.

Humani Generis and the new intellectual environment

By 1950, however, the Catholic effort at communication and dialogue had
become so "polyvalent," not to say amorphous, that Pius XII felt obliged to
issue his encyclical, *Humani Generis*.[23] In their effort to solve the "crisis in
human beings" some Catholic thinkers (or at least their less-competent popular-
izers) seemed to have embraced existentatialism without adequate reservations
or qualifications. It was this modern mindset, particularly its revisionist attitude
toward theology, which the encyclical focused on. *Humani Generis* did not,
however, address the central problem behind the problems: "How, in an intellectual atmosphere of universal evolutionism, can we safeguard transcendental
truth?"[24] Pius XII might have cut some of the ground out from under this
highly academic question had he responded: "Did it every occur to you that an
intellectual atmosphere of universal evolutionism is a large part of the crisis
in human beings? How about using a few of your transcendental truths to
develop a few *practical* models of healthy human living? There is more to
communication and dialogue than mere talk!" As it was, however, the encyclical
stayed on the purely academic level. It merely rejected many of the styles of
thinking and dialogue then in vogue: i.e., unmitigated evolutionism, absolute
historicism, and any type of existentialism leading to epistemological or moral
relativism. Rhetorical, if not factual, tendencies in this direction had crept into
Catholic thinking via Bultmann, Heidegger, Sartre, Marx, and others.

In his sane and balanced way Fr. Gustave Weigel, SJ, provided American
scholars with a benign and irenic analysis of the intellectual background and
issues of this religious controversy.[25] The American Church became sensitized

to some new theological developments taking place in Europe, and everything settled back to "normal." But what such analysts — progressives and
conservatives — missed at the time was that socio-political events on the world
scene had already reduced such intellectual and theoretical problems to secondary importance.[26] With the destruction of Hiroshima on August 6, 1945, the
world of the *status quo antea* had come to an end, and history had already
moved into a uniquely "new moment."[27] The overriding issue was now the very
pragmatic one of human survival. And it was *that practical problem* and the
religious formation program necessary to grapple with it in a constructive
way that became the focus of the great pastoral renewal program of the Second
Vatican Council.

Aggiornamento in the new moment of human history

One of the least appreciated and most popularly misconstrued concepts in the
Church today is what Pope John XXIII meant by *aggiornamento*. Here, for
example, is how several reputable American thinkers formulated this complex
matter back in 1964:

> For the Holy Father the *"aggiornamento"* was to have two dimensions:
> first, an internal renewal of the Church that would bring out sharply the
> features it had when it first came from the hands of Christ; second, a
> revitalization in the Church's approach to the modern world, which
> would make the Church better understood and more attractive, and put
> her in a position to bring the Gospel more effectively to twentieth-century
> man.[28]

The *first* point must be denied outright as representing the mind of John
XXIII. In *Humanae Salutis*, the apostolic constitution whereby he convoked the
Council, the Holy Father stated that the Church was already "in great part
transformed and renewed."[29] As a religious organization it had kept up with
the times socially, intellectually and spiritually.[30] From a merely internal point
of view there was really no need for any "updating" (*aggiornamento*). If anything, the pope could easily have been accused of triumphalism every time he
made a public utterance about the moral beauty and attainments of the Church
as he appreciated it![31] The *second* point takes on a certain painful quality
if we see it in relationship to the authentic biblical model inspiring the Holy
Father's "opening to the world." Was the Good Samaritan interested in "re-
vitalizing" his approach to the Jews when he tended the wounded man lying by

the roadside?[32] Was he thinking of making himself better understood and more attractive, and thus put himself in a better position to proselytize the Jews of that era? Or was he not primarily interested in performing a much-needed human service prompted by his religious values and some very dire circumstances?

Even today, however, it remains difficult to "prove" which of the two opposed opinions of *aggiornamento*, listed above, is the correct one. A long list of papal statements could be cited favoring either interpretation, at least in an unimaginative, philological sort of a way. The major weakness of the first opinion, proffered by the Editors of the Pope Speaks, is that it is formulated within the preconceptions of the *status quo antea*: mankind has not yet moved into a substantially "new moment" of human history.[33] The academic mindset manifested here is basically that of the French scene (1930–1950) described previously. Only as this outlook gradually erodes – as it inevitably will in our world of ongoing crises – will the ecclesial community abandon its naive formula of *aggiornamento* suggested by the first opinion. In other words, there must be an intellectual growth process whereby internal renewal is seen in dynamic relationship with the dire human needs of the modern world. This is what John XXIII wanted to express for the pastoral enrichment of the Church, but even he (along with the bishops at the Council) had to go through a growth process before achieving the sensibilities, insights and communication process necessary to orchestrate such complex ideas in an adequate and vital way. Consequently, much of our discussion on phenomenology, as used at Vatican II, will be aimed at assisting this growth process in ourselves.

John XXIII as an observer of human behavior

Before embarking on our discussion of how John XXIII grew into his concept of *aggiornamento* we must have some notion of the historical influences shaping his personality.[34] Although he was by nature a simple man, he was capable of handling some very complex ideas, and that in a very creative way. (1) His spirituality was, in the main, a product of the Italian Counter-Reformation.[35] This means it was shaped by seventeenth-century "devotional humanism" deriving from writers like St. Francis de Sales, St. Charles Borromeo, St. Philip Neri, Baronius, and others who tried to adapt gospel values to everyday life in society.[36] (2) His social theories were shaped by Leo XIII's *Rerum Novarum* updated, of course, by the later teachings of Pius XI and XII. The best evidence of this is John's own encyclical, *Mater et Magistra*.[37] (3) From his earliest contact with the subject Roncalli expressed a strong aversion toward theological modernism.[38] He always remained a staunch defender of the unity of doctrine, and his first encyclical, *Ad Petri Cathedram*, emphasized this point.[39]

There is a final talent possessed by John XXIII which must be stressed: his ability to *look*. The only other man, to my knowledge, who possessed this skill in a way comparable to John's, is the ethologist, Konrad Z. Lorenz. Such men are naturalists, observers of animal behavior; their vocation consists largely in *looking*.

> They [watch] with an affection and absorption that ultimately [begins] to break down the barriers that exist between species. They [begin] to see the objects of their interest not as they have always looked to people but as they look to each other. Here are the first glimmerings of true knowledge. And if your observer is also a scientist, a man with an orderly and inquiring mind, he may hit on the rarest of rare commodities, a principle governing the behavior of living beings.[40]

One time when Lorenz had quickly learned to differentiate fourteen almost identical jackdaws, he was asked how he had acquired such a skill.

> The secret is looking, says Lorenz. "It is the peasant urge," he told a visitor recently. "Those who have it want to look at animals, want to own them, to breed them. To really understand animals and their behavior you must have an esthetic appreciation of an animal's beauty. This endows you with the patience to look at them long enough to see something. Without that joy in just looking, not even a yogi would have the patience.
> "But," he went on, "combined with this purely esthetic characteristic, you must have an analytic mind. These two things rarely go together, and I think this is why there are so few [good naturalists] ."[41]

In describing his natural fascination with his subject matter Lorenz takes his stand at a junction in human reflection where empiricism, phenomenology, and scholasticism meet.[42] In the first place, his above account formulates in a non-technical way the basic elements of the phenomenological method: analysis of "the things themselves," eidetic intuition, and the apprehension of essential relationships among essences. Lorenz is, however, focusing his attention on a distinctive class of empirical phenomena: *living* things appreciated as *whole systems*. Like Husserl his analytical mind inclined toward the scientific; a more humanistic cast of mind (e.g., Scheler, John XXIII, or Sartre) might have produced a system of morals, a religious renewal program, or even a novel. Secondly, Lorenz's description also echoes the scholastic notion of *connatural knowledge*.[43]

This is not the usual knowledge gained through concepts and logical demonstration. Rather, it is an experiential wisdom mirrored in a person's *affective* inclinations: i.e., the interplay of his mind and will, knowing and loving, sensitivity and affectivity. It reflects his whole *attitudinal* stance toward reality and the *motivational* pattern shaping his very being.[44] In scholastic theory such knowledge is especially relevant in ethics, mysticism, art, and esthetics.[45] It is, in short, a practical discernment process which focuses on data ranging from the empirical to the transcendent. As a scholastic, however, John XXIII applied this type of knowledge in a new way to a psycho-social analysis of contemporary mankind appreciated as a whole system. Hence, we should make a few remarks about how this approach to human existence came to maturity in John's life.

While Lorenz specialized in animal behavior, Roncalli attended to human behavior. This is first seen in his *Journal of a Soul* which is a meticulous reflection on his own life. His early priesthood was also shaped by a deep personal involvement in "Social Catholocism," the theory of which was formulated by Pope Leo XIII and the practical meaning of which was exemplified by Roncalli's bishop, Radini Tedeschi. From 1906 until 1959 Roncalli did historical research into the reform efforts of St. Charles Borromeo at Bergamo in 1575; in this way he honed and systematized his analytical skills according to modern professional standards.[46] Lastly, his diplomatic career (1925–1953) in Bulgaria, Turkey, Greece, and France forced him — almost of necessity — to be a perceptive observer of men and their societies on the international level. Roncalli was not merely a shrewd psychologist. In a quite intuitive way his analytic mind perceived a unique convergence of trends in modern human and social dynamisms, and from this reflection on empirical data he derived a "principle governing the behavior of living beings." This will become more apparent later on, particularly when we discuss his opening speech at the Council and his encyclical, *Pacem in Terris*. Like Lorenz, then, John XXIII had a mindstyle that naturally leant itself to the phenomenological method in his particular field of interest, human beings.

Summary

This chapter has concentrated on the prevailing intellectual atmosphere found in Europe at midcentury. The point has been emphasized that this academic mindset is a direct-line development from the late nineteenth century. In spite of the sense of urgency displayed by Husserl's *Crisis* this midcentury outlook displayed no widespread awareness of the "new moment" of human history occasioned by nuclear weaponry. Such preconceptions, even today, affect many Catholics since they entertain a rather simplistic comprehension of the meaning of *aggiornamento*.

In the European Catholic community the two dominant mindstyles were either scholasticism or phenomenology; occasionally it was some combination of the two or scholasticism well-seasoned with existentialism. Such approaches to religious and human reality were not easy bedfellows, as Pius XII's encyclical, *Humani Generis*, has indicated. This chapter did not deal with a third important mindset, that of the historians. Since historical methodology falls into the category of the "sciences," its connection with our topic will be discussed as occasion offers in the book. This is particularly true of chapter ten which deals with the council document on revelation.

Lastly, this chapter tried to touch on those intellectual characteristics of Pope John XXIII whereby his essentially scholastic, but pastorally oriented, outlook naturally tended to approximate the phenomenological approach to reality. His ongoing development in this regard will be the subject of the next chapter.

NOTES

1. See Spiegelberg [1982], pp. 74–76.
2. Husserl's life was shaped by a quest for a philosophy of science, yet he is virtually unknown in comparison with Mach, Duhem, Poincaré, and Russell. Americans concerned about the relationship between science and philosophy have probably read Whitehead and Polanyi, but not Husserl. His phenomenology was developed somewhat in individual isolation, and retrieving his authentic thought today involves a certain philological as well as philosophical archaeology. In our American environment Husserl's thought often enough needs to be extensively interpreted before it is really understandable. This complexity in his thought opens the way for serious distortions, as seems to have been somewhat the case when Freud was first introduced to Americans. See Bettelheim [1983]. A naive understanding of Husserlian themes can inadvertently lead to the type of reductionism which he rejected in "Philosophy as a Rigorous Science." See McCormick and Elliston [1981], pp. 166–197. His notion of historicity, for example, can easily be equated with a new version of absolute historicism. For Husserl's phenomenology to have a constructive role it must be interpreted within the theoretical strictures which he assigned to it, and this is doubly true if we are to imply that this methodology had a formative influence on Vatican II.
3. If ever a teleological-historical study is written of the phenomenological movement, its philosophical coherence will probably pivot around *intentionality* in its multiple meanings and uses. The notion derives from Thomistic epistemology which is quite realistic and objectivistic in focus. See Maritain [1959], pp. 112–118. Its meaning was drastically narrowed in empirical psychology to "reference to an object," when Brentano used it to point out the distinctive character of psychic phenomena. See Spiegelberg [1982], pp. 36–37 and note 19, pp. 47–48. With Husserl the term gradually evolved from "directedness toward an object" to an acceptance of even non-intentional experiences, and finally to intention as seemingly constituting, by

genetic phenomenology, the intentional object itself. See Spiegelberg [1982], pp. 97–99, 130–132. In spite of these and other meanings associated with intentionality over the years, there has been a core-meaning throughout all these adaptations: the world *as meant*, the being of the object *for me*. See Carr [1974], pp. 15, 26–27. If we may assume the Western intellectual environment is today a pluralistic and inner-directed one, the Church – at least for serious dialogical purposes – would have no great difficulty adapting to a style of reflection committed to an authentic pursuit of intentionality. In important epistemological controversies, however, it may also be surmised she would ease back into her objectivistic and realistic orientation to being.

4. Husserl's slogan went through a shift of meaning as his thought matured: from a "turning to objective realities in the world outside" to a subjective reflection on phenomena in one's own insights. See Spiegelberg [1982], p. 109. Later there was a perceptible shift from the idealities of the scientific world to make allowance for history and the preconceptions of the life-world. In the first half of the twentieth century many Catholic scholars went through something of the same shift, particularly in historical research. Early in this century there was a "Back to the Sources" (*resourcement*) emphasis among theologians due to interest in scripture, patristics, and liturgy. (For the secular historical context within which this development occurred see Landgrebe [1966], pp. 102–122.) The field of scripture, however, was one of the first to experience the impact of phenomenology due to the writings of Rudolph Bultmann, a student of Heidegger. Prominant in this "hermeneutical revolution" was Bultmann's technique of "demythologizing" (i.e., bracketing) the historical non-essentials in order to get at the bible's contemporary kerygma (i.e., its existential sense *for me* in my quest for authenticity). See Smart [1979], pp. 61–69, 98–106. By the 1930s the influence of phenomenology began to be felt in other fields of theological reflection. See Farley [1975], pp. 235–272. We may round off this reflection by a quotation from P. Koestenbaum which sums up the European situation as of 1975:

Research on Husserl today is found, above all, in Catholic centers of learning. This fact is perhaps evidence for the current awareness that Husserl philosophized in the tradition of metaphysics, particularly scholastic and realistic ontology. The connection between Husserl's position and metaphysics is therefore of the first importance.

See Husserl [1975], pg. LXXIII.

5. For "Operationalism," *q.v.*, G. Schlesinger in Edwards [1967], Vol. 6, pp. 543–547. The vast majority of technical terms and philosophical thinkers mentioned in this book may be found in the Index of this encyclopedia. Use of this encyclopedia is especially informative for appreciating the cultural gap between Husserlian ideas and contemporary American ones.

6. For the contemporary American outlook on the relationship of philosophy and the natural sciences, see Suppe [1977], pp. 617–730.

7. See George Miller, "The Background to Modern Psychology," in Miller [1983], pp. 14–28.

8. See Ricoeur [1967], p. 89. This is quite understandable since the supreme genus for Husserl is meaning, not substance and certainly not being. See Carr [1974], p. 9.

9. See Spiegelberg [1982], pp. 404–409, 575–580. For serious reasons, however, many professional phenomenologists do not agree with this evaluation of Spiegelberg.

10. Cited by Spiegelberg [1982], p. xxiii.
11. See Spiegelberg [1982], pp. 425–447, where the important German influence of Heidegger is also mentioned.
12. The literature on this topic from O. Spengler to J. Ellul is enormous. One of the more perceptive early works, however, was Benda [1928]. For a handy critical reader dealing with the intellectual roots of this malaise see Friedman [1964].
13. Anthropology, both philosophical and theological, is a topic of growing importance in the post-conciliar period. Spiegelberg displays an acute insight into this new development when he traces its phenomenological roots to Heidegger's shift of focus from the epistemological aspects of human consciousness to its ontic dimensions. See Spiegelberg [1982], pp. 362–365. However, the modern intellectual context of the anthropological question was set by Kant at the beginning of the 19th century. See Schrag [1980], pp. 30–31.
14. For a balanced view of the differences between "Husserl's Phenomenology and Sartre's Existentialism" with some of the historical antecedents leading into this new approach to reality see Spiegelberg [1981], pp. 51–61.
15. Much of this "anti-scientific" animus was directed toward the rigidly Cartesian mindstyle then dominant in French philosophy and science, and personified by Léon Brunschvicq. See Spiegelberg [1982], pp. 429–430, 483–484, 487, 547.
16. On "Phenomenology and Existentialism" with special reference to Jaspers and Heidegger see Spiegelberg [1982], pp. 436–440.
17. For a popular, extended treatment of this melange of developments see Tymieniecka [1962]. The book is of interest as a presentation of a dominant academic mindset on the eve of Vatican II. For a sympathetic view of these developments from a Neo-Thomistic point of view see Dondeyne [1962].
18. See Spiegelberg [1982], p. 433. This important incident can be appreciated fully only in the context of Excursus V on Anthropology under the subheading, "The radical nature of Vatican II's reflection." In the light of our previous comments on the rise of existentialism in France around 1944 we should emphasize that Thomism, as such, has a tremendous theoretical investment in the concept of existence, both philosophically and theologically. Aside from the multiple works of E. Gilson see especially Carlo [1962]. However, for the development of the act of existing in Thomistic philosophy just prior to Vatican II see John [1962].
19. For an insightful interpretation of the European social scene in the 1930s, see Drucker [1939]. This book in turn had an important, if now forgotten, influence on American psycho-social theorizing inasmuch as it led to the paradigm of Psychological Man which epitomizes much of the functional "anthropology" in America today. See Tolman [1958]. It would be no exaggeration to say that what the existentialist type of phenomenology was trying to accomplish within the speculative, academic mindstyle of Europe, Tolman's psycho-social theorizing was trying to accomplish within America's more pragmatic, behavioralistic environment. What should be first noticed here, however, is the enormous "culture gap" between these two approaches to human problems. Secondly, for the practical implementation of their ideas, such theorists generally turn to the dominant politico-economic force operative in their environment: e.g., Marxism, National Socialism, or Capitalism. Both Husserl and Christian Personalists are distinctive in not having identified with any of these socio-political formulas. What I am saying is that they were both intent on a *renewal* program aimed primarily at the human consciousness but with derivative social effects.

20. See Carlen [1981], Vol. 3, pp. 415–443.
21. See Mounier [1938]. This should be read in conjunction with Mounier [1948], which provides the context of "existentialist" humanism. For the perduring influence of the Personalist Movement see Hellman [1980–1981] and Woznicki [1980]. One of the handicaps of Christian Personalism is that the Thomistic concept of "person" is a *metaphysical* one; it does not serve well as a key-idea of any popularly-based socio-political movement. For short-range purposes there is a tendency to reinterpret this concept in psychological terms – with a consequent danger of psychological reductionism and its accompanying fragmentation. See Paul C. Vitz, "Empirical Sciences and Personhood: From an Old Consensus to a New Realism," in Moraczewski [1983], pp. 189–212. What originally attracted Christian Personalists to phenomenology was the adaptability of the "transcendental ego" to their concept of "person" and the *via media* which Husserl's method provided between "person" as an epistemological subject in philosophy and as a psychophysical object in psychology. See Ricoeur [1967] in his Index under "Person." More especially, "the person is related to his world not causally but through *motivation*." See Carr [1974], p. 197: emphasis added. This important insight will assume increasing importance as our reflections on Vatican II develop.
22. For an overview of the era's non-cognitive tendencies see Alexander [1942], Barrett [1962], Camus [1960], Lunn [1931], and Rauschning [1939]. See also L.W. Beck, "German Philosophy" and H. Kuhn, "German Philosophy and National Socialism," in Edwards [1967], Vol. 3, pp. 291–309 and pp. 309–316.
23. See Carlen [1981], Vol. 4, pp. 175–184.
24. See Vollert [1951], p. 8.
25. See Weigel [1951]. In an interview in the *National Catholic Register* 60:18 (Apr. 29, 1984) 1, 6, Hans Urs von Balthasar confirms Weigel's statement that there never was a "nouvelle theologie." For further comments on this era and its aftermath see Congar [1968], p. 10 sq. and Connolly [1961]. It should be emphasized that the perspectives, just mentioned, are those of *academicians.* I have no difficulty with such observations as part of "intellectual history," but they seem empyrean and overly theoretical in terms of the "social history of ideas." Such technical diagnoses seem to lack a practical, pastoral sense both toward the world at large and toward the normally anticipated consumers of their ideas. In such a turbulent, postwar context *Humani Generis* was a consummately pastoral document: a harbinger of problems under development in the Church.
26. For the on-going radical shift in the American spectrum of progressive Catholic thought see O'Dea [1958], [1967], and [1968]. Roche [1968] was one of the first American journalists to describe the developing phenomenon. For two bemused Catholic historians contemplating the impact of renewal on the American Church see Gleason [1979] and Hitchcock [1980].
27. For an early perceptive analysis of the "new moment" in human history see Hutchins [1952], pp. 57–58. A virtually contemporaneous analysis by a respected European commentator would be Jaspers [1961]. For the presentday socio-political implications of this situation see Schell [1982], Brown [1981], and Ward [1976]. The *moral* challenge implicit in these problems is discussed by Schumacher [1973], pp. 293–297 and Laszlo [1972], pp. 281–290. What complicated American sensitivity to such awesome problems in the world *ad extra* in the 1960s is that a large portion of our "baby boom" generation was going through a psycho-social cultural crisis *ad intra.* In

the late 1960s Drucker offered this analysis: ". . . many of the young Americans now in college and graduate school are searching for an ethic based on personal (if not spiritual) values, rather than on social utility or community mores – what one might call an Ecumenical Ethic . . . there is a passionate groping for personal commitment to a philosophy of life. Above all, a new inner-directedness is all the rage in this group." See Drucker [1971], p. 94. One of the more perceptive, if somewhat disturbing, analyses of this new psycho-social trend was provided by Rieff [1966]. No one at the time, however, was suggesting that one of the purposes of Vatican II was to fuse these *ad extra* and *ad intra* developments into a constructive global enterprise.

28. See Staff of the Pope Speaks Magazine [1964], p. 382. Comparable ambivalence is also displayed by Christopher Butler, OSB, "The Aggiornamento of Vatican II," in Miller [1966], pp. 3–13. From this point on the confusion simply accellerates on the American scene: see O'Malley [1971], Greeley [1982], Novak [1982], and Rahner [1979].

29. See Abbott [1966], p. 705.

30. On John XXIII's evaluation of the "Present Vitality of the Church" (i.e., 1961) see Abbott [1966], pp. 704–705.

31. For John XXIII's glowing description of the Church see Abbott [1966], pp. 705–706.

32. The Good Samaritan model of the pastoral intent of Vatican II derives from two facts emphasized in *Humane Salutis*: the *problem*, i.e., critical global social problems and the *resource*, i.e., a Church "in great part transformed and renewed." See Abbott [1966], pp. 703–706. In his final address to the bishops at Vatican II, Dec. 7, 1965, Paul VI affirmed that the Good Samaritan had provided the biblical model for the pastoral intent of the Council. See Paul VI [1966], p. 61.

33. In the West the intellectual preconceptions shaping secular society derive from the Enlightenment. See Gay [1954], [1976] and Nisbet [1980]. As the world crisis continues, these secular assumptions and values will come under a critical reassessment in order to formulate a workable strategy to cope with these problems. The same adjustment faces all cultural and social systems, even the non-Western ones. The Church has already entered upon this course of change and adaptation by reason of Vatican II. In view of these larger common problems all parties, both secular and religious, should be working toward some sort of coexistence and collaboration for the wellbeing of mankind.

34. Aside from official papal documentation the only direct access to the mind of John XXIII for English-speaking readers is his spiritual diary. See John XXIII [1965]. His secretary, Capovilla [1964], stays within this spiritual framework when reflecting on the pope. Some speeches from Roncalli's assignment in France (1944–1953) have also been translated. See John XXIII [1966]. The best available English biography is Hebblethwaite [1985]. Other books meriting attention would be: Editors of Herder Correspondence [1965], Hales [1965], Lercaro and De Rosa [1966], Gorresio [1970], and Zizola [1978]. None of these studies can be considered critical, historical biographies of John XXIII. The two Italian journalists, Gorresio and Zizola, reflect a better grasp of the practical implications of John's thought than most theologians, but they lack an ability to integrate John's ideas into any larger religious vision. One journalist who displays a maturing grasp of the modern Church is Nichols [1981], which displays an awareness not found in Nichols [1968], nor in Martin [1972].

35. See Zizola [1978], pp. 276–279.

36. See Zizola [1978], pp. 279–284.

37. See Carlen [1981], Vol. 5, pp. 59–90. Roncalli's early priesthood was strongly shaped by his contact with Bishop Radini Tedeschi of Bergamo, a leader of Social Catholicism as inspired by Pope Leo XIII. See Lercaro and De Rosa [1966], pp. 30–51, 62–70.

38. See Zizola [1978], pp. 285–328. For a recent comprehensive treatment of theological modernism see Daly [1980].

39. See Carlen [1981], Vol. 5, #69–70, pp. 11–12. In spite of all that has been written by and about Pope John XXIII, his life and ideas are still very much in need of critical reflection and analysis. I heartily endorse the sentiments expressed in Giacomo Lercaro's "Suggestions for Historical Research." See Lercaro and De Rosa [1966], pp. 7–29.

40. See Lorenz [1952], pp. vii–viii. (Within a phenomenological purview, of course, Husserl and Schutz also displayed similar talents.) At this early stage of the essay I am – in a very preliminary way – laying the groundwork for a *practical discernment* process focused on an empirical *a priori*, but broad enough to embrace both John XXIII and the sophisticated style of reflection employed by modern theologians. This discernment process will be unified *objectively* because all the parties concerned are trying, in an epistemologically responsible way, to correlate a religious life-world with a multiplicity of natural life-worlds. This same discernment process will be unified *subjectively* by the fact that the participants share a corporate religious experience shaped by a *concrete* universal paradigm unifying their religious and human reality. "We find ourselves here at the frontier between two languages, that of the philosophy of 'consciousness' and that of the philosophy of 'being.'" See Frossard [1984], pp. 94–95. At this early stage of the essay it is much easier to get a felt-sense of John XXIII's analytic focus by comparing him with Lorenz rather than Husserl. But, as this essay moves into the more complex aspects of ecclesial reflection, Husserl's style of bringing together the various sense-contents of concrete mental states (*Erlebnissen*) will become more relevant, and his perceptive grasp of "the being of the object *for me*" will be appreciated within the context of religious *kerygma*, i.e., the ecclesial proclamation of the Good News. See Carr [1974], p. 15.

41. See Lorenz [1952], p. ix.

42. In making this preliminary statement about how empiricism, phenomenology, and scholasticism may conceivably share a common ground in their methodological approach to reality, I realize I am in danger of losing some of my professional readers. For example, how can a pre-scientific philosophy like scholasticism be correlated with empiricism and phenomenology? Or, how can phenomenology, which does not use induction (unless it be in a very nuanced sense), be correlated with empiricism which does? See P. Koestenbaum in Husserl [1975], p. xxv. Hopefully, any professional reader who realizes I am aware of such technicalities will have the forebearance to follow the cumulative development of this essay. In its use of phenomenology scholasticism is flexible enough to allow for a complementary "methodological idealism." (See Footnote 44, *infra*) It also appreciates the authentic sense behind Husserl's remark: "It is we who are the genuine positivists." See P. Koestenbaum in Husserl [1975], p. xli.

43. For a brief introduction to connatural knowledge see Faricy [1964] and Moreno [1970]. On such "love-knowledge" in St. Thomas see Gilby [1963], pp. 126–131.

44. A phenomenologist will immediately recognize the relationship of connatural knowledge to his field of study by our reference to attitude and motivation. See Carr [1974], pp. 20–21, 35–36 and p. 197 respectively. Such a congenial rapprochement between scholasticism and phenomenology is possible when dealing with the human act. See

Wojtyla [1979a] or T.P. Brinkman, "John Paul II's Theology of the Human Person and Technologized Parenting," in Moraczewski [1983], esp. pp. 356–363.

45. For the ethical/mystical applications of connatural knowledge see Maritain [1959], pp. 260–263. For its artistic/mystical application see Maritain [1953], pp. 117–145. The relevance of connatural knowledge to religious and philosophical thought is emphasized by Pius XII in *Humani Generis*. See Carlen [1981], Vol. 4, #33, p. 181. In view of the artistic/esthetic achievements of Vatican II (see "The new religio-social hierophany" in Chapter 8, *infra*), which our essay perceives as a product of connatural knowledge used in conjunction with phenomenological techniques, the following passage from A. Solzhenitsyn sums up the role of the artist-bishop-theologian at the Council:

> The task of the artist is to sense more keenly than others the harmony of the world, the beauty and the outrage of what man has done to it, and poignantly, to let people know. Art warms even an icy and depressed heart, opening it to lofty, personal experience. By means of art we are sometimes sent dimly, briefly, revelations unattainable by reason, like that little mirror in the fairy tales. Look into it and you will see not yourself but for a moment, that which passes understanding, a realm to which no man can ride or fly and for which the soul begins to ache.

A. Solzhenitsyn, '*One Word of Truth* . . .': The *Nobel Lecture on Literature*. London: The Bodley Head, 1978. Cited in Muggeridge [1980], pp. 46–47.

46. Angelo G. Roncalli (with Don Pietro Forno), *Gli Atti Della Visita Apostolica Di S. Carlo Borromeo a Bergamo, 1575*. 2 vol. in five books. Fontes Ambrosiani (Vol. 13–17). Fiorenze: L.S. Olschki, 1936–1957. There are only five known copies in the U.S. It is difficult to locate sources in English referring to this prolonged research by John XXIII. One convenient reference is Lercaro and De Rosa [1966], pp. 70–81.

CHAPTER 2

FROM *HUMANAE SALUTIS* TO THE OPENING OF THE COUNCIL

There is one time in John XXIII's writing when his Catholic historical consciousness became so aligned with phenomenological method that the tumblers
of both systems naturally fell into place. I am not suggesting here that the Holy
Father *consciously* employed the phenomenological method, but that his
approach to empirical humanistic concerns, his practical goals and expectations,
became substantially aligned with those of any reputable phenomenologist –
especially the Husserl of the *Crisis*. What may have begun, however, in a somewhat unwitting or eclectic fashion was eventually cultivated in a more conscious
way as time progressed. When European religious thinkers began to see Husserl
and John XXIII correlated at the practical level by their common focus on
renewal, such intellectuals were not slow to perceive the possibilities for an
"ecumenical" collaboration at the theoretical level. Our present reflections
on John's style of practical thought is an important segment in the over-all
development of this essay.[1] To the extent we comprehend it, our understanding
of Vatican II's use of phenomenology will be facilitated. The point to be emphasized here, however, is the *alignment* of scholastic method with phenomenological method. In this instance both are so naturally coordinated that
scholasticism, preoccupied as it is with contemporary renewal, unconsciously
"backs into" or allows for the use of phenomenology without either system
being compromised.

The strategic vision of *Humanae Salutis*

On December 25, 1961, Pope John XXIII issued an apostolic constitution,
Humanae Salutis, which convoked the Second Vatican Council to begin on
October 11, 1962.[2] The very title of this much-neglected document sets it
within the context of the "crisis in human beings." John's view of these problems is essentially a global one, and he rapidly summarizes them as the background for his statements pertaining to the future work of the Council. Worldwide
humanity today is afflicted with two basic problems: the danger of nuclear war
and the ongoing dehumanization of men by atheistic materialism, affluent
hedonism, or abject poverty.[3] Important as these observations are for setting

the practical and pastoral context for the work of Vatican II, my focus here
will be on the developing alignment between scholasticism and phenomenology
as evident in this apostolic constitution and even as clearly perceived at that
time by shrewd observers of the Council. The two passages which we are about
to consider are part of one long paragraph in *Humanae Salutis*, and the second
passage needs some rather technical explanation.

The first quotation is quite traditionalistic in tone, and its ethical realism
may be traced back to the Epistle of St. James (2:26), the last judgment scene
in Matthew (25:31—40), or the social encyclicals of Leo XIII and Pius XI. In
the English translation I have italicized certain words simply to assist in the
easy understanding of the passage.

> Verumtamen supernus ordo ad alterum ordinem, temporis finibus
> artatum, qui, pro dolor, saepenumero unus hominum curas eorumque
> anxias sollicitudines occupat, maxime efficax sit oportet.[4]

> This *supernatural* order must, however, reflect its *efficiency* in that
> other order, the *temporal* one, which on so many occasions is, unfor-
> tunately, ultimately the *only* one that occupies and worries man.[5]

Scholastic presuppositions of the strategic vision

While the previous quotation simply reaffirms traditional Catholic ethics, it
places such constructive action in a context more comprehensible to modern
men: utilitarianism, pragmatism, empiricism, and historicity.[6] The pope, however, is not frenetically pursuing social relevance for an irrelevant Church,[7] nor
is he precipitating Catholicism into materialistic relativism.[8] Only John XXIII's
scholastic preconceptions can explain why he expected religion to confer such
empirically discernible psycho-social benefits. In scholastic theory all levels of
existence, as created by God, are harmoniously interrelated in a mutually
beneficial way. If functioning as God intended, such ordered entities — whether
natural or supernatural, subjective or objective — can never work at odds with
one another. Rather, they can only work for each others enhancement or enrichment.[9] Therefore, the supernatural order is expected to confer manifest
benefits on the natural, temporal order. Any authentically human enrichment
of the natural order should, at least by way of dispositive causality, redound
to the benefit of the supernatural order. Such ontological and teleological presuppositions underlie any concept of Christian humanism and would naturally
shape John's "therapeutic" approach to the "crisis in human beings."[10]

Yet, we must admit that Pope John does display some pastoral daring in this new mode of evangelizing. He wants to establish an empirically discernible linkage between invisible supernatural causes and their visible effects. In this type of venture the pope cannot expect too much help from his scholastic peers. As theologians or academicians they work mainly with principles and ideas derived from a pre-scientific methodology, and so they do not function comfortably at this down-to-earth level of thought.[11] Presumably Pope John expected the Council, as a gathering of bishops with on-the-scene practical experience in pastoral leadership, to provide the needed prudent advice. But this empirical milieu, this concrete life-world, is the natural habitat of phenomenology, both in its philosophical and broader sense.[12] So, when the Holy Father formulated his strategic vision of *aggiornamento* at the level of usefulness, practicality, verifiability, and temporality, he eased over — imperceptibly, if not unwittingly — into the domain of phenomenology.

The new communication process intended by the strategic vision

In the quotation which follows I have again italicized portions of the English translation for ease of understanding.

Quamvis Ecclesia ad terrestrem finem in primis non contendat, tamen in itinere suo nequit abesse ab iis quaestionibus, quae de bonis temporalibus sunt, vel labores, qui haec progignunt, neglegere. Novit profecto, quantopere prosint immortalibus animis ea adiumenta et praesidia, quae apta sunt ad humaniorem efficiendam singulorum hominum vitam, quorum aeterna salus procuranda est. Novit eadem se, cum Christi luce homines collustret, id conferre, ut iidem se ipsi penitus agnoscant. Nam illuc eos perducit, ut intellegant, quid ipsi sint, qua dignitate excellant, quem finem prosequi debeant.[13]

Though not having direct earthly ends, [the Church] cannot, however, in its mission fail to interest itself in the problems and worries of here below. It knows how beneficial to the *good of the soul* are those means that are apt to make the life of those individual men who must be saved more *human*. It knows that by *vivifying the temporal order* with the light of Christ it *reveals men to themselves*; it leads them, therefore, to *discover in themselves their own nature, their own dignity, their own end.*[14]

A brief technical excursus on the key-sentence

Although not a literal translation in every respect, the above English translation
is really a brilliant one in rendering "sense for sense." The key-line of the Latin
passage is:

> Novit eadem se, cum Christi luce homines collustret, id conferre, ut
> iidem se ipsi penitus agnoscant.

Literally: That same [Church] knows [that] when [she] illumines on
all sides [the total reality of actually existing] men [by means of] the
light of Christ, she [thereby] brings it about that these same [men]
recognize themselves [i.e., their true selves or their authentic humanity]
from [their] innermost depths [i.e., by their inherent, God-given natural
capacity; or, through and through, thoroughly, completely, wholly,
entirely, utterly].[15]

More simply: The Church knows that when she illumines human
existence with the light of Christ, she enables men to recognize their
authentic humanity by a sort of natural empathy on their part.[16]

The final redaction: It [i.e., the Church] knows that by vivifying
the temporal order with the light of Christ it *reveals men to themselves*.[17]

Connatural knowledge and phenomenology in alignment

As I have mentioned previously, this final redaction (i.e., "reveals men to themselves") is a brilliant *tour de force* on the part of the translator, but it takes a
little explanation to understand what he has done. In the first place the translator
recognized that the phrase, "*se ipsi penitus agnoscant*," drawn from scholasticism,
referred to connatural knowledge as commonly understood in that philosophy.[18]
In this approach to reality, where all levels of existence are harmoniously interrelated, Christ is the most exalted expression of this order. When any man, made
in God's image, is confronted with the authentic moral beauty of Christ, his
natural response should be, "That man is *you*!" (i.e., he expresses my true self
as I experience it from my innermost depths). This judgment, although welling
up from the subjectivity of a man's whole interior, is a necessarily true one,
since it is authentically resonating with the truth of the God-given order.[19] Our
translator, then, adroitly recast this scholastic expression of subjectivity by using
an English phrasing which suggested the more contemporary sense of phenomenology but meant the same thing. As a result, he has integrated both closely

related ideas into a modern historical context which makes eminently good sense to both schools of philosophy.[20]

The final redaction, as cited above, was published in 1966. It expresses the easy flow in academic circles between scholasticism and phenomenology which was particularly evident by the close of the Council. This was especially true for that type of scholasticism known as Transcendental Thomism. For the most part this was a constructive and wholesome development, but as Paul VI observed in *Ecclesiam Suam*, the methodology was not without its dangers.[21] Nevertheless, in 1967 W.E. May briefly summarized the historical antecedents for such a development:

> The emphasis on intersubjectivity in recent existential and phenomenological thought has helped redirect inquiry into this subject [i.e., connatural knowledge]. Interest in it is reflected in J.H. Newman's distinction between notional and real knowledge, a distinction further elaborated by M. Blondel, and in H. Bergson's opposition of the knowledge characteristic of scientific inquiry to that achieved in intuition.[22]

The rapproachment to phenomenology in its historical context

The perception that the authentic intent of John's thought is the revelation of man to himself inserts his program neatly within the *European* context of the history of ideas which has impinged most intimately on Catholic thought over the past century and a half. In the mid-nineteenth century, for example, Ludwig Feuerbach's overt purpose was "the revelation of religion to itself."[23] Early in this century Edmund Husserl formulated his phenomenological method in order to achieve "the revelation of consciousness to itself."[24] The common denominator in both of these Post-Kantian developments is an approach to the problems under consideration by way of subjectivity. Pope John's intended "revelation" is, therefore, understood as a creative adaptation in this ongoing intellectual controversy. This interpretation of the Holy Father's thought has the obvious merit of soliciting all interested parties in the academic community to dialogue about the "crisis in human beings" on the basis of a methodology respected by all.

This line of thought, congenial as it may be to the European style of philosophizing, does have some built-in liabilities. The intellectual harmonization provided by the history of ideas, as outlined above, expresses the tidiness and coherence demanded by the academic mind. Pope John's outlook on the world scene, however, was more influenced by the social history of ideas; here theories can be distorted beyond all recognition over the course of time by social forces.[25] The above academic mindset, furthermore, need not necessarily imply any discontent with the secular *status quo* of the modern world.[26] For John that world had been rendered obsolete by the "new moment" of human history. Lastly, academics are primarily concerned with the *speculative* order; John, for his part, is primarily concerned with shaping human affairs in a *practical* and pastoral way.[27] Over the past twenty years the liabilities of this European intellectual framework have become even more manifest. Some Catholic intellectuals have turned to the Orient for their religious inspiration; others have approriated Marxist thought-categories in order to draw out better the political implications of gospel values. Nonetheless, the fact remains that the two dominant Catholic academic mindsets in 1961, when John wrote *Humanae Salutis*, were — in one form or another — scholasticism and phenomenology.

John XXIII's practical ideas and preparation for the Council

John XXIII had no easy task in impressing his practical and pastoral formulary of the Council's goals on those curial administrators in charge of the preparatory work for this great event. They went about their work as professional theologians with a theologian's academic concerns for the theoretical comprehensiveness and accuracy of the doctrinal issues to be discussed. Vatican II, presumably, was to carry out the unfinished business of Vatican I, and the approach to doctrinal statements at that council had simply been a fine-tuning of procedures used at the Council of Trent. This is not to say such preconceptions were unreasonable ones: after all, John himself agreed that these concerns and customary procedures had produced a modern Church "in great part transformed and renewed."[28] The point is, however, that such administrators were over-focusing on the speculative concerns of academic theologians and the result of their work was really missing the practical objectives being contemplated by John's pastoral program. Had this trend continued unabated, Vatican II may have become the doctrinally-fixated type of Council which the pope neither wanted nor needed. Since he genuinely desired the conciliar participants to arrive at their conclusions in a corporate and free way, he did not interfere substantially in the preparatory process.

But as the opening date of the Council approached, the three years of preparatory work had resulted in a morass of over seventy schemata, or semi-developed topics, for conciliar discussion.[29] From the untoward fate some of these suffered during the first session (e.g., the documents on the Church and on Revelation), we may surmise the majority of these schemata were formulated in such a rigidly scholastic way as to be out of step with new trends intent on wide-ranging pastoral adaptation, ecumenism, and a return to biblical simplicity. Certainly these documents did not meet the practical purposes of John XXIII.[30] Almost in desperation and somewhat by way of solemn warning, the pope delivered an important radio broadcast on September 11, 1962, dealing with a broad spectrum of world problems to be considered by the Council, but which were not found in the proposed schemata![31] These last-ditch efforts of the Holy Father did have some impact. In their first session the Council Fathers did issue a "Message to Humanity" which explicitly identified itself with the main principles of the papal broadcast and focused its attention on the *problem of peace.*[32]

The paradoxical optimism of John's opening speech

Yet, it must be admitted that when John XXIII gave his opening speech at the Council on October 11, 1962, the problem of peace had been so toned down as to be virtually non-existent. Indeed, the pope made a pointed reference to "those prophets of gloom," people he met in the daily exercise of his office, "who are always forecasting disaster as though the end of the world were at hand."[33] Such men, presumably Catholic and probably including Roman Curia members, "behave as though they had learned nothing from history, which is, none the less, the teacher of life."[34] For his part, John chose to emphasize the happy circumstances under which the Council was beginning and gave his interpretation of contemporary history and the important lesson to be drawn from it:

> In the present order of things, Divine Providence is leading us to a new order of human relations which, by men's own efforts and even beyond their very expectations, are directed toward the fulfillment of God's superior and inscrutible designs. And everything, even human differences, leads to the greater good of the Church.[35]

Eleven days after this optimistic prognosis on the future the Cuban missile crisis hit the headlines, and shortly thereafter John XXIII with the knowledge and approval of President Kennedy sent Norman Cousins on a secret peace mission to Khrushchev.[36] This crisis had been underway since the previous July when the Russians had decided to ship the missiles. By August the launching sites were already under construction in Cuba. It is hard to believe that the Vatican, the listening-post of the world, was uninformed of these developments. Why did Pope John deliver a radio broadcast on September 11 emphasizing the

peace problem and exactly one month later play it down? In his opening address, then, was the Holy Father trying to defuse as much as possible what was
really a very critical situation in world events? His years in the field of diplomacy
might have taught him that. Or, did he believe that by avoiding the urgency of
the peace issue and by emphasizing the positive, the religious, and the pastoral
he would better achieve his purposes? We may never really know. But it is
interesting to note an historical comparison. A good hundred years after Marx,
John XXIII is here offering his analysis of the historical dialectic in the modern
world. If so, on what is his judgment based?

Connatural knowledge: The basis for John's optimism

Were John forecasting simply as an historian in our Post-Hiroshima Age, then
his futurology would have a decidedly utopian cast about it. History, both
secular and religious, affirms that war has been with men from the very beginning. Even the most orthodox Marxist, who maintains a necessary dialectic
for the historical process, would admit that as atomic weapons multiply around
the world, the statistical probability of their usage is creating a monstrous
antithesis which could annihilate the very historical process itself. To the extent
the Holy Father refers to Divine Providence we know he is viewing social reality
from a religious vantagepoint. Even though St. Paul said that all things work
together unto good for those who love God (cf. Rom. 8:28), no professional
theologian or scripture scholar today would make specific predictions on that
basis about social progress. They have the further *caveat* that Christ said his
kingdom was not of this world (cf. Jn. 18:36). Christ's gift of hope may sustain
Christians during some very apocalyptic times, but it does not warrant their
making predictions about a new *earthly* order of human relations. Yet, with
calmness and conviction John discerns a future in which the natural actions of
men will unwittingly collaborate with divine providence to achieve God's purposes. In so doing, he can only be expressing a holy man's or mystic's affective
grasp of reality by *connatural knowledge*.

This preliminary statement of John's intuition into social reality is very interesting from a phenomenological point of view. Similar to Lorenz's approach, it
derives from an affectionate contemplation of empirical data, i.e., human
behavior. Yet, as these phenomena take on meaning in the pope's life-world,
he apperceives that two seemingly disparate horizons of humanity are falling
into alignment. The authentic human values of the City of Man are so rotating
under the gravity-forces of modern global problems as to become ever more in
conjunction with the genuine values of the City of God.[37] For John this is a

unique moment in both human and salvation history. Is the Holy Father constituting this new eidetic essence of humanity-under-formation in his consciousness? Yes, but only in the sense that his affective dispositions are set in resonance with those human trends consonant with his own sensibilities. In a sense, John's personality is acting as a magnifying glass bringing into focus the truths and values of his larger religious world to concentrate on and selectively illumine human trends under development. (As we shall see shortly, the integral truths and values of this larger religious world are not to be tampered with in any substantial way.) Since the Holy Father's *applied* religious insight is not the product of scientific reflection derived from some secular or religious area of study, it prescinds from and transcends the academic problem of intellectual pluralism. His spiritual methodology, finally, provides the bishops with a rudimentary demonstration-model for pastoral reflection at the Council. Since each of them individually represents a religious life-world, he is inviting them as an intersubjective community to reflect on and share their personal experiences in a non-technical, affective, and dialogical way.

The art and bipolar dialectic of the pastoral challenge

In employing the term, "non-technical," in the sentence above, I am referring to a quite specific, largely scholastic tradition within which conciliar statements have been formulated over the centuries.[38] All the bishops were acquainted with this methodology and probably expected to use it at Vatican II. As with constitutional or corporation law in this country, this is a domain of specialists, and in its ongoing development professional theologians necessarily play a key-role.[39] John XXIII was *not* inviting the bishops to travel once more that well-worn road of the past. Rather, in view of the uniquely "new moment" of human and salvation history the pope was inviting the bishops to embark on a great *artistic* enterprise.[40] Just as Michaelangelo took the story of the bible and produced the glory of the Sistine chapel in an art-form expressive of the humanistic and religious ideals of the Renaissance, so John wanted the bishops to reinterpret Christianity in a comparable way for our era. The medium to be used, however, would not consist of paints and oils, but be an enriched perception of experience that would operate from *within* men to shape their minds, attitudes, and values.[41] In this "updated" way the traditional doctrines of Christianity would become more efficacious in training balanced citizens of two worlds: i.e., men who could integrate the authentic purposes of the City of God and the City of Man in a harmonious and constructive way.

In his opening speech John XXIII displayed a good grasp of the essential pastoral challenge, although he was not yet sure of the final methodology for meeting that challenge. He continued to grow in this regard, and his mature reflections may be found in *Pacem in Terris*.[42] So too, the bishops had to go through a growth process both at the Council and even after it. At this introductory stage, however, John XXIII placed two major, bipolar concerns before the Council: doctrinal integralism and the need for a more contemporary expression of doctrine in order to shape the whole man in a more effective way.[43] In this bipolar relationship doctrinal integralism was a necessary precondition for any effective teaching of doctrine. To precise the issues involved, we now cite and comment on some pertinent passages in John's speech.

> The greatest concern of the Ecumenical Council is this: that the sacred deposit of Christian doctrine should be guarded and taught more efficaciously. [. . .]
> In order, however, that this doctrine may influence the numerous fields of human activity, with reference to individuals, to families, and social life, it is necessary first of all that the Church should never depart from the sacred patrimony of truth received from the Fathers.[44]

The problem of doctrinal integralism

For many Catholic intellectuals the very word "integralism" sets their teeth on edge.[45] Such men are suffering from "flashbacks" occasioned by the excesses of the Integralist Movement, a Catholic form of vigilantism in the early twentieth century directed against theological modernism. While the simpliste outlook associated with the Integralist Movement may have caused inconvenience, and even suffering, for certain historical and biblical scholars until midcentury, we cannot jettison a word with serious cognitive content in theology simply because of some noxious historical associations. In the Catholic religious ontology we must understand that doctrinal integralism is not merely the necessary precondition for effective evangelization. Even more basically, it is the necessary presupposition for theological discernment, both at the theoretical level and that of connatural knowledge.[46] On this axiomatic principle the Church's magisterium has in the past exercised either a favorable or unfavorable judgment on the teachings of theologians, mystics, or reputedly holy people. The importance of this topic, therefore, warrants a rather long quotation from John XXIII in order that we may appreciate his own conviction on this matter.

> The manner in which sacred doctrine is spread, this having been established, it becomes clear how much is expected from the Council in regard

to doctrine. That is, the Twenty-first Ecumenical Council, which will draw upon the effective and important wealth of juridical, liturgical, apostolic, and administrative experiences, wishes to transmit the doctrine, pure and integral, without any attenuation of distortion, which throughout twenty centuries, notwithstanding difficulties and contrasts, has become the common patrimony of men. It is a patrimony not well received by all, but always a rich treasure available to men of good will.

Our duty is not only to guard this precious treasure, as if we were concerned only with antiquity, but to dedicate ourselves with an earnest will and without fear to that work which our era demands of us, pursuing thus the path which the Church has followed for twenty centuries.

The salient point of the Council is not, therefore, a discussion of one article or another of the fundamental doctrine of the Church which has repeatedly been taught by the Fathers and by ancient and modern theologians, and which is presumed to be well known and familiar to all.

For this a Council was not necessary.[47]

Three points are worth noticing in regard to the above statement: (1) It rejects the idea of "historical primitivism" (i.e., a return to a Golden Age) as a norm for the anticipated renewal of the Church;[48] (2) The axiom of doctrinal integralism was later explicitly endorsed by the bishops in their "Message to Humanity," issued during the first session of the Council as an expression of their corporate intent;[49] (3) Pope John seems to be suggesting that whatever "new theology" the Council might produce should simply be the old theology "in a new key." In the context, then, of adapting the *whole* doctrinal heritage of the Church to the contemporary needs of the *whole* man the Holy Father goes on to say:

[. . .] But from the renewed, serene, and tranquil adherence to all the teaching of the Church in its entirety and preciseness, as it still shines forth in the Acts of the Council of Trent and First Vatican Council, the Christian, Catholic, and apostolic spirit of the whole world expects a step forward toward a doctrinal penetration and a formation of consciousness in faithfull and perfect conformity to the authentic doctrine, which, however, should be studied and expounded through the methods of research and through the literary forms of modern thought. The substance of the ancient doctrine of the deposit of faith is one thing, and the way in which it is presented is another. And it is the latter that must be taken into great consideration with patience if necessary, everything being measured in the forms and proportions of a magisterium which is predominantly pastoral in character.[50]

The scope and challenge of the conciliar pastoral goal

There is much to admire about the technical accuracy with which the Holy Father is describing the anticipated renewal program. The Council intends to take the authentic substance of Catholic doctrine and present it in a new *modality* more apt to meet the needs of contemporary humanity.[51] Even at this stage we can appreciate that such an adaptation will involve a most demanding *artistic* process. What the bishops are really faced with is essentially the same challenge which confronted the apostles after Pentecost. At that time these men had to sort out their memories of Christ in order to present them in a way that would meet the human and religious needs of their first-century world. So too, the bishops were being called upon to sort out the Church's historical consciousness of Christ in order to adapt his truths and values to the needs of a twentieth-century world at a turning point of human history. Before the bishops could ever hope to achieve such an enormous project, they themselves as a corporate group would have to achieve their own "doctrinal penetration and formation of consciousness." As part of their reflective and creative process they were being expected, of course, to use the "methods of research" and "the literary forms of modern thought." The ultimate purpose of all this work, as the pope later remarks, is to prepare and consolidate "that unity of mankind which is required as a necessary foundation, in order that the earthly city may be brought to the resemblance of that heavenly city where truth reigns, charity is the law, and whose extent is eternity (cf. St. Augustine, Epistle 138, 3)."[52]

The above presentation does, however, have one great *weakness*. Albeit technically correct, it is largely abstract and ahistorical. In *Humanae Salutis* of a year previously John had set the projected renewal within the specific context of world problems, one of which was the danger of nuclear war. His radio broadcast of September 11, 1962, had emphasized the problem of peace. Yet, here in his opening speech the pope has, either deliberately or for reasons of prudence, chosen not to emphasize the *acute urgency* of the Catholic renewal program in today's world. "The Bomb" is the extrinsic historical factor which lends intelligibility and relevance to the internal renewal program of the Catholic Church.[53] Without that extrinsic historical factor *aggiornamento* becomes merely a program of spiritual and human enrichment. This naive evaluation of things can have disastrous consequences. (1) It projects the Council as an unnecessary and extremely costly program for a Church "in great part transformed and renewed." (2) It imparts a utopian tonality to Pope John's pastoral program when, in fact, it is a product of the "new realism."[54] (3) It exposes zealous Catholics intent on remedying terrible social evils to the danger of relegating such an enrichment program to mere religious introversion and self-preoccupation.[55] John himself would eventually see the need of returning to the peace problem, and he did this in his encyclical, *Pacem in Terris*.

Summary

This chapter dealt with two periods just prior to Vatican II.

The *first* was from *Humanae Salutis*, December 25, 1961, to the radio broadcast of September 11, 1962. The tone of this period was one of urgency for pastoral renewal since concern for peace and other world problems loomed large in the Holy Father's thinking. In *Humanae Salutis* John XXIII formulated a new strategic vision for renewal in which supernatural truths were expected to have empirically discernible results in the natural order. This pastoral program would also require a new communication process which would "reveal men to themselves." While this type of thinking derives from scholasticism, its emphasis on subjectivity brings it into alignment with phenomenology and the European history of ideas dating from about 1850. John had a difficult task in impressing his pastoral ideas on the work of the Preparatory Commission. This led to the radio broadcast of September 11, 1962 stressing world problems and peace.

The *second* period was simply October 11, 1962, on which John delivered his opening speech to the Council. The tone of this period, which will carry throughout much of the Council, is set by the somewhat paradoxical optimism of the pope's opening speech. John's vision of humanity working in unwitting collaboration with the purposes of Divine Providence is again a product of his connatural knowledge. But as he unfolds his pastoral concept of the Council's work, we begin to appreciate some of its problem-areas: doctrinal integralism, the artistic scope of the anticipated adaptation, and the need for a real growth process both on the part of John and the bishops in Council.

The next chapter will reflect on this growth process on the part of the bishops.

NOTES

1. Over the next three chapters I will try to develop some teleological-historical reflections on John XXIII in the same way Husserl analysed the role of Galileo in the *Crisis*.

See Husserl [1970], #9, p. 23 sq. Starting with the fact in his own day of the mathematization of nature by the natural sciences, Husserl traced the intentional origin
of this mindset back to the basic notion of Galilean physics which viewed nature as
a mathematical universe. Such an "intentional history," of course, provides some
formidable problems for professional historians. Some would say the project is not
even theoretically possible. Others more sympathetic to a philosophy of history might
trace the *idea* of the mathematization of nature as far back as Thomas Bradwardine
(c. 1290–1349) or one of the later Ockhamists. More critical historians in this area
might point out that for three hundred years Galileo has been seriously misinter-
preted: in reality, he was a developmental Aristotelian in his natural philosophy. See
Wallace [1977], [1983a], [1983b]. In spite of such technical historical difficulties
there is an important element of truth in Husserl's intentional connection of an evident
cultural *fact* with the catalytic influence of Galileo. Whatever may have been Galileo's
individual ideas on scientific method, the later tradition of mathematicizing scientists
had so interpreted the intentional gestalt of his cumulative work that they acknowledged him as their authentic progenitor in both theory and method. It was only after I
had become aware of the *fact* that Vatican II was a demonstration-model of the phenomenological method that I was also enabled to trace its intentional connection with the
efforts of John XXIII.

2. The complete English text may be found in Abbott [1966], pp. 703–709. The official
    text may be found in Latin Texts [1966], pp. 839–853. The working-papers used in
    preparation of this constitution have been consigned to the Vatican archives and are
    not yet available to scholars. Only Zizola [1978], p. 249 attributes to this constitution
    an importance comparable to my own estimation of it.

3. See Abbott [1966], pp. 703–704: "Painful Considerations." See Kobler [1983] and
    Nichols [1981], esp. pp. 70–71, 77. It would be too facile to read John XXIII's state-
    ments against the notion of religious decline familiar to European intellectuals. See
    F.R. Lipsius in Pelikan [1969–1970], Vol. 2, pp. 282–286. If anything, his remarks
    should be read against a background of the "Better World Movement" in Italy which
    had been endorsed and encouraged by Pius XII. See Lombardi [1958]. Consequently,
    as we gradually hope to make clear, the pope's diagnosis is pertinent to a uniquely "new
    moment" of human history. From a *phenomenological* point of view the pope is really
    presenting the "horizon" within which he is viewing the global events of our contem-
    porary historical and cultural world (i.e., the natural lifeworld(s) of global mankind).
    Inasmuch as the intentional ground of the pope's horizon is constituted by his religious
    and moral principles, it differs radically from the optimistic horizons dominant in most
    secular societies of 1961. He offers this altered horizon in order to stimulate a much-
    needed transformation of attitude on the part of mankind. For "The Five Evils of the
    Age" as viewed by Pope John Paul II see Johnson [1981], pp. 65–165.

4. See Latin Texts [1966], p. 846.

5. See Abbott [1966], p. 706 (emphasis added). This principle is drawn out of the social
    philosophy of Pope Leo XIII, who – as Paul VI says – "devoted himself whole-
    heartedly to finding a Christian solution to the problems of this modern age." See
    Carlen [1981], Vol. 5, #67, p. 150. John XXII simply appropriates Leo XIII's "Social
    Catholicism" as elaborated within the context of the industrialized West and re-
    presents its enlarged challenge within the context of the contemporary global scene.
    (On the Leonine influence on the young Roncalli recall Chapter 1, footnote 37.)

6. By implication John XXIII is insisting that the Church today must reflect its efficiency

in the temporal order, if only to maintain its *human* credibility. Stated in this abstract way, this principle could easily be interpreted as a selfserving one. Its authentic sense, however, derives from the "crisis in human beings," perceived by Husserl [1970], Heidegger [1976], Jaspers [1961], and others, and further crystalized by the Parable of the Good Samaritan which became the operative model for conciliar reflection. See Paul VI [1966], p. 61.

7. We are, of course, speaking here only of the mindset of John XXIII. The quest for social relevance, however, has always posed an important problem for Catholic intellectuals excluded from influence in secularized societies. Since he was papal legate in France from 1945 to 1953, Roncalli would have had first-hand knowledge of one of the more serious European examples of such overt discrimination. Such problems were not seriously voiced in America to any great extent until after Vatican II and – somewhat surprisingly – after a Catholic president had been elected in this country. Two of the first Catholic voices were Callahan [1967] and Novak [1967]. Up until that time the quest for social relevance had largely been associated with Protestantism. Various aspects of the problem are discussed by Rieff [1966], Mascall [1968] and Caporale and Grumelli [1971].

8. Relativism in matters of truth, as this is commonly understood in intellectual history, is so far from the traditional Catholic consciousness that comparatively little has to be said about it. The mind of John XXIII is staunchly in the mainstream of this tradition. His markedly orthodox views are reflected in his first encyclical, *Ad Petri Cathedram.* See Carlen [1981], Vol. 5, #9–11, #17–19, pp. 6–7.

9. The well-known concept of "order" in Catholic scholastic theology views the cosmos as structured and functioning somewhat along the lines of a comprehensive "ecological system." (As this book develops, however, we shall move much beyond this elementary analogy.) John XXIII, for example, begins *Pacem in Terris* (See Carlen [1981], Vol. 5, pp. 107–108) with a summary of these ideas, and the encyclical itself is an extended meditation on the implications of order among men in the modern world. Within this classical view of things all levels of existence, objectively speaking, complement one another in a harmonious way which contributes to the common good. In the subjective order which refers to human consciousness, authentic personhood, and the pursuit of happiness the above matters must be more carefully nuanced. Here the Christian comprehension of the created order must factor in the problem of fallen human nature, the requirements of holiness, and the moral value of suffering accepted with the dispositions of Christ. The faith-evaluation of all these complex matters (other than sin itself) is optimistic. The biblical foundation of this optimism ranges from God's judgment on the goodness of creation in Genesis (1:31) to the New Testament gospel as "good news." The unifying principle throughout all these reflections is God as creating through His Logos and as redeeming through His Logos made flesh. See Frossard [1984], pp. 91–95, 101, 133. In the context of Vatican II one theologian who has appreciated this centrality of creation would be Wojtyla [1980], pp. 19, 38, 45–48, 50–52, 55. In 1966 Landgrebe [1966], p. 168 still appreciated the majority of Neo-Thomists as philosophizing within this tradition, whatever may have been their use of phenomenological method. We shall return to this topic again in Chapter Ten where we discuss the objects (noemata) in the consciousness of the Church. For a contemporary philosophical context more familiar to Americans and treating ideas of such comprehensive order see Laszlo [1972], pp. 8–12.

10. For the immediate impact of such ideas on John XXIII and some of the postconciliar Catholic developments see Gremillion [1976], pp. 8–10. One of the earliest (1936) thinkers to grapple extensively with the speculative aspects of this pastoral problem was Maritain [1973]. Vatican II's less than clear handling of Pope John's pastoral intent has created a practical, pastoral vacuum into which others were quick to enter. Important postconciliar developments, for example, have centered around the formulation of functional pastoral theologies based on particularized psycho-social, or even political, concerns: e.g., liberation theology, feminist theology, etc. These are all interpreted within the context of today's turbulent world and as harbingers of a "postmodern theology" in Cox [1984]. However, what I have understated as the "crisis in human beings" Landgrebe [1966], pp. 19, 121, 160 more accurately catalogues as "the crisis of reason" or "the crisis of nihilism."

11. It should come as no surprise that the theologians at Vatican II – both conservative and progressive – appropriated John's pastoral goals only after they had *theologized* them according to their own preconceptions. Some of the Curialist pattern in this regard had been set by the fact that preparations for a Council had begun under Cardinal Ottaviani as early as February 24, 1948. This preparatory work tended toward a sweeping condemnation of errors in the modern world; after reviewing the material Pius XII consigned this work to the Vatican archives. See Gorresio [1970], pp. 234–247. In 1962 Fr. Ciappi, John XXIII's personal theologian, predicted Vatican II would promote "a huge doctrinal program." How frustrating all this was to John's pastoral purposes should be quite evident by the end of this chapter. Even after the "progressive" wrested control of the Council from the hands of the Curia, this theologizing trend continued. The new trend was away from the static, conceptual "objectivism" of scholasticism toward a more experiential and evangelical, dynamic handling of doctrine. In European academic circles that could only be a melange of phenomenology and existentialism as this had been appropriated by Catholic scholars over a generation. As Chapter Ten, however, will attempt to show, the pastoral concept in the minds of the theologians never matured much beyond its doctrinal and kerygmatic dimensions. On Pope John as a "theologian" see Zizola [1978], pp. 265–266.

12. Life-world (Lebenswelt): See Excursus I.

13. See Latin Texts [1966], p. 847.

14. See Abbott [1966], p. 707, emphasis added. In discussing the life of Angelo Roncalli, Gabriele De Rosa mentions that at twenty-two years of age the young seminarian experienced something of a revelation of himself to himself. This occurred under the spiritual direction of Fr. Francesco Pitocchi. Roncalli realized he must give up his slavish imitation of the details of saints' lives; rather, he must "[absorb] the vital sap of their virtues and [turn] it into [his] own life-blood, adapting it to [his] own individual capacities and particular circumstances."

   Not that at this point he set aside all those formulae of post-Tridentine peity . . . , but from this moment onwards they were observed with greater freedom, with an ever more tranquil Christian spirit, and with that fidelity to his own nature which he sought more and more earnestly to express, until the moment of self-revelation came during the brief but triumphant season of his pontificate.

   See Lercaro and De Rosa [1966], pp. 49–50.

15. This is my own translation simply to rough out the literalist sense.
16. This is my own translation within the context of scholastic theory. In this sense it implies a certain commonsense realism, natural law theory, and the correlation of the natural and supernatural orders. Although John XXIII is not excluding spiritual discernment here, he is primarily alluding to a process of *natural* discernment available to all men. In such a context it is but a short step to a phenomenological reflection on the self as incarnate body-subject. In both scholasticism and phenomenology the discernment of authentic self-identity is a necessary, preliminary step toward understanding authentic *social* relationships. Both systems of thought rely heavily on an elemental sense of *empathy*. See F.A. Elliston, "Husserl's Phenomenology of Empathy," in Elliston and McCormick [1977], pp. 213–231. In the deliberative processes of Vatican II it is most fascinating to follow the conciliar reflection which starts from a base of empathy and by a process of consensus-formation gradually constitutes its *corporate* sense of the ecclesial self as incarnate body-subject (i.e., the People of God in *Lumen Gentium*).
17. See Abbott [1966], p. 707, emphasis added. The phrase, "reveals man to himself," will later appear in the pastoral constitution, *Gaudium et Spes*, #22; see Abbott [1966], p. 220. This is a dominant idea in the thought of Pope John Paul II. See Wojtyla [1980], pp. 75, 309; the encyclical, *Redemptor Hominis* in Carlen [1981], Vol. 5, #25, p. 251; and the following statement from Frossard [1984], p. 67: "When God reveals himself and faith accepts him, *it is man who sees himself revealed to himself and confirmed in his being as man and person.* " (Emphasis in text.)
18. The connatural knowledge understood here is primarily the type referring to natural ethics, although that referring to esthetics, art, and even mysticism is not excluded.
19. This is simply common Catholic doctrine. A good summary statement of this may be found in Abbott [1966], pp. 220–222: "Christ as the New Adam."
20. One reason why an influential segment of the bishops was interested in seeking such a rapproachment with phenomenology is that John's pastoral challenge easily leant itself to the way of subjectivity, by which we mean "an enrichment of faith [. . .] expressed in terms of consciousness and attitudes." See Wojtyla [1980], pp. 203–206. In such a context the Council became intent on, not new doctrinal definitions, but on a new style of doctrinal penetration (and development) with increased potential for a more contemporary catechesis, spiritual formation, and relevant witness (kerygma). The *enrichment* of the faith sought by the Council has to be understood in two ways:

    [. . .] as an enrichment of the content of faith in accordance with the Council's teaching, but also, originating from that content, an enrichment of the whole existence of the believing member of the Church. This enrichment of faith in the *objective* sense, constituting a new stage in the Church's advance towards the "fulness of divine truth," is at the same time an enrichment in the *subjective, human, existential sense*, and it is from the *latter* that realization of the Council is most to be hoped for.

    See Wojtyla [1980], p. 18: emphasis added. The context of the above statement is totally phenomenological. Consequently, "objective" signifies "a new [methodological] stage," etc., and "subjective" is self-explanatory.
21. See Carlen [1981], Vol. 5, #28, p. 140. In this paragraph Paul VI does not mention phenomenology or any of its derivatives by name, but he is obviously referring to them since they constituted the dominant academic mindstyle in Europe at that time.

22. See May [1967], p. 228, col. 2, middle.
23. See Feuerbach [1957], p. xli.
24. See Ricoeur [1967], p. 17.
25. For a brief but concise differentiation between intellectual history and the social history of ideas see Gay [1954], pp. ix–xi. John XXIII's sensitivity to social influence on ideas over the course of time is best displayed in *Pacem in Terris*. See Carlen [1981], Vol. 5, #159, p. 125.
26. This type of apparent complacency in the face of serious global problems may also be projected indirectly and unwittingly by focusing on doctrinal theory in such an academic way that pressing human problems become, in effect, secondary. In retrospect this may be one of the critical problems today of Vatican II as an ostensibly *pastoral* Council. See Cox [1984]. For the recent European historical background for this academic fixation and its pattern of concerns see Schoof [1970], and for three examples see Schillebeeckx [1967], Lindbeck [1970], and Bouyer [1982]. The inevitable logic of this fixation on the speculative may be found in Tracy, Küng, and Metz [1978].
27. The "mind of John XXIII" will not be completely clarified in this essay until Chapter 4: The Influence of *Pacem in Terris*.
28. See Abbott [1966], p. 705. Pope John's pastoral evaluation of the Church's Post-Tridentine development is reasonably accurate on a global scale if one employs purely institutional criteria. See Durant [1968], pp. 23–24. Under the surface, however, a complex intellectual problem with serious pastoral implications was festering, and no adequate institutional means had been developed to process these difficulties in a constructive way. By recasting Pope John's pastoral concerns as *theological* concerns according to the paradigm set by Trent and Vatican I the Roman Curia provided an opening whereby Vatican II became a battleground between the three major intellectual camps of Catholic theologians. These alignments were: (1) the neoscholasticism inspired by Leo XIII and favored by the Roman Curia; (2) Transcendental Thomism as developed in Northern Europe and best represented by such theologians as Rahner and Lonergan; and (3) historical theology represented mainly by scripture scholars and the Tübingen faculty of theology. The Transcendental Thomists and historical theologians are all familiar with phenomenological method (especially as used by Heidegger) and employ it in various ways. For the historical background of the Neo-Thomistic program see McCool [1977], esp. pp. 241–267. The central issue at the heart of this *theological* controversy is the legitimate nature and scope of theological (and ethical) pluralism in the Catholic Church. As this essay later hopes to show, the *pastoral* style of religious reflection used at Vatican II *bypassed this theoretical issue entirely*!
29. See Latin Text [1960–1961].
30. If we are to believe Gorresio [1970], pp. 255–256, Pope John assigned his secretary, Loris Capovilla, the task of making a large number of telephone calls to bishops arriving in Rome for the opening of the Council. The purpose of these calls was to inform the bishops about the Pope's true feelings regarding the way the Roman Curia had prepared for the Council.
31. The text of this broadcast may be found in Anderson [1965–1966], Vol. 1, pp. 18–21. The translation is not a good one, but the substance of the pope's social concerns is clear. One of the first to appreciate the significance of this broadcast was Bea [1967], p. 4. For a belated recognition of the importance of this broadcast see Cox [1984], pp. 110–111.

32. See Abbott [1966], pp. 3–7, esp. "Two Issues of Special Urgency Confront Us," pp. 5–6.
33. See Abbott [1966], p. 712. By 1977, however, Paul VI was sounding very much like a "prophet of gloom." See Nichols [1981], p. 51.
34. See Abbott [1966], p. 712.
35. See Abbott [1966], pp. 712–713. See also Footnote 37, *infra*.
36. See Cousins [1972].
37. This interpretation of Pope John's spiritual discernment process is shaped by ideas and valuejudgments made explicit only later in *Pacem in Terris*. See Carlen [1981], Vol. 5, pp. 107–129. This is in accord with our purpose of writing an intentional history of Pope John's conceptual development.
38. The sense of "non-technical" will go through a gradual change of meaning in this essay on its way to effectively achieving Husserl's peculiar type of first reduction, a *suspension of science*, in order to get insight into the (religious) life-world and its structures. In the first session of the Council the bishops interpreted John XXIII's opening speech as an exhortation to avoid the static conceptualism of scholasticism. See Vorgrimler [1967–1969], Vol. 1, pp. 108, 110. This rather wholesale reaction against (though really not an abandonment of) scholastic intellectualism freed the bishops from the rigid restrictions of the one "scientific" tradition most of them shared in common. This attitudinal change, however, necessitated more reliance on their personal experiential sense of their Catholic identity and on their "connatural knowledge" for prudential judgments regarding faith, morals and pastoral decisions. (The fuller implications of this break with their scholastic foundations will be taken up in the next chapter when we discuss the bishops' reflective process on the Sacred Liturgy.) Throughout the Council, however, the bishops had to cope with an on-going dilemma: i.e., the discrepancy between their pastoral intent and their doctrinal obligations. See Vorgrimler [1967–1969], Vol. 3, p. 169. In the document on Revelation (*Dei verbum*) the bishops' doctrinal reflection came face to face with the technical problems of historical methodology, which can serve here as an exemplary case for all the modern positive sciences. This difficulty was resolved by a further application of a *suspension of science* (i.e., historical science) in order to get needed insights into the religious life-world and its structures. As a matter of fact, however, this process was operative throughout the Council, although it only becomes most apparent with the suspension of the *positive* sciences in the document on Revelation. (See Chapter Ten of this essay.) Viewing the Council retrospectively, however, the key to this suspension of the sciences (both positive and philosophical) may be found in the centrality of the concept of *mysterium* (*sacramentum*), which is at the heart of the major conciliar documents on the Liturgy, Church, and Revelation. See Vorgrimler [1967–1969], Vol. 1, pp. 9–13, 111, 139–140; Vol. 3, pp. 171–172; Vol. 5, pp. 196–197, 220–221. Once it is grasped that the primary (reified) analogue of *mysterium* (*sacramentum*) is the Plan of God (see Vorgrimler [1967–1969], Vol. 1, p. 111) and that this Plan is perfectly "hominized" in the Word made flesh, then the exclusively religious nature of the Council's style of reflection becomes apparent and manifests the corporate consciousness of the ecclesial life-world.
39. One needs to be acquainted with scholasticism in its role of juridical interpretation to appreciate the complexities involved. However, a quick sense of this may be acquired by glancing at Morrisey [c. 1975] which lists nine types of documents typically issued by the Holy See. My essay focuses on the religious substance of Vatican II in order

to discern later what might be authentic post-conciliar goals and values, particularly as these may be reflected in the new code of canon law.

40. The challenge of this *pastoral* artistic enterprise is essentially given in *Humanae Salutis*. In this project, however, John XXIII's role approximated that of Husserl in esthetics: i.e., he laid out the theory of the enterprise, but its implementation was left to others. For example, John XXIII laid out the ontological relationship of act-object in *Humanae Salutis* in its first goal of renewal: to display the *efficiency* of the supernatural order in the temporal one. He also endorsed the path of subjectivity in his second goal of renewal: that this process enable men to discover *in themselves* their own nature, dignity, and end. What the Council did for John XXIII, Spiegelberg [1982], pp. 223– 233 suggests that Roman Ingarden (*q.v.* in bibliography) did for Husserl. In this context, however, three other sources may be profitably consulted: O'Meara [1981], Dufrenne [1973], and Landgrebe [1966], pp. 123–144: "The Philosophic Problem of Art."

41. The writer who displays the best practical grasp of this point is Wojtyla [1980], pp. 201 sq.

42. This topic is more extensively treated in Chapter 4 of this essay.

43. The key *philosophical* problem which Pope John imposed on the Council in its search for a more contemporary expression of doctrine is that for almost *six hundred years* the understanding of *integral* doctrine had been formulated in terms of the objectivist thought-categories of scholasticism. How does one move out of such a realist epistemology without precipitating the Church into absolute relativism?

44. See Abbott [1966], pp. 713–714.

45. For one such reaction from a rather mild philosopher see Maritain [1968], pp. 160–162. For all of his animosity toward the historical aberration of Integralism this did not prevent him from writing an important book, *Humanisme Intégral*. See Maritain [1973]. I employ "integralism" much in the same way as Maritain does and with no connection with the historical fanaticism at the turn of the century.

46. Doctrinal integralism, as employed here, has an intrinsic relationship to the fact and function of creeds in the history of Christianity. Objectively speaking, creed structures belief and is indicative of an ontology permeating the vertical and horizontal relationships consequent upon belief. For the essentially credal structure of Vatican II see Wojtyla [1980], pp. 36–41, 57 *et passim*. An intriguing phenomenological analysis of "The Creed as Expression of the Structure of Faith" may be found in Ratzinger [1969], pp. 56–64.

47. See Abbott [1966], p. 715. The basic thesis of this essay is that the 21st Ecumenical Council not merely drew upon "the effective and important wealth of juridical, liturgical, apostolic and administrative *experiences*," but made them the apriori emperical basis for its phenomenological analysis.

48. See O'Malley [1971], pp. 592–595. O'Malley's historical reductionism is essentially incapable of grasping the meaning of Vatican II, as his evaluation of the Council as a "revolution" indicates. See O'Malley [1983], pp. 393–395.

49. See Abbott [1966], p. 4. "We shall take pains so to present to the men of this age God's truth in its *integrity and purity* that they may understand it and gladly assent to it." (Emphasis added.)

50. See Abbott [1966], p. 715. In this quotation it is quite apparent Pope John is, in principle, endorsing *methodological flexibility* on the assumption it will not infringe on authentic doctrine. Although he does not yet know what that new method will be, he is entrusting this choice to the prudence and experience of the Council Fathers.

51. By implication this task is undertaken to meet the *authentic* needs of humanity, not its myths, preconceptions, assumptions, or wants. One of the notorious weaknesses of O'Malley [1983], pp. 392–393 is his uncritical acceptance of the new "historical consciousness." A comparable naive optimism is displayed by Cogley [1968]. For a more realistic outlook on critical historical method see E. Kasemann's remarks in Vorgrimler [1967–1969], Vol. 3, p. 193. In spite of the serene and irenic image projected by this opening speech John's pastoral intent is, in the reality of things, focused on the rather grim contemporary "crisis in human beings" described at the beginning of *Humanae Salutis*. See Abbott [1966], pp. 703–704.

52. See Abbott [1966], p. 719. John XXIII's efforts to promote the unity of mankind by way of Vatican II's religious undertakings have to be read in correlation with an important *socio-political* judgment which he expressed in *Pacem in Terris*:

> Today the universal common good presents us with problems which are world-wide in their dimensions; problems, therefore, which cannot be solved except by a public authority with power, organization and means co-extensive with these problems, and with a world-wide sphere of activity. Consequently the moral order itself demands the establishment of some such general form of public authority.

See Carlen [1981], Vol. 5, #137, p. 122. However, in an address in St. Peter's on June 3, 1960 – a year and a half before he wrote *Humanae Salutis* – the Holy Father developed the same idea out of the religious exigency of Catholicism itself:

> [. . .] This is now a principle that has entered into the spirit of everyone who belongs to the Holy Roman Church: that is, to be, and to consider oneself truly to be, by virtue of being Catholic, *a citizen of the whole world*, just as Jesus is the adored Saviour of the whole world: *Salvator Mundi*. This is a good exercise of true universality, which every Catholic should take note of and turn into a precept for the guidance of his own mind, and as a principle for his conduct in religious and social relations.

See Lercaro and De Rosa [1966], p. 119; emphasis added.

53. The implication of "The Bomb" have been reasonably well-handled by Schell [1982]. It is, however, merely the "tip of the iceberg" for today's global problems which involve population growth, ecology, poverty, economics, and a host of other problems. These have been discussed in such well-known works as Ward [1976], Mische [1977], and Brown [1981]. The distinctive contribution of John XXIII to the assessment of these global problems is the recognition that their humane solution could be achieved only by a *moral* renewal of mankind and the restoration of the natural and human order which he made the central focus of *Pacem in Terris*. See Carlen [1981], Vol. 5, #167–168, p. 126.

54. Reasonable query regarding the utopianism of John XXIII's religious renewal has surfaced in Lercaro and De Rosa [1966], p. 25 and Zizola [1978], esp. pp. 363–370. For a balanced Catholic appraisal of this in the post conciliar era see Gremillion [1976], #37, p. 502 and #138–139, p. 555. The "new realism" of Christian morality in contrast to the "crackpot realism" of self-centered materialism is discussed in Schumacher [1973], pp. 293–297. Schumacher is a significant modern example of a man who over a lifetime grew into the spiritual and pastoral sense of Vatican II without ever realizing it. His life may be found in Wood [1984].

55. See Cox [1984], pp. 138–145, 159–169.

CHAPTER 3

THE DEVELOPING CONSCIOUSNESS OF THE BISHOPS IN COUNCIL

As is well known, on October 13th, two days after John's opening speech, the majority of the bishops by an adroit parliamentary maneuver wrested effective control of the Council out of the hands of the Roman Curia.[1] Of necessity the Curia is a quite internationalminded body when it comes to the flux of human relationships involved in political diplomacy and the tactics of survival in a secular, if not hostile, world. For the pastoral thrust of the Council to have fallen into the hands of men preoccupied with local needs and the decentraliz- ation of authority implied by collegiality and subsidiarity need not be viewed as any great leap forward to "that unity of mankind," requested by John XXIII.[2] The bishops did, however, understand and endorse the ideal of renewal which the pope presented to them in his opening speech. It should come as no surprise that they initially appropriated it in the narrowly religious, abstract, and ahis- torical way in which he presented it. By "ahistorical" I mean divorced from contemporary, secular global history. In such a context Vatican II suffered an overload of *religious* history: i.e., two thousand years of a developing historical consciousness, the strains of critical historical method, and the internal parochial concerns of Northern European pastors and theologians since the turn of the century.[3]

Religious over-focus in need of redemption

Since the reign of St. Pope Pius X no pastoral topic in the Church has received more professional and religious attention than that of the Liturgy.[4] Somewhat naturally, then, the bishops placed this topic first on the agenda of the Council. While dealing with this exclusively Catholic and very spiritual subject-matter, some of their religious over-focus managed to find its way into the opening paragraph of the document on the Liturgy:

> It is the goal of this most sacred Council to intensify the daily growth of Catholics in Christian living; to make more responsive to the require- ments of our times those Church observances which are open to adap- tation; to nurture whatever can contribute to the unity of all who believe in Christ; and to strengthen those aspects of the Church which can help

summon all of mankind into her embrace. Hence, the Council has special reasons for judging it a duty to provide for the renewal and fostering of the liturgy.[5]

This goal-statement, formulated in the abstract as a spiritual and human enrichment program for the faithful, cannot be faulted as a theoretical religious statement. But it lacks any sense of urgency or special pertinence to our critical era. The values expressed are more typically those of the priest and the levite rather than those of the Good Samaritan. (Cf. Lk. 10:31–32) Near the end of the Council an attempt to reintroduce the topic of the liturgy into "The Church in the Modern World" failed; had this move succeeded, perhaps the above-mentioned imbalance might have been rectified. In the structural logic of the Council, as this essay later hopes to make clear, the Constitution on the Liturgy is one of the documents which should have been formulated near the end. Instead, it became the consensus-formation vehicle of the bishops as they moved toward the mature methodology which would ultimately shape the Council's thought. The above goal-formulation does, however, have a saving grace. Any religious reflection intent on the authentic values modeled by the life of Christ has a built-in exigency, or "dialectic of return," to be incarnated in the realities of human existence. Just what those realities are in today's world would constitute, as the Council progressed, the supreme challenge for the bishops' spiritual discernment and growth in consciousness.[6] Once we appreciate this point, then the conciliar style of reflection – so akin to contemplation in its "over-spiritualized" tendencies – starts to assume an understandable pattern.

From the ahistorical to anamnesis

The above style of reflection can not only abstract from contemporary history, but also from past history as we commonly view it.[7] Any profound religious reflection has this tendency to abandon, or at least suspend, profane time for a much more exalted view of the historical process. This tendency was not immediately apparent during the first session, but Oscar Cullmann, a Protestant observer, noticed one of its more obvious side-effects during the second session.[8] Anyone familiar with modern critical historical method would be prone to notice this anomaly in the conciliar style of reflection. What seems to be a somewhat less-than-careful use of historical source material need not be a necessary adjunct to the formulation of conciliar thought. However, care for the historical accuracy of religious source materials is really a specialized discipline distinct from the analytical and genetic style of reflection employed by Vatican II. (What is under development here is a rerun of the Husserl-Dilthey controversy.) Cullmann, a renowned scripture scholar, is high in his praise of how the liturgy document draws its inspiration from biblical sources.[9] But what is his surprise when the *De Ecclesia* document seems to be a tissue of *proof texts* "added as after-thoughts in order to establish a rather exterior relation between a pre-fabricated schema and the bible."[10] Evidently a new dimension of the conciliar style of reflection is now manifesting itself here, and Cullmann with a scholar's preoccupation with technical, historical methodology seems to be missing the important transformation which has taken place. The pastoral reflective process, grounded as it may be in an ancient historical experience, now seems to rise superior to the primitive empirical data as critically retrieved, uses it largely as a supplementary adjunct, and factually dominates it for larger religious purposes. Somehow the reflective process has metamorphosed into a *transhistorical* one!

This bishops' extended reflection on the liturgical constitution must have been a quite liberating experience for the vast majority of them. As they groped for a "doctrinal penetration and a formation of consciousness" adequate to their pastoral concerns, they entered the world of Christ's Paschal Mystery i.e., they returned to the primordial ontology at the heart of the Church's historical consciousness.[11] This is the realm of Sacramental Time, where past, present, and future fuse into an "eternal now." Here profane chronological time has no meaning except in terms of the *economy of salvation*, God's Plan hidden from all eternity. (Cf. Eph. 3:5–11) This is the realm of the primordial "salvation history" whose successive events are intelligible only as orchestrated by messianism, redemption, and eschatology.[12] One enters this world not by subjective memory or by merely recalling it psychologically, but by way of *anamnesis.*[13] This means that by way of Word, Sacrament, and Prayer the conciliar effort at pastoral reflection was transformed gradually into an "objective memorial directed Godward, releasing Christ's personality and power afresh."[14] Implied in the very process is "an experience of a fellowship with Christ" in his eternal Paschal Mystery.[15] Such an experiential awareness is something distinctively and exclusively characteristic of the religious life-world of Catholics and Orthodox Christians. Since at this point the bishops are now judging things primarily on the basis of their connatural knowledge as holy people and mystics do, they are formulating an *Erlebnis* theology of the Church (i.e., an *experiential* theology with strong conceptual overtones),[16] rather than one with a non-cognitive tonality and more properly to be called existential.[17] It may be called an "existential" theology, if by that we mean the type of reflection whereby we *commit* ourselves to a certain interpretation of the "sense" of experience as it presents itself to us.[18] As a corporate group, then, the bishops are, in effect, composing their own and the modern Church's *Journal of a Soul*.[19] From this point on at least, pastoral reflection at the Council is quite evidently a loving celebration of Christ's living presence in the Church.

Pastoral reflection and theological safeguards

In spite of Cullmann's warranted technical observations we must not rashly conclude that the bishops' handling of the sacred scripture was either casual or non-theological. A legion of professional theologians was on hand to prevent that, and I will discuss the technicalities of this issue in Chapter Ten dealing with the document on Revelation. The point is that the bishops were not intent on analysing the contents of the bible as critically retrieved by historical method, but on analysing the contents of their own Christian experience. Their critical, historical accuracy here somewhat resembles a fond husband's recall of his wife's old love letters. As mentioned in the last chapter, the bishops were doing in a careful and prayerful way what the apostles did after Pentecost: recalling their personal memories of fellowship with Christ, organizing them in a pastoral way to preach the Good News, and thus serve the needs of the faithful. By doing this in a corporate and collaborative way the bishops were manifesting the historical consciousness of the modern Church, today's memory of the Risen Christ vitally alive in the midst of humanity. As a *living* memory this is ordered, proportioned, integrated, and three-dimensional. Karl Pribram would describe it as a "holographic memory."[20] As a *healthy* memory, there is operative in it a certain homeostasis, or vital balance:[21] formally, that would be the Holy Spirit (cf. Jn. 14:25 sq.) and, materially, the resulting religious ontology, the teleological-historical coherence, which his influence structures and maintains.[22] The operative axiom throughout this whole reflective process is that of doctrinal integralism.

The pastoral reflective process and phenomenology

The pastoral reflective process, just discussed, at this stage shows some interesting similarities to phenomenology and some differences. *The similarities*: (1) The bishops, as an intersubjective community, are reflecting on their corporate life-world. (2) They are applying Husserl's "Back to the things themselves," and not the technical *resourcement* of the theologians with its heavy reliance on critical historical method. (3) The objects, derived from a religious faith, have phenomenological legitimacy even though belief about their reality in the external, material order has been suspended.[23] (4) The purpose of the reflection is not scientific clarification for its own sake (e.g., early Husserl) but renewal (e.g., later Husserl). (5) This life-world is permeated with a universal teleology.[24] (6) A complex christocentric (i.e., hominized) type of intentionality seems to be operative on three levels: i.e., toward the Glorified Christ, towards human dispositions/acts with an obediential potency to mirror Christ, and toward signs/symbols apt to correlate dimensions of Christ to human beings. (It is in this last area, as part of structuring a communication process, that the Council will achieve one of its most creative breakthroughs.)[25] *The differences*: (1) Since the technical thematization of the bishops' reflections is done by the theological commissions of the Council, all descriptive and analytical techniques are used in a corporate way, rather than as typically used by individual phenomenologists.[26] (2) An analogous concept of being is operative, rather than the univocal one customarily understood by phenomenologists.[27] (3) The religious ontology of the Council involves a hermeneutics of temporality and historicity differing from that of most philosophical phenomenologists. (4) The affectivity of connatural knowledge has an important role in shaping the mode of phenomenological constitution.[28] This quick sketch has been offered here for two reasons. First, to sensitize the reader to the somewhat natural alignment inherent in the phenomenological style of reflection and that employed by the Council. Secondly, to suggest to professional phenomenologists that Vatican II may offer some new horizons for their methodological considerations.

Of all the points mentioned above, the role of a religious ontology as the stable backdrop for pastoral reflection at the Council needs the most emphasis. Unlike Heidegger or Merleau-Ponty the bishops were not searching for an ontology;[29] they were searching for ways of making it practically effective in the modern world. On one occasion, however, their flexibility of expression seemed to compromise an aspect of this ontology. This occurred on November 14, 1964, when Paul VI felt obliged to demand an "authentic" (i.e., technically correct) interpretation be given specific points in *Lumen Gentium* (Dogmatic Constitution on the Church) *before* its final vote by the bishops.[30] The following principle was at stake: "Without hierarchical communion, the sacramental-ontological office [of a bishop], as distinct from its canonical-juridical aspect, *cannot* be exercised."[31] This is not the only time Paul VI displayed his solicitude in this regard. When a significant number of the bishops at the Council seemed intent on demanding a *technical* review of the birth-control issue, Paul VI withdrew the topic from the essentially *pastoral* agenda and gave it to a special commission for technical review.[32] Lastly, on June 30, 1968, he promulgated the *Credo of the People of God* at the solemn closing of the Year of Faith.[33]

In this way he was trying to lace the Council's "new" description of the Church into the ancient credal (ontological) tradition of Christianity. The common denominator rendering all these actions of the pope intelligible is his solicitude for doctrinal integralism: i.e., the religious ontology or coherent intellectual system ordering Catholic religious truths and values.[34]

The ongoing development of the Council's methodology

Within such a clearly defined context and within the religio-social scope of its reflection Vatican II provides us with a very fine demonstration-model for a study in *pure methodology*. When I say "methodology" here, I am simply objectifying or reifying the extraordinarily complex, yet controlled, approaches which the human mind can take to any reality under consideration. By implication I am also suggesting that the notion of intentionality presented by scholastic and phenomenological writers is far more complex than these authors ordinarily imply. The methodology finally achieved at the Council was elaborated only with great difficulty. Even today it is still poorly understood. Up to this point we have seen it develop in, at first, an abstract and ahistorical way, then suddenly metamorphose into a transhistorical style of reflection. We know from *Humanae Salutis*, however, that John XXIII originally viewed his pastoral renewal program within the specific context provided by the modern world's global crises, although in his opening speech at the Council he, for some reason, chose not to focus on such problems.

At the present time, consequently, I would like to resume our reflection on the ongoing development of the Council's methodology since its fully matured form is not yet apparent. Two important factors, both of Johannine inspiration, contributed to its completed form. The first was the distinction, *ad intra/ad extra*, formulated prior to the Council but not consciously appropriated by the bishops until toward the end of the first session. The second was, of course, the great encyclical, *Pacem in Terris*, issued by John XXIII on April 12, 1963. The discussion of the *ad intra/ad extra* distinction will round out this chapter, and *Pacem in Terris* will be the topic of the next chapter. In discussing both of these Johannine influences I intend to treat their sometimes complex historical background in only a brief way. The burden of such details will be borne by the footnotes. In following this procedure I hope to be able to focus rather exclusively on the important contribution these two factors made to the conciliar methodology.

The *ad intra/ad extra* distinction

In his important radio address of September 11, 1962, John XXIII first employed the *ad intra/ad extra* distinction relative to the forthcoming work of the Council.[35] Canon Charles Moeller quotes the pertinent text and lists some of the topics about which the Holy Father was concerned:

> "The Church must be sought as it is both in its internal structure – its vitality *ad intra* – in the act of representing, above all to its sons, the treasures of illuminating faith and of sanctifying grace . . . . Regarded in relation to its vitality *ad extra*, that is to say the Church in face of the demands and needs of the nations ... feels it must honour its responsibilities by its teaching: *sic transire per bona terrena ut non amittamus aeterna.*" A list follows of some of the problems which will form the essentials of *Gaudium et Spes* [i.e., Pastoral Constitution of the Church in the Modern World]: the fundamental equality of all nations in the exercise of their rights and duties; defence of the sanctity of marriage; social responsibility; the underdeveloped countries, where the Church must show itself to be the Church of all, and especially of the poor; disorders of social life; the right to religious freedom; peace between nations.[36]

It took a great deal of caucasing by many bishops to get the social dimension of religion once again to the forefront of conciliar reflection. The intense involvement of the majority of the bishops with such an overtly religious and parochially practical topic, such as the liturgy, exposed them to falling into an excessive "spiritualism" typical of such introverted reflection. Not until late in the first session was there a breakthrough by the more social-minded bishops.[37] Here is how Canon Moeller sums up the scene:

> On 4 December, [1962], Cardinal Suenens made a speech proposing to group the schema round two poles: *ad intra, ad extra*; this won the approval of the Council fathers. The next day Cardinal Montini emphasized the bond between Christ and the Church and went on to express his own agreement with the proposed schema on the Church and the world. On 6 December, Cardinal Lercaro emphatically insisted on the necessity of speaking about the Church of the poor.[38]

The dialectical implications of this distinction

As presented above, the *ad intra/ad extra* distinction seems to be simply a handy way to organize a multitude of ideas swarming around the theme of the Church both in itself and in the modern world. But there is *already operative* at the Council a double dynamic which will breathe life into this distinction and transform it into a spiritual dialectic.[39] Any christocentric truth or value of Catholic doctrine operates in a bipolar field of theocentric and anthropocentric relationships: this is the basis for the biblical commandment of love of God and neighbor. An aspect of this interrelationship was expressed by Montini's emphasis on *Logos* immediately correlated by Lercaro's emphasis on Shepherd.[40] Both are biblical themes, and salvationhistory becomes unintelligible if we omit God's concern for the *anawim*.[41] From such a "natural" correlation and exigency derive the two great models of theocentric holiness: Mary (christocentric) and Martha (anthropocentric). The second dynamic is the pastoral mindset operative in the majority as *local* bishops: i.e., *pontifices* or "bridgebuilders" between two worlds, theologizing either to enrich the lives of their people back home or to serve their needs.[42] *In foro concilii populus ore episcopi et corde loquitur.* This would especially be the case for bishops being guided by the sensitivity and affectivity provided by connatural knowledge. Out of this factual confluence of religious ontology and dialogue, both with their built-in dialectic, there will arise in the historical consciousness of the bishops their practical sense of *communio*: i.e., a "co-presence" with the living Christ, with their people, and among themselves. This vital unity of minds and lives may be called "realized" intersubjectivity. On this foundation there will follow a further outreach to other Christians and humanity as a whole.

Summary

This chapter has reviewed the ongoing development of the bishops' reflective process at the Council. In the beginning it seemed quite over-focused on spiritual matters. With time this mode of reflection became transhistorical, involving anamnesis and a different outlook on temporality as commonly understood by men today. As radicated in such a transcendent religious life-world, the endproduct of such reflection might better be called an *Erlebnis* theology rather than an existential one. Professional theologians at the Council kept this theology from wandering beyond the confines of academic responsibility, and after he became pope, Paul VI was vigilant about its ontological moorings. Although the reflective process had not yet reached its full maturity, we pointed out its similarities and differences with phenomenological methodology at this stage of our discussion.

After mentioning that Vatican II provides a good demonstration-model for a study of pure methodology, we introduced the next important development in the conciliar mode of religious reflection: i.e., the *ad intra/ad extra* distinction. Although originally introduced merely as a convenient cataloguing device, we began to appreciate its potential as an ongoing dialectic recapitulating all the dynamic intellectual forces operative at the Council.

The next chapter will deal with the impact of *Pacem in Terris* on the continuing development of the Council's method of religious reflection.

NOTES

1. See Wiltgen [1978], pp. 15–19. For a very perceptive socio-cultural analysis correlating this Vatican II "revolt" against the curial power structure with the Berkeley student riots see Drucker [1971], pp. 101–102.

2. For some sound observations on this point from the theological view of *communio* see Kress [1967], p. 123: "Sacrament of Communio."

3. At this early stage of the Council it is quite evident that the intellectual leadership is dominated by bishops and theologians from what is called the "European Alliance." See Wiltgen [1978], pp. 15–19, 65, 80 *et passim*. The most respectable formulation of this mindset of which I would be aware is Walgrave [1972], pp. 13–16. Some sort of organized opposition to this dominance did not develop until the third session (1964). See Wiltgen [1978], pp. 148–150. My negative remarks here should be interpreted within the context of the *early* stage of the Council. As this essay continues, the reader will have an opportunity to study the growth in consciousness which all the bishops underwent in the course of the Council.

4. For a compact history of liturgical reflection since the turn of the century see J.A. Jungmann, "Constitution on the Sacred Liturgy" in Vorgrimler [1967–1969], Vol. 1, pp. 1–8. The historical context in which the modern liturgical movement began and its search for adequate principles of renewal are well handled in Franklin [1975], [1976], [1977], [1979]. Some of the complex involvements of the twentieth-century movement may be found in Quitslund [1973].

5. See Abbott [1966], #1, p. 137. Jungmann's commentary on articles 1–2 of this constitution in Vorgrimler [1967–1969], Vol. 1, pp. 8–9, briefly presents a balanced interpretation of this text as understood at that time. Although the constitution on the liturgy was composed prior to *Lumen Gentium* and *Dei verbum*, it must be interpreted within their larger doctrinal framework and phenomenological structure. Assuming, for a moment, that *all* of Vatican II's documents can be integrated into a coherent religious paradigm, there is a larger background problem which we must never forget: How does this structuring of religious truths relate to the *ultimate practical goal* of the Council which John XXIII formulated in *Humanae Salutis*?

6. This topic has been well handled by Canon Charles Moeller in Vorgrimler [1967–1969], Vol. 5, esp. pp. 8–12. Murnion [1984] manifests a maturing consciousness

in the U.S. regarding the relationship between the problems of today's world and liturgy.

7. From a phenomenological (and retrospective) point of view this is the first manifest example at the Council of the suspension of a "science" (i.e., modern historiography). The reduction of scholastic methodology, alluded to the previous chapter, might be more properly classified as a philosophical reduction, if only on the basis of the prescientific origins of scholasticism. One of the reasons this "first reduction" largely went unnoticed during the early stages of the Council was due to a widespread *academic assumption*: so much historical study had been done in the field of liturgy that the conciliar reflections were interpreted as the direct outgrowth of that historical research. The living consciousness of the Church, however, transcends its empirical historical antecedents. Vatican II was not an academic but a *pastoral* council. The bishops there were intent on the transcendent realities symbolized by the liturgical phenomena, and they were operating out of a mindset which in America we would tend to describe as "symbolic realism." In this outlook there are — in addition to the "objective symbols" of the empirical sciences — another whole category of "nonobjective symbols": i.e., symbols

that express the feelings, values, and hopes of subjects, or that organize and regulate the flow of interaction between subjects and objects, or that attempt to sum up the whole subject-object complex or even point to the context or ground of that whole. These symbols, too, express reality and are not reducible to empirical propositions.

See Robert N. Bellah, "Between Religion and Social Science" in Caporale and Grumelli [1971], p. 288. Access to this *religious* level of reality is not available by way either of subjective or objective "scientific" knowledge. One enters this primordial religious world only by assuming a distinctively different time-consciousness with its accompanying attitudinal stance known as *anamnesis*. Further attention will be given to each of these ideas as they appear in the course of this chapter.

8. See Cullmann [1964].

9. See Cullmann [1964], p. 249. Cullmann belongs to the tradition of "historical realism." See Robert N. Bellah in Caporale and Grumelli [1971], p. 282. This historicist mindset is basically a form of psychological reductionism.

10. See Cullmann [1964], p. 249. It goes without saying that because of the extreme importance of the *De Ecclesia* document (i.e., *Lumen Gentium*) to the central ideas of the Second Vatican Council, far more care was exercised on its use of scripture than ever given to the document on the Liturgy.

11. In Vatican II's Constitution on the Liturgy the Paschal Mystery (i.e., the Glorified Christ, liturgically viewed as vitally operative under the threefold dimension of his death, resurrection, and ascension) is treated in relationship to: (a) the history of salvation (i.e., God's Plan), #5; (b) the celebration of liturgy, #6; (c) sacraments and sacramentals, #61; and (d) the celebration of the saints, #104. See Abbott [1966], pp. 139–140, 158, 168. "For it is through the liturgy, *especially the divine Eucharistic Sacrifice*, that 'the work of our redemption is exercised'." See Abbott [1966], #2, p. 137, emphasis added.

12. On Sacramental Time-Consciousness see Excursus II.

13. On "anamnesis" see Excursus II.

14. See Brunner [1967], p. 476. On "The Communion of Life" see Excursus II.

15. See Brunner [1967], p. 476.
16. *Erlebnis* ("experience") is a word with rich historical connotations, especially since the period of the German Romantic Enlightenment. In the context of the social history of ideas Peter Gay remarks: "The Germans, noting the intimate relation of experience to poetry in Goethe, called him their *Erlebnisdichter. Voltaire was an Erlebnispolitiker.*" Gay [1954], p. 60. In this same sense Pope John XXIII was an *Erlebnistheolog.* How the historical reflection of German Romanticism influenced thinking on the nature of the Church has been well-treated by O'Meara [1982]. This strain of *erlebnis*-thinking derived from Schelling, whereas by mid-twentieth-century Husserl had opened a whole new development radicated in *Erlebnisse* (concrete experiences). See Carr [1974], p. 8 sq. How this style of thinking infiltrated into Vatican II may be found in Excursus III. Unlike the Schelling-Husserl genesis of *erlebnis*-thinking, Vatican II is not the product of any one great thinker, but an expression of the *corporate* experience of the bishops. In the collision at Vatican II of scholasticism, historical experientialism (as described above), and phenomenology only the strong ontological convictions of Catholic thought could have held such disparate tendencies in any collaborative working-order. The burden of this task, both during and after the Council, fell most heavily on the shoulders of Paul VI, as this book hopes to make clear.
17. The Sartrean type of existentialism would be the primary example of this non-cognitive tendency, but the issue is much broader than Sartre. See Barrett [1962], Mounier [1948], pp. 23–24, and Rieff [1966], esp. p. 9. One of the most concise differentiations between existentialism and phenomenology is that provided by Gary B. Madison in Elliston and McCormick [1977], p. 257:

> What the "existentialist" experiences in wonder is the *fact* of the world's being, the world's *facticity*, and he experiences this fact as something fundamentally *opaque*. For Husserl, however, as for rationalism in general, the fact is essentially *transparent*; the fact is but an *instance*, an exemplification of a universal law or *essence* which is the task of reason to uncover and lay bare. It is impossible for a rationalist, for one looking for the *essence* or nature of something, ever to fully recognize what an "existentialist" calls the "facticity of the fact," for to do so would require abandoning the goal of science, which can exist only so long as one presupposes the intelligibility, the "essentiality," of what-is. Husserl thus naturally maintains that "all the rationality of the fact lies, after all, in the apriori." He says: "'Fact,' with its '*irrationality*,' is itself *a structural concept within the system of the concrete apriori.*" Or, as Berger said in his exposition of Husserl's philosophy: "*Fact* in its very opacity and in its historicity is still – just like nothingness or the absurd – a constituted reality." And even more concisely: "There is no radical unintelligible."

18. See Mounier [1948], pp. 55–60: "The Concept of Personal Conversion."
19. See John XXIII [1965]. The type of religious journal reflected by the major documents of Vatican II seems to be a quite sophisticated one. For example, the fact that the bishops' experiential sense of *communio* at the Council first grew out of their shared reflection on liturgical symbolism and its inherent *telos* to shape the ecclesial community raises a number of important points which may be clarified only as this essay develops. (1) The bishops' reflection on traditional religious symbolism (i.e., both as word and sacrament) may be the most decisive factor shaping the development of conciliar thought and provide a pastorally oriented topology of the corporate Catholic consciousness. (2) In such an essentially contemplative process modern advances in

academic theology or historical research would have only an extrinsic, ministerial role in safeguarding the process from error. (3) This topology, as shaped by pastoral purposes, would be a functional one, but developed out of the primordial ontology structuring the life-world of the Church. (4) The topological changes in the corporate consciousness of the Church, as endorsed at Vatican II, seem to provide the elements for constructing a field theory of the ecclesial consciousness. (5) This field theory would deal with two complimentary dimensions of the Church's consciousness: *ad intra*, the inherently religious noetic field, and *ad extra*, the social field. (6) The corporate religious consciousness, viewed *ad intra*, is really a bipolar field with a subjective pole (*Lumen Gentium*) and an objective pole (*Dei Verbum*). (7) In the *ad extra*, social field the Roman Catholic Church as a corporate entity has a missionary *telos* which orients her to be a religious *ecumene* transcending the limited social fields of consciousness associated with culturally or otherwise restricted local churches. For collateral reading see Voegelin [1978], pp. 200–205, and Caporale and Grumelli [1971], pp. 286–295.

20. See Pribram and Goleman [1979].

21. The concept of homeostasis, originally developed by Claude Bernard as a physiological idea, was popularized in America by Cannon [1932]. The concept has since been constructively applied in psychology. See index references in Menninger [1963] and Frankl [1967]. The concept is anything but a static one, and in this book should be viewed as a preliminary step in introducing the *isomorphic* character of human consciousness.

22. The role of the Holy Spirit is well-known in Catholic theology and was obviously part of the thinking at Vatican II. See index references in Wojtyla [1980]. For the *humanistic* appreciation of the role of Christ's Spirit and contemporary reality see Royce [1968]. This latter work should be read in relationship to the pastoral goals set by Pope John XXIII for Vatican II.

23. "Phenomena are objects of intentional acts. 'Objects' here are not taken as real entities or events; they are whatever present themselves by way of the acts of perception." See Natanson [1973a], p. 13.

24. See E. Husserl, "Universal Teleology," in McCormick and Elliston [1981], pp. 335–337.

25. This essay will discuss this point more extensively in Chapter 8: "The New Ecclesial Hermeneutics."

26. Whether the vast majority of the bishops were aware that the phenomenological method was being employed at the Council is a debateable issue. They knew they were employing a descriptive method avoiding, for the most part, the technical intellectualism associated with scholasticism. They also knew that this descriptive data was being redacted in a competent fashion by highly skilled bishops (e.g., Bea, Montini, Wojtyla, etc.) and theologians (e.g., Rahner, Congar, de Lubac, etc.), who also conducted informative seminars and discussion-groups to keep the bishops abreast of what was going on. It is somewhat difficult to believe that this phenomenological style of reflection was not public knowledge. While the fact may have been known and taken for granted, there is little indication that the vast majority of the bishops had any real appreciation of the practical implications of this new style of theologizing. It goes without saying, of course, that the redaction of the commissions is done in a way that does not seriously contravene or undercut the traditional scholastic formularies of previous Councils. This had to be, since – as in all previous Councils – much of the discussion at Vatican II was focused on consensus-building among the bishops. See

Ratzinger's observations in Vorgrimler [1967–1969], Vol. III, pp. 159–164. Late in the Council, however, when the bishops dealt with the Church in the Modern World (*Gaudium et Spes*), it was fairly general knowledge that phenomenology had shaped its formulation of ideas. See Miller [1966], p. 429. Some of this development should be more understandable after the next chapter dealing with *Pacem in Terris*.

27. Inasmuch as philosophical phenomenology focuses on human consciousness, or human being, its understanding of being is typically univocal, whereas in Catholic theology which deals with the correlation of the natural and supernatural orders the notion is typically analogous.

28. Although Vatican II has a rich conceptual content, the selection and orchestration of this content are shaped by the broad *pastoral* needs of the Church as appreciated by the bishops. Such pastoral needs, in turn, strongly influenced the affective and volitional basis on which the bishops connatural knowledge was operative.

29. See Spiegelberg [1982], pp. 401–407, 574–580.

30. See Ratzinger, "Announcements and Prefatory Notes of Explanation" in Vorgrimler [1967–1969], Vol. I, pp. 297–305.

31. See Abbott [1966], p. 101. For this "ontological" view as applied to the whole Church see John Paul II, *Redemptor Hominis*, #87 in Carlen [1981], Vol. 5, p. 268.

32. See Paul VI, "The Year Behind and the Year Ahead." (June 23, 1964) *The Pope Speaks* 9:4 (Spring-Summer, 1964), esp. pp. 355–356. See also Paul VI, "The Genesis of 'Humanae Vitae'." *The Pope Speaks* 13:3 (Summer-Autumn, 1968) 206–210.

33. See Paul VI, "The Credo of the People of God." *The Pope Speaks* 13:3 (Summer-Autumn, 1968) 273–282.

34. It is readily admitted that Pope Paul VI worked out of a strongly objectivist mindset. This topic will be discussed at some length early in Chapter 5 of this essay.

35. The *ad intra/ad extra* distinction was originally formulated by Cardinal Suenens in 1956 in a book later published in English as *The Gospel to Every Creature*. Preface by Cardinal Montini. Westminster: Newman Press, 1965, p. 4. For the further history of how the ideas of Cardinal Suenens and his distinction found their way into the September 11, 1962, radio broadcast of John XXIII see Charles Moeller's brief history in Vorgrimler [1967–1969], Vol. V, p. 8. The English translation made available at the time of the broadcast is not clear in its translation of the *ad intra/ad extra* distinction. See Anderson [1965–1966], Vol. 1, p. 19. The same translation appeared in *The Irish Ecclesiastical Record* 98 (Oct., 1962) 149–155. Hence, the need to quote from Canon Moeller's clearer text.

36. See Vorgrimler [1967–1969], Vol. 5, p. 8. Pope John XXIII, as we may recall, spoke glowingly of the "Present Vitality of the Church" in *Humanae Salutis*. See Abbott [1966], pp. 704–705. In the same apostolic constitution, however, the pastoral challenge was to display the *efficiency* of this vitality *ad extra* in the *temporal* order. See Abbott [1966], p. 706. How all these ideas factually coalesced in the first session of the Council to become a working unity may be found in Gerard Philips' History of the Dogmatic Constitution on the Church. See Vorgrimler [1967–1969], Vol. 1, esp. pp. 107–110. The first draft of the document on the Church was characterized by a certain "scientific reductionism" because it was formulated within the strictures of scholastic theology and the then-existent canonical mindset. See Bouyer [1982], pp. 164–166. The bishops, however, wanted the document to be more expressive of the spirit of the bible and the early Church Fathers. Worthy as this new move may have been, it too had its danger of falling into an "historical reductionism," such as

might have pleased Cullmann's tastes. As this essay hopes to show, the technique of the "scientific reduction" was employed at the Council to avoid both pitfalls.

37. See Vorgrimler [1967–1969], Vol. 5, pp. 10–11.
38. See Vorgrimler [1967–1969], Vol. 5, p. 11. The three speeches may be found in Latin Texts [1970–1980], Vol. 1, pars iv, pp. 222–227 (Suenens), pp. 291–294 (Montini), and pp. 327–330 (Lercaro). While these three speeches did much to focus the Council's train of thought, they did not immediately resolve the theoretical and pastoral issues under discussion. For the general contours of the debate see Vorgrimler [1967–1969], Vol. 1, pp. 107–110. It may be noted, however, that the pastoral challenge of Pope John XXIII is voiced in a' somewhat modified way by Cardinal Lercaro. He views the mission of the modern Church, its sanctifying role and the magisterium, in terms of a three-fold presence of Christ in the poor, in the eucharist, and in the hierarchy. As a precondition for authentic renewal the Council must formulate a tripodal ontological connection between these dynamic realities in order to present a unified presence of Christ in the historical actualities of modern human existence. This style of thinking, admirable as it may be, never developed beyond doctrinal penetration and kerygma. To this extent, Vatican II simply refined the strategic vision of John XXIII by way of further religious conceptualization and a preliminary statement of new apostolic directions. Much of the purpose of this essay is to clarify the fuller meanings of such ideas; possibly such spadework will be groundbreaking for some thought about a much-needed pastoral management theory.
39. See Excursus III: Concrete Human Relationships and Cardinal Suenens.
40. The bipolar dialectic inherent in this Logos-Shepherd complementarity left a distinctive stamp on the Conciliar style of reflection. In what amounts to a description (in religious terms) of the objectives of phenomenological method Ratzinger remarks in Vorgrimler [1967–1969], Vol. 1, p. 299:

[...] The Council has laid down no new dogma on any subject. But this does not mean that all the Council says is mere edification, binding no one. Its texts, according to their literary form, have serious claims upon the conscience of Catholics; their pastoral dispositions are based on doctrine, and their doctrinal passages are suffused in concern for men and for a Christianity of flesh and blood in the world of today. The Council is "pastoral" in its *fusion of truth and love*, "*doctrine*" *and pastoral solicitude*: it wished to reach beyond the dichotomy between pragmatism and doctrinalism, back to the biblical unity in which practice and doctrine are one, a unity grounded in Christ, who is both *Logos* and the Shepherd: as the *Logos* he is our Shepherd, and as our Shepherd he is the *Logos*. [Emphasis added.]

41. The term is customarily translated as "The Poor of Yahweh." See "Poor" in Léon-Dufour [1973], pp. 436–438.
42. No one has incorporated this sense of doctrinal penetration and kerygma into his integral understanding of the Council better than Wojtyla [1980], pp. 15–18.

CHAPTER 4

THE INFLUENCE OF *PACEM IN TERRIS*

The next great methodological influence on Vatican II after the *ad intra/ad extra* distinction was the encyclical, *Pacem in Terris*.[1] As mentioned previously, this was occasioned by the Cuban missile crisis, and the encyclical was issued between the first and second sessions of the Council. As his last great legacy to the Church, the pope returned to the problem of world peace which had been a major concern of his in both *Humanae Salutis* and the radio broadcast of September 11, 1962. Almost immediately this encyclical stirred up a good deal of positive public opinion on both sides of the Iron Curtain.[2] Two years later world opinion was brought to a focus at the United Nations where a "Symposium of world problems of peace in the light of the teaching of John XXIII in the Encyclical *Pacem in Terris*" was held, February 17–20, 1965. To my knowledge, the best commentary on this encyclical was issued on its tenth anniversary (April 11, 1973) by Cardinal Maurice Roy.[3] I have no intention here of repeating the observations of this very careful study. My purpose is far more limited: simply to *nuance* some of the cardinal's insights into the pope's unique methodology which has proven the most creative and lasting impact of the encyclical.

John XXIII's methodology and focus

In introducing John's methodology in its totality Cardinal Roy zeroes in on its pastoral originality as a *comparative* method correlating the spiritual and the empirical.[4] As in quantum physics, John's methodology and the workings of the larger religious ontology shaping his outlook are largely incomprehensible unless we recognize at work an important Principle of Complementarity.[5] In his encyclical John dealt with certain broad themes: nature, order, the interrelationship between truth, justice, love, and freedom, the role of the historical process, and the signs of the times. Included under one or another of these themes would be such important issue as: faith, reason and human nature; the dignity of man and universal human rights; God's eternal law and natural law; the connection between peace and development; and the convergence of global consensus and collective convictions. John's comparative method, accordingly,

brings these relevant events – or these well-established invariables – face
to face with Christian Revelation and the doctrinal tradition or teaching of
the Church. And it seeks to find, under the surface of the collective
phenomena observed, a certain searching for God.[6]

The phrase, "a certain searching for God," is the key to understanding John's
methodology in its integrity. None of the themes or issues, mentioned above,
"searches for God," only *men* do. This is not a precious distinction, but one
essential to comprehend what John is looking *at* and looking *for*. All of the
themes and issues, mentioned above, represent the mind's tendency to reify
or objectify what are really symptoms, or *indirect* indicators, of the human.
When Konrad Lorenz studies a nest, for example, this purely instinctual product
becomes intelligible only to the extent it tells him something about its maker,
the bird, which is the *direct* object of his observation. So, too, with John XXIII,
except that his religious vision focuses on two correlated objects. The first is
the Logos-Christ, the Everlasting Man. The second is human beings created
ontologically in the image of God and who are in the Second Creation, or
redemption, once again restored to this ontological order as more precisely
and concretely set by the Divine Paradigm of the Integrated Man, Christ the
New Adam.[7] Social systems, laws, ideologies, customs, products of technology
and art can only be *indirect* indicators of what is going on in human minds,
hearts and attitudes.[8] The same thing must also be said for the "signs of the
times," as indirect indicators of the human.[9] Human thoughts, actions, and
attitudes as correlating in one or another degree with the dispositions of Christ
are the proper object of the Holy Father's analysis. In such an analysis, we must
again emphasize, connatural knowledge plays a major role in the discernment
process.

The anthropology of John XXIII

Now Cardinal Roy is perfectly aware of the distinctions I am making, but occasionally his terminology does not make this clear. For example, he categorizes
the encyclical as a "phenomenology of peace."[10] Indeed, it is a phenomenology
inasmuch as it is based on empirical data, employs an analytical method, suspends the modern sciences, and arrives at a contemporary expression of eidetic
essences. The encyclical is, however, only indirectly a phenomenology of peace.
Directly it is a phenomenology of the twentieth-century *peacemaker*, which
sets John's reflections within the biblical context of the Beatitudes (cf. Mt. 5:9).[11]
His methodology, furthermore, is not merely analytical, but *analytico-genetic*

as rising to a meaningful, new synthesis of corporate human existence in the modern world.[12] Historically, this places John's reflections within the context of the "crisis in human beings." Again, Cardinal Roy is aware of all this, although he prefers to call attention to it by alluding to the encyclical's impact on *Gaudium et Spes*, the conciliar document on the Church in the Modern World:

> *Gaudium et Spes.* It is on *Gaudium et Spes* that the Encyclical exercised an undeniable influence. This is evident in the chapter devoted to war and peace (Part II, Chapter 5); but it is equally clear in the very inspiration and structure of this "pastoral constitution." In these two documents peace is not equated with the absence of war or with the techniques of coexistence or of development. It goes much further than the suppression of the causes of conflicts. It is an *anthropology*, a total vision of the human condition in the world today; it is a reflection on the personal and collective action of humanity that considers the paschal mystery and eschatology as the origin and end of peace.[13]

What the Cardinal is saying here, first of all, is that John's anthropology is the product of a phenomenological hermeneutics, but since the Holy Father's spiritual discernment is radicated in the paschal mystery (i.e., a religious ontology), his anthropology is also a theological hermeneutics.[14] In other words, Pope John is offering us a quite complex, split-level type of anthropology.[15] At both the religious and human levels it provides a "revelation of men to themselves,"[16] and as "a total vision of the human condition in the world today," it is also a Vision of Hope for all of mankind.[17] Since Pope John's analysis, however, is formulating a *proleptic* anthropology (i.e., one in an embryonic but developing form), Cardinal Roy is quite right to situate it within the perspective of religious eschatology. Again, this emphasizes that the Holy Father's spiritual discernment is radicated in the ontological time-frame of salvation history. But this anthropology, grounded as it also is in contemporary empirical data, likewise implies a split-level eschatology where religious and human eschatology complement one another and work in collaboration.[18] In such collaborative efforts the supernatural order is offered the opportunity to display its *efficiency* in the temporal order. To the extent John approves this new human ideal in the process of self-creation, he implies that its inherently wholesome dynamics should, if not irretrievably disrupted, arrive at a *realized* eschatology here on earth. In the modern world's crisis John XXIII discerns under actual development the ethical ideal which Josiah Royce discerned only in principle: man's distinctive capacity to transform an evil situation into an even *greater good* by his loyalty to truth and goodness and by the power of creative love.[19] This prospective resolution of the "crisis in human beings" incarnated for both Royce and Pope John the essential values of Christ's saving mission (i.e., the paschal mystery — in the less-than-satisfactory religious shorthand of Vatican II).[20]

John XXIII, Marx, and Teilhard

We should not miss an important historical allusion here. What Marx did for the nineteenth century, John XXIII was attempting for the twentieth. Both men, reflecting on the critical problems of their era, were intent on deciphering the dominant evolutionary dynamisms shaping mankind's historical process. At the speculative level each beheld a new *humanistic anthropology* under development in society, and this new psycho-social construct would provide the working myth, or paradigm, for mankind's future progress and development.[21] Marx drew his interpretive principles from the Enlightenment, and John from his religion. Both, however, were quite practical-minded men. They wanted to discover those working-principles whereby men could use the evolutionary process in a constructive way. However diverse their focus, each was intent on psycho-social renewal. Each was in search of a new anthropology, or science of man, which would serve as a demonstration-model for mankind as it moved into a future of growing complexity. Starting from a mechanistic conception of material evolution, Marx discerned in the prevalent economic structures of the industrialized societies a deterministic pattern leading to class warfare until a global classless society emerged. The fact of nuclear weaponry has made this scenario a highly dubious one today.[22] Starting with men made in the image of God, John discerns a new counter-cultural dynamic at work beneath the surface of the world's turmoil. It is a dialectic of truth and love, justice and freedom.[23] This dialectic, by implication, exemplifies the Principle of Complementarity operative at the heart of *communio*. This freely chosen dynamic, as assisted by God's grace and the work of the Church, will ultimately lead to the unity of mankind. The stance of both Marx and John, each in his unique way, intended to be both prophetic and sapiential.

The "missing link" between Marx and John XXIII was, in my estimation, the aborted religious effort of Pierre Teilhard de Chardin.[24] His "scientific" Grand Vision was grounded empirically in the evolutionary process of matter.[25] His phenomenological reflection on this experience was, however, the product of his connatural knowledge as priest-poet-mystic. Probably his greatest religious difficulty derived from the fact that he seemed to be constructing ontological hierarchy from the ground up. If not, then his major difficulty was essentially that of Galileo: while he had a legitimate idea, he lacked the capacity to explain it adequately in its religious context.[26] However, through his uniquely original writings Catholic thought — willingly and unwillingly — was exposed to some new horizons by his cosmotheandric paradigm of reality. This would be especially true for his insights into "the convergence of global consensus and collective convictions."[27] His writings constitutes a sort of *Menschheitgeschichte*: i.e., the cosmic process of hominization whereby the phenomenon of *man* rises to the transcendent *person*.[28] The following quotation from Teilhard's *The Vision of the Past* might easily have found a place either in *Pacem in Terris* or in John's opening speech at the Council:

> In us and around us, almost beneath our eyes, a psychological phenomenon of great magnitude is developing (born hardly a century ago!) which might be called: *the awakening of the sense of humanity*. In a positive sense, men began to feel themselves bound together, all united in a great task, and captivated, in an almost religious sense, by its progress. To know more, to be able to do more. Although many still take these words in a utilitarian sense, for the great majority they are already tinged with sacred value. In our days people constantly devote their lives to 'the progress of the world.' Thus in actions more substantial than any speculation they show their implicit recognition of the phenomenon of man.[29]

Vatican II as a strategic vision

While both Marx and John XXIII each had their own Grand Vision of the really real, they were not armchair theorists like Hegel, Feuerbach, or de Chardin. Both were men intent on the practical action necessary to accomplish the "great task," i.e., to make their Grand Vision a productive and functioning guide to men's lives. They were, accordingly, men of strategic vision. Marx authored *The Communist Manifesto* and *Das Kapital*, and founded the Communist Party. The Holy Father wrote *Mater et Magistra* and *Pacem in Terris*, and convoked the Second Vatican Council. These men well appreciated that axiom of John Naisbitt: "Strategic planning is worthless — unless there is first a strategic vision."[30] Men preoccupied with a strategic vision and its implementation do their work on the conviction, or assumption, that their Grand Vision is essentially valid and not to be questioned. This is an extremely important point if we are to comprehend the pastoral intent of John XXIII and the strategic work of adaptation carried out by the Council.[31] In this light John's opening speech at the Council, insisting on doctrinal integralism, is really stating a fundamental

precondition necessary for a pastoral adaptation to be *clearly understood* both
before and after such a strategic move. This would be doubly true if this discernment process involved the use of connatural knowledge, which approximates
a non-cognitive approach to reality. In every instance, then, the methodology
of the Council and its products stand under the judgment of the Grand Vision,
described by John XXIII as "the common patrimony" of the Church.[32] The
bishops, clearly in accord with the Holy Father's pastoral conception of the
Council, also understood his preconditions for it and endorsed doctrinal integralism in their "Message to Humanity."[33]

Summary

Pacem in Terris was a return to the problem of peace, which had been one of
John's major concerns prior to the Council. It also was the mature expression
of his pastoral goals and method. His focus in the encyclical was two-fold with
an implied hierarchy between the objects under consideration: on Christ and
on human behavior in correlation with this christocentric paradigm. This analysis
resulted in a theological hermeneutics best described as an anthropology of the
peacemaker. But as a phenomenologically derived anthropology, it acquaints
us with the split-level type of concepts peculiar to John's style of pastoral reflections: i.e., where the religious and human levels of existence are seen in a
complementary relationship and working in mutual collaboration. All of this
is a development of ideas originally only sketched in *Humanae Salutis*: i.e.,
the revelation of men to themselves and the contemporary opportunity for the
supernatural order to display its *efficiency* in the natural order. An historical
parallel is drawn between the work of Marx and John XXIII, and Teilhard de
Chardin is seen as something of a "missing link" in this conceptual history.
Since John's pastoral method, goals, and work are component parts of his
strategic vision for the Church and mankind, his undergirding doctrinal integralism is once again stressed. In spite of its seeming clarity this type of pastoral
reflection, especially when yoked with phenomenology, does have its ambiguities.
That is the topic of the next chapter.

NOTES

1. For the complete text see Carlen [1981], Vol. 5, pp. 107–129. A compact, journalistic history of the encyclical's origins may be found in Zizola [1978], pp. 11–24. The
   conciliar document on the Church in the Modern World (*Gaudium et Spes*) was influenced by the encyclical in many passages. See "Pacem in Terris" in the Subject

Index of Vorgrimler [1967–1968], Vol. 5, p. 405. The encyclical also influenced the Council's Declaration on Education and the Declaration on Religious Freedom, but to a lesser degree. See Vorgrimler [1967–1968], Vol. 4, pp. 45, 64, 72, 77. One of the best extended reflections on the development of Catholic social teaching from 1961 to 1975 is Gremillion [1976].

2. For the negative reaction in much of the Italian press see Zizola [1978], pp. 162–163, 173–180.

3. See Gremillion [1976], pp. 531–567.

4. See Gremillion [1976], #57, p. 542. Unlike scholasticism, which is for the most part deductive, John XXIII's comparative approach is "inductive," at least on its empirical side. See Gremillion [1976], #56, p. 542. However, the sense of induction in phenomenology must be carefully nuanced. See Merleau-Ponty in Natanson [1973b], Vol. 1, pp. 65, 76–81; Allen [1978], pp. 196–199; and Spiegelberg [1982], note 56, p. 155.

5. On the Principle of Complementarity see Teller [1980], pp. 105–107; Heisenberg [1971], pp. 79–81, 209–210. Jerome Bruner, the psychologist, tells the story of how Niels Bohr finally came to accept the Principle of Complementarity when faced with a personal *moral* dilemma: "Could you," [he said], "have both love and justice in the same psychological system?" See Miller [1983], p. 36. Recently, the International Theological Commission employed such complementarity in discussing the question: "What is the relationship between Christology and the problem of the revelation of God?" See *Theology, Christology, Anthropology.* Washington, DC: United States Catholic Conference, 1983. In Ladner [1959], pp. 433–442 his "Excursus II: Metahistorical Preconceptions" has a good reflection on the Principle of Complementarity from a historian's point of view.

6. See Gremillion [1976], #57, p. 542.

7. This religious mindset of John XXIII is also reflected in the major council documents, as this essay hopes to make clear in the course of its development.

8. This outlook on human artifacts is essentially the same as Giambattista Vico's "*Verum et factum convertuntur.*" See Collingwood [1946], esp. pp. 64–65. It also assumes the fundamental principle of the Church's social teaching as formulated by Pope John XXIII in *Mater et Magistra* (see Carlen [1981], Vol. 5, #219, p. 83).

This teaching rests on one basic principle: individual human beings are the foundation, the cause and the end of every social institution. That is necessarily so, for men are by nature social beings. This fact must be recognized, as also the fact that they are raised in the plan of Providence to an order of reality which is above nature.

9. On the "Signs of the Times" see Excursus IV.

10. See Gremillion [1976], #56, p. 542.

11. John XXIII's phrase for this notion was derived from *The Imitation of Christ*, book II, Chap. III: *De bono homine pacifico.* See Staff of the Pope Speaks Magazine [1964], p. 497.

12. In using the term, analytico-genetic, I am not taking back my previous remarks about John XXIII's use of induction. I am, however, understanding induction in the same sense as Merleau-Ponty does. See Natanson [1973b], Vol. 1. esp. pp. 77–78. This gives a priority to an eidetic intuition of the essence, which illumines the empirical experience (data) under consideration. As the product of a quite selective and optimistic discernment process, Pope John's hermeneutics stands *midway* between the turbulent human dynamisms on collisioncourse in the *objective* world of social reality and his own *subjective* religious life-world. Inasmuch as the pope's hermeneutics is directed

to *all* men of good will, it does not express the totality of values inherent in his religious ontology. At most it expresses an "ecumenical ethics" for the global social order, inasmuch as his hermeneutics provides a functional paradigm of religio-social dynamisms which complement one another and can provide a common basis for constructive collaboration in the buildings of peace and humanity.

13. See Gremillion [1976], #33, pp. 537–538. The comprehensive Christian vision formulated by John XXIII has an "ecumenical" counterpart derived from the field of comparative religious studies:

> The *homo religiosus* represents the "total man;" hence comparative religion must become a total discipline, in the sense that it must use, integrate and articulate the results obtained by the various methods of approaching a religious phenomenon. In other words, it must become a *total* and creative *hermeneutics*, since it is called to decipher and explicate every kind of encounter of man with the sacred, from prehistory to our days. We do not doubt that this "creative hermeneutics" will finally be recognized as the royal road of the history of religions. Only then will its role in culture begin to show itself to be important. Such a "total discipline" can open new perspectives to Western thought, to philosophy properly speaking as well as to artistic creations.

M. Eliade, "Comparative Religion: Its Past and Future," in Ong [1968], p. 251.
14. For a discussion of "anthropology" in general see Excursus V.
15. The "split-level" type of both anthropology and theology, which John is suggesting, goes back to his *pastoral* goal as formulated in *Humanae Salutis*: i.e., where the upper-level truths of the revealed order display their *efficiency* in the lower-level temporal order. See Abbott [1966], p. 707. By implication, at least, John XXIII's notion of pastoral theology is one which demands that the spiritual and temporal orders are viewed in a comparative, correlated, and complementary way. See footnote 4, *supra*. A phenomenologist would say that the two orders are presumed, in John's outlook, to be "isomorphic."
16. See Abbott [1966], p. 707. The anthropological vision provided by *Pacem in Terris* appealed far beyond the confines of the Catholic Church, as its original popularity indicated. See Gremillion [1976], pp. 534–536.
17. In the context of Vatican II the message of hope, projected by *Pacem in Terris*, has both its strength and weakness. As you may recall, *Humanae Salutis* called attention to the danger of nuclear war and the on-going dehumanization of people in the world today. Within such a "horizon" of the global, natural life-world, so markedly different from the optimism of secular Western societies, *Humanae Salutis* projected a sense of *urgency* about the work of the Council and tried to stimulate a much-needed *transformation of attitude* on the part of mankind. *Pacem in Terris* reflects on the *same* horizon projected by *Humanae Salutis*, but in his encyclical Pope John now chooses to focus on the hopeful trends which he sees developing under God's Providence. The point to be emphasized here is that both of these documents deal with the *same* horizon constituted by the religious and moral principles of the Holy Father; hence, their messages are meant to *complement* one another rather than diverge from one another. To seize on the optimism of *Pacem in Terris* at the expense of the realism involved in *Humanae Salutis* is incompatible with John XXIII's intended sense. These observations are important for "the Formation of Attitude." See Wojtyla [1980], pp. 201–418.

18. For "eschatology," see Excursus II on Sacramental Time-Consciousness. However, since the period of the Enlightenment there has been operative in Western society a secular "eschatology" under the rubric of "progress," and this is particularly true of the ideologies influenced by Hegelian thought (e.g., Marxism). See Nisbet [1980]. By entering into this flux of human dynamics religious eschatology becomes "incarnated," but only to the extent such dynamisms have an "obediential potency" to be conformed to authentic Christian values.

19. See Royce [1968], pp. 180–181.

20. See Gremillion [1976], #154, p. 562. See also "The Church in the Modern World," in Abbott [1966], #4–10, pp. 201–209.

21. For "anthropogony," see Excursus V.

22. The same critical problems which occasioned the Church's *aggiornamento* have not been without their impact on Marxist intellectuals. See A. Gibson, "Christian Crossroads and Atheist Aggiornamento," in Shook [1968], Vol. 1, pp. 313–328. We shall return to the correlation of Marxism and Vatican II more extensively in our closing "Epilogue."

23. See Carlen [1981], Vol. 5, #35–36, pp. 110–111. In this context the Holy Father is viewing human society as being "primarily a spiritual reality." Such an intersubjective reality is today expressed by the term, *communio*, in both phenomenology and ecclesiology.

24. See H. de Lubac, SJ, "Teilhard de Chardin in the Context of Renewal," in Shook [1968], Vol. 1, pp. 208–235.

25. The focus of John XXIII on the empirical dynamisms operative in the world was markedly different from that of Teilhard. The pope's intuitive grasp was fixed exclusively on contemporary human dynamisms, and not on the evolutionary process as Teilhard conceived of it as a scientist. John XXIII's methodology, like Husserl's in the *Crisis*, implies a first reduction: i.e., a suspension of science. Teilhard's methodology does not.

26. In all of intellectual history no incident is more instructive for the partisans of both religion and science than the Galileo Case. Today there are "two Galileos": the Standard Galileo of the textbooks and the New Galileo. As regards the cultural and scientific impact of the *Standard Galileo* on modern thinking see Husserl [1970], #9, pp. 23 ff.: "Galileo's mathematization of nature;" for a balanced appraisal of the historical data by a renowned scientist see Teller [1980], pp. 33–38. The *New Galileo* surfaced in 1983 at the International Galileo Conference marking the 350th anniversary of his trial. William Wallace formulates the new view thus: ". . . Galileo stood in considerable debt to Aristotle for his science; and . . . this debt was mediated to him through a progressive Aristotelianism coming directly from Thomas Aquinas, without which modern science – science as we know it – would not be the reality it now is." For fuller information see Wallace [1977], [1983a].

27. See Gremillion [1976], #56, p. 542.

28. The *Menschheitgeschichte* of which I am speaking is intended to be a religio-scientific alternative to *Heilsgeschichte* in biblical theology. Each has its proper complement of eschatology. Teilhard's strategic vision, it seems, was to correlate in a quasi-academic fashion the dynamics of revelation with the unconscious forces of cosmic evolution. His theories, from a doctrinal point of view, stand in need of great clarification. Such a clarification is imperative today when global human and ecological concerns are being viewed more and more as "a gigantic biological process." See Muller

[1982], pp. 16–18. For a sample of two Catholic authors grappling with these ideas see Thomas Berry and Joseph B. Gaven in Eigo [1981], pp. 1–24 and 105–137. Furthermore, John XXIII's and Vatican II's almost exclusive focus on *human* dynamisms, inspired by their paradigm deriving from the biblical origins story, leaves their legacy open to the charge of blindness to both ecology and the origins story of cosmic evolution. While the Catholic teaching on natural law, reiterated in *Gaudium et Spes*, should moderate such a charge, that teaching is today being brought into question by a significant segment of Catholic intellectuals. A clarification of Teilhard's theories, particularly as correlated with the substance of traditional natural law theory, would greatly assist the pastoral renewal program of the Church. Perhaps the linchpin between the two theories would be some form of systems philosophy. See Laszlo [1972]. If we can allow for a developmental type of Aristotelianism, then we should extend the same courtesy to Teilhard.

29. See Teilhard de Chardin [1966], pp. 172–173.
30. See Naisbitt [1982], p. 94.
31. This problem has been well stated by A. Gibson in Shook [1968], Vol. 1, p. 321:

> The crossroads at which Christianity stands today, the crossroads to which Christianity has been brought by the radical swing of the pendulum in the direction of humanism, is a crossroads of *identity*. Shall and can Christians, individually and as a group, proceed to a collaboration with the world, in abstraction from the primordial and radical commitment to the person of Christ, the incarnate God-Man? Can we make a tactical compromise at least so as not to outrage an unbelieving world? Can we quietly endeavor to apply Christian principles in a collaboration with other men of good will who share these principles insofar as they are generically human principles? The answer is clear from Christ's own words: "Apart from me, you can do nothing!" It is simply erroneous and disloyal to ontological facts and theological dogmas to [de]sert the Christ who came to satisfy man's deepest longings: for that Christ himself said that for *this* reason was he born and for *this* cause did he come into the world, *to bear witness to the truth*. And his other equally solumn declaration makes this proposition reflexive, for he said, "I am the Truth!"

32. See Abbott [1966], p. 715.
33. "We shall take pains so to present to the men of this age God's truth in its integrity and purity that they may understand it and gladly assent to it." See Abbott [1966], p. 4.

PART II

AMBIGUITIES, TECHNICALITIES AND ADJUSTMENTS

CHAPTER 5

THE AMBIGUITIES: INTEGRALISM, PLURALISM AND COMMUNICATION

Paul VI and integralism

About a year after the release of *Pacem in Terris* another encyclical was issued by the Holy See on August 4, 1964. In it the problem of peace, while still of special urgency, was subsumed under a set of overriding concerns more properly spiritual. The document displayed a perceptible shift of focus: from John's practical (*ad extra*) solicitude for humanity to a speculative (*ad intra*) concern for theological accuracy. I am, of course, referring to Paul VI's encyclical on the Church (*Ecclesiam Suam*),[1] issued just four months prior to the Council's dogmatic constitution on the same subject (*Lumen Gentium*). The pope's letter had no intention of preempting the forth-coming conciliar statement. Under an umbrella-statement, however, of the broad religious policies which would shape his future efforts, he once again repeated the "rules of the game." In doing so he revealed himself as a man of a theologically meticulous, integralist mindset. The encyclical is something of a "Driver's Manual for Pastoral Renewal," as composed by a theological engineer. Two points of focus in the document highlight this solicitude for abstract principle and technical accuracy: (1) the care taken to ground the *aggiornamento* in a totally spiritual matrix;[2] and (2) the incipient anxiety expressed that such a pastoral program could occasion serious internal problems for the Church (e.g., resurgent theological modernism, false irenicism, over-accommodation to secular values, etc.).[3]

The mind of Paul VI *ad intra* and *ad extra*

Now, if Paul VI felt obliged to take his stand at the *ad intra* end of the religious spectrum, I can only infer that as an informed participant in the Council he was reading some intellectual signs of the Catholic times and trying to restore the vital balance necessary to the healthy life of the Church. His three broad policy concerns may be viewed as his resolve to continue in his papacy dynamics already under development at the Council. Hence, he hopes to foster: (1) the Church's own self-awareness as the Mystical Body of Christ; (2) the spiritual renewal and adaptation appropriately flowing from such a consciousness-raising process; and (3) dialogue with the world.[4] It is in his extended reflection on dialogue that he displays a good, if highly intellectualized, grasp of John's pastoral intent.[5] In his encyclical Paul displayed no great anxiety about phenomenological method, as long as it was "carefully coordinated with that habit of mind whereby a man discovers objective truth."[6] Yet, Paul's irenicism in this regard was not long-lasting since his pontificate was wracked by a series of theological controversies from left and right, all impinging on the axiom of doctrinal integralism.

Coerced by circumstances, then, into an ongoing defensive posture, Paul VI's public utterances on pastoral renewal often seemed narrow, technical, and over-spiritualized — somewhat redolent of his etherialized image of the Church as the Mystical Body of Christ.[7] Only when liberated from the strictures imposed by an exclusively Catholic audience did he give us an insight into the fuller dimensions of his thoughts. The first time this occurred in any extended way was on October 4, 1965, when the Holy Father addressed the General Assembly of the United Nations.[8] In his concluding remarks he explicitly stated the "civilization on trial" theme in its moral and human context.[9] Two years later, on March 26, 1967, he laid out his basic ideas on The Development of Peoples (*Populorum Progressio*).[10] But much of the impact of these creative pastoral statements was diminished by the controversy surrounding *Humanae Vitae* in 1968 when Catholics themselves brought into question the credibility of the papacy as a teacher of modern morality.[11]

Pluralism, discernment, and the communication problem

The above problem developing toward the end of Paul VI's reign was, for Catholics, essentially a conflict between corporate and individual discernment. Historically Catholicism has always stood for *corporate* discernment of its revealed patrimony. Outside of this context Vatican II and the Catholic notion of "Church" itself make virtually no sense whatever. But by trying to dialogue with the world of the twentieth century, the Church entered an environment dominated by intellectual pluralism. Since at least 1850 most theories of knowledge and science have been dominated by some form of psychologism. This creates an environment of moral relativism in which each *individual* must face up to reality *as he sees it* and make his own responsible decision.[12] This intellectual stance, as reinforced by the theories of Darwin and Freud, is mainly characteristic of affluent Western democracies. It will be shaken only to the extent that our world becomes even more destabilized, and people see the need for corporate moral commitment and collaborative efforts for peace. By recognizing the "crisis in the sciences" caused by ongoing intellectual fragmentation,

Husserl sought to restore philosophy as a rigorous science and reopen the time-honored channels of communication among intellectual leaders in society. Somewhat in the same vein, the bishops' rapproachment with phenomenology was one attempt among many to open new channels of communication in a pluralistic age. Unlike Husserl they did not think that the technique just in itself would solve the "crisis in human beings." Rather, their usage of phenomenology was an "ecumenical" outreach toward our "separated brethren," the modern intellectuals, and represented the Church's first effort at some very highlevel "acculturalization."[13] Once these points are appreciated, the ambiguities and imperfections of the system can be seen in perspective and gradually worked out by all interested parties.

The communication problem in a phenomenological perspective

Any bishops at the Council familiar with phenomenological method also recognized its hazards. Yet, they could not afford to be intimidated by such problems since the ongoing crises in the modern world made it absolutely imperative to open new channels of communication. Consequently their rapproachment with this methodology was both informed and controlled. They knew, for example, that they were not practicing transcendental phenomenology in a way identical with that of Husserl, but in a corporate, developmental way commensurate with his practical purposes of renewal.[14] John XXIII had left the bishops an inspiring illustration of this approach in *Pacem in Terris*; the ground rules had been set by the axiom of doctrinal integralism; and they could, in an unobtrusive way, use their own scholastic philosophy and theology to double-check the results of their reflections. By fostering such methodological flexibility the bishops hoped to open a *multilevel* communication system[15] for the ideas expressed at the Council and provide Vatican II's own demonstration-model for enriched theological reflection in the future.[16] The incentive for such creative procedures traces back to the pastoral nature of Vatican II as conceived by John XXIII.[17] In this concrete context the religious reflection of the Council would have proven useless unless it got people to *do* something. That may have been the bishops' ultimate practical goal, but as God's salesmen they knew that consummate *artistic*[18] skill would have to be employed to overcome the sales-resistance to their ideas in the modern world.[19] They would, accordingly, have to point out their product's merits, how it would meet the customer's needs or wants, and how it would enrich his life or that of his loved ones. No salesman can do any of these things unless he first communicates with his prospective customer. Here, then, in compact form are the progressive steps which the bishops hoped to take: (1) communication with the people of this age; (2) to show them how their lives might be enriched; (3) in order to influence their attitudes; (4) so that they would *do* something.[20]

Today, however, communication is somewhat differently understood than in the past. In our era of psychologism it is generally conceded that it is the *hearer* (or the prospective customer) *who is the real communicator*! The salesman is, in reality, only sending out signals which he thinks are appropriate. The hard realities of the marketplace inform him whether or not he is successful. It is, however, the hearer who *interprets* these signals and *tells himself* what is being communicated. Quite literally he *reveals the message to himself*. If we may assume such a psychologistic frame of reference, then it is but a short step to Pope John's pastoral goal of the revelation of man to himself. By reason of the complexity of this communication process (in which non-verbal elements and the esthetic "packaging" of a product often play an important, if not dominant, role) we can appreciate why John XXIII downplayed an exclusively conceptual approach to modern men in favor of a demonstration-model correlating authentic religious and human values. Scholasticism, while long on theoretical concepts, is short on the practical psychological techniques needed to work within human consciousness and influence attitudinal change. On the European scene phenomenology provided the most respected methodology for such access to consciousness, and the scholastic theory of connatural knowledge allowed for a virtually seamless alignment with that method. Once such a methodological correlation had been established, the whole conciliar process could, in theory, be interpreted within either a scholastic framework or the more "existentialist" style of reflection typical of phenomenology. Later on, however, we shall see that the conciliar process is best appreciated when these two methodologies are viewed as *fused*.

The unrealized potential of the conciliar process

The next chapter intends to provide a detailed reflection on phenomenology in the context of Vatican II. Here I would only like to point out some of the missed opportunities existent in our own day regarding the innovative communication efforts of the conciliar process.

The general run of scholastic thinkers, particularly those classified as Transcendental Thomists, today display a fair awareness of some of the phenomenological dimensions of the Council, but they seem nowhere near an integrated comprehension of its work.[21] This would be especially true regarding the anthropology sketched in principle by the bishops. After twenty years of disarray the more classical style of scholastic thinkers seem to be regrouping, so their positive contribution to conciliar thought and development is yet to be felt.[22] Non-scholastic thinkers in the Catholic Church are, in large part, preoccupied with epistemological problems centering on methodology and reductionism.[23] Such theoretical controversies have hindered the development of wide-ranging pastoral programs other than quite parochialized types and have fostered an introverted conception of renewal modeled almost exclusively on innerdirected, psychological "personalism" and *ad hoc* social activism.[24] Among contemporary theologians only B. Lonergan shows some awareness of what the modern theological enterprise should involve, but his vision is shaped more by his own academic method rather than the pastoral goals and needs of Vatican II.[25]

Professional phenomenologists, on the other hand, display no great awareness of the value of Vatican II for their specialized line of study. This lack of sensitivity is not in the creative tradition of Husserl, who reached across disciplines to derive inspiration for his concept of the life-world from Lévy-Bruhl's *Primitive Mythology*.[26] At the very time when the Council was in session (1962–1965) H. Spiegelberg was energetically laboring to develop a new way into phenomenology by a *workshop* approach.[27] Yet, Vatican II was an international demonstration-model of this methodology as used by an intersubjective community in a corporate and constructive way for renewal purposes in the best tradition of Husserl. Spiegelberg's co-subjective and empathetic approach has, regretfully, not had much impact on phenomenologists. Perhaps interest in such a collaborative practice of phenomenology would be stimulated if the community of professional phenomenologists were to again take seriously the theme of "renewal" fostered by Husserl. In this regard, as you may recall, he found that the *facts* of a real life-world exceeded anything that could be achieved by a free variation in the imagination![28]

The problem, which I am alluding to here, goes beyond merely the theologians and phenomenologists. In our critical age all intellectuals and educators ought to view such projects as Vatican II, NASA, and the United Nations as "signs of the academic times." The age of the philosophes has been rendered obsolete by the practical problems of a turbulent world. A project, such as Vatican II, may be viewed as one huge corporate brain.[29] The participants in its dialogical self-analysis were like nerve-ends: passing information back and forth in the system, processing it, and ultimately synthesizing it as heightened self-comprehension affirmed and celebrated. This ecclesial process may serve as a model for our individual innerdirected quest for self-identity in today's world in two ways: first, by illustrating that genuine self-knowledge is achieved only in a context of larger interpersonal relationships, and secondly, by emphasizing such self-introspection is but a preliminary phase for grappling with

the comprehensive practical problems in that world outside ourselves. Out of
this achievement of self-identity and goal-clarification comes the spirit of hope,
indeed the enthusiasm, for the practical tasks at hand. Vatican II, as a corporate
demonstration-model of applied phenomenology, displays how professional
phenomenologists could play an important role in any such collaborative enterprise.

Summary

This chapter is something of a small watershed in the development of this essay.
It marks the dividingline between the *ad extra* pastoral focus of John XXIII
and the *ad intra* doctrinal preoccupations of Paul VI. Furthermore, the chapter
provides the comprehensive framework within which the next several chapters
are developed.

The framework of this chapter embraces two broad problem areas: (1) doctrinal integralism ("ontology") on collision-course with an age of intellectual
pluralism; and (2) the challenge of developing an adequate communication
system in such an ambivalent environment. *Doctrinal integralism* was reflected
upon on the basis of Paul VI's preoccupation with objective truth. *Intellectual
pluralism* was viewed in terms of its impact on the discernment process, both
corporate and individual. Here the use of phenomenology at the Council was
appreciated as a high-level acculturalization process for religious thought in a
pluralistic age. Lastly, the *communication problem* was formulated within the
context of a pluralistic and psychologistic environment. This led to an appreciation of the internal dispositions and attitudes of the hearer, as communicator to
himself, and the utility of the phenomenological method in constructing a
communication process to meet the hearer's needs. The chapter concluded
with some random observations, directed mainly to scholastics and phenomenologists, on the untapped potential of the conciliar process for their respective
fields.

The next chapter will deal with some technical aspects of phenomenology
pertinent to the Council's reflective process.

NOTES

1. See Carlen [1981], Vol. 5, pp. 135–160. In this encyclical Paul VI's basic spiritual
   priorities are made quite clear: "Thus before embarking on the study of any particular
   problem and before considering what attitude to adopt vis-a-vis the world, the Church
   must here and now reflect on its own nature, the better to appreciate the divine

plan which it is the Church's task to implement." See Carlen [1981], Vol. 5, #18, p. 138.

2. See Carlen [1981], Vol. 5, #18–25, pp. 138–139; #34–40, pp. 141–143; #41–42, pp. 143–144; #45–46, pp. 144–145, *et passim.*

3. See Carlen [1981], Vol. 5, #26–28, pp. 139–140; #47–49, pp. 145–146; #88; p. 153.

4. See Carlen [1981], Vol. 5, #8–15, pp. 136–137.

5. See Carlen [1981], Vol. 5, #58–118, pp. 148–159. For "dialogue," see Excursus VI.

6. See Carlen [1981], Vol. 5, #28, p. 140. Although Paul VI does not mention phenomenology by name, what he meant by the "modern bent of mind" is quite clear. Recall Spiegelberg [1982], p. xxiii and Farley [1975], pp. 235–272. What is so extremely important here is that, while maintaining his own *objectivist* mindset, he is at the same time allowing for a *methodological idealism* which some have attributed to phenomenology. See Carr [1974], p. 39. In this sense Paul VI has already moved beyond Pope John XXIII, who in his opening speech at the Council simply advocated *methodological flexibility* in general.

   A major *academic* problem, however, still remains: doctrinal integralism is still viewed in *objectivistic* terms. Paul VI gives no indication of jettisoning his own and the Church's heritage of scholastic realism. This problem, reaching back through John XXIII to Pius XII and *Humani Generis*, recalls once more Vollert's *academic* question: "How, in an intellectual atmosphere of universal evolutionism, can we safeguard transcendental truth?" For John XXIII, more concerned about the "crisis in human beings," this was really a *non-problem.* His answer to this problem would have been that of *enlightened praxis*: i.e., to show the *efficiency* of the Church's transcendent moral truths in the temporal order! Paul VI, however, was more sensitive to the theoretical dimensions connected with the "crisis in human beings." Consequently, in a rather broadminded way he endorsed the methodological idealism implicit in the Catholic use of phenomenology and encouraged dialogue at all levels. As regards any enlightened praxis, he expected that program would, in substance, be developed by the Council.

7. See Carlen [1981], Vol. 5, #35, pp. 141–142 *et passim.* Anything which Paul VI says about the Mystical Body in *Ecclesiam Suam* should be viewed as simply an extended commentary on the speech which he made as Cardinal Montini on the floor of the Council, December 5, 1962. See Latin Texts [1970–1980], Vol. I, pars IV, esp. p. 292. What Paul VI is saying in *Ecclesiam Suam* is that the Mystical Body, phenomenologically speaking, always remains – at the *horizontal* level – the intentional ground of the Church's concrete experience of its own body-phenomena. This topic will be taken up in Chapter Eight. However, the term, *Mystical* Body, is also comprehensive enough to embrace the intentional ground of the *vertical* dimension of the Church. That topic will be taken up in Chapter Ten when we deal with Divine Revelation (*Dei verbum*).

8. See Gremillion [1976], pp. 379–386.

9. See Gremillion [1976], #31, p. 386.

10. See Gremillion [1976], pp. 387–415. Cardinal Roy sees Paul VI's theological development of *Pacem in Terris* exemplified particularly in the following major documents: *Ecclesiam Suam, Populorum Progressio,* and *Octogesima Adveniens.* See Gremillion [1976], #35, p. 538; #150, pp. 561–562. However, the comprehensive overview of Catholic social teaching provided by Gremillion [1976], pp. 5–138 is the best general index of the practical contribution of Paul VI to the work of John XXIII and Vatican II's renewal program.

11. A balanced commentary on the Holy See's attitudes toward "birth regulation and population policy" may be found in Gremillion [1976], pp. 96–103. For the humanistic values implicit in these policies see Lucas Moreira Neves, "'Humanae Vitae' – Ten Years Afterwards Towards a More Human Civilization" in Schall [1984], pp. 426–435.

12. The responsibility for self engendered by psychologism is not to be identified with the sense of responsibility engendered by Husserl's phenomenology. As Natanson [1973], p. 11 writes:

   Radical certitude is Husserl's goal; radical certitude must be phenomenology's method. The person who strives for such certitude must turn to himself as the locus of ultimate rigor, for all of the translations made of history and of the deeds of fellow men in the worlds of spirit and politics must finally be made by the individual for whom reality exists to be comprehended. Past any cheap "subjectivism" and beyond all merely idiosyncratic attitudes, the egological structure of experience stands as the last criterion for philosophical accountability.

13. The principle of "acculturalization," first endorsed in the document on the Liturgy, was appropriately reaffirmed throughout the other documents of Vatican II. See Abbott [1966], #37–40, pp. 151–152; and in the Index under "Adaptations" and "Culture," Abbott [1966], pp. 749, 761–762. The point to be made here is that Vatican II's phenomenological style of reflection, inasmuch as it has been applied to matters of religious substance (e.g., *Lumen Gentium* and *Dei verbum*), displays a type of *quasi-philosophical*, or intellectual, acculturalization operative on a much higher level than that typically implied in the conciliar documents. However, the quite comprehensive description of acculturalization found in the "Decree on the Missionary Activity of the Church" allows for such a sophisticated adaptation. See Abbott [1966], #22, pp. 612–613. All of this should be viewed in correlation with the endorsement of *methodological idealism* given by Paul VI in *Ecclesiam Suam*. In other words, acculturalization is accepted as a methodological principle, and only to the extent the cultural detail in question has an obediential potency to be conformed to authentic Christian values. The importance of these reflections may be surmised by the fact that on May 20, 1982, Pope John Paul II established a new Pontifical Council for Culture for the evangelization of cultures and for the defense and promotion of the cultural inheritance of mankind.

14. As the pioneer of phenomenological theory and method, Husserl never got beyond the "solipsistic" dimension in his practice. His theorizing, however, saw all of this as a necessary first stage on which would be founded a final stage of intersubjective phenomenology. Out of this approach there would develop a phenomenology of transcendental intersubjectivity, as the ground for a universal transcendental philosophy. See Carr [1974], pp. 102–103. The *corporate* practice of phenomenology, as reflected by the finalized documents promulgated at Vatican II, represents the above type of intersubjective phenomenology anticipated but never practiced by Husserl.

15. Once Pope John XXIII endorsed the principle of methodological flexibility in his opening speech at the Council, the bishops gradually became sensitized to the acute communication problem which confronted them. Any attempt to have tailored their message to all levels of intelligence in their anticipated *global* audience would have been impossible, so the bishops were forced to handle the communication process in

a *selective* way. It is important to focus on the fact that they selected *educated* people as their target audience. In the pastoral outlook of the bishops there was at least a vague awareness of the need for collaborators, drawn from all segments of social leadership, in order to carry out the pastoral purposes of Vatican II. Implicit in any collaboration with educated people is the need for a certain "collegiality": i.e., a recognition of subsidiarity and the prudent delegation of responsibility in order to capitalize on their initiative and creativity. But among such educated people (as within the Church itself) there are *levels of consciousness* concerned with widely diverse "regions of reality" (e.g., physical, psychic, spiritual or cultural). The surface-meaning of the conciliar documents is directed toward the moderately educated, who will read them out of some sort of "natural attitude." The phenomenological substructuring of the Council's documents is directed toward highly sophisticated intellectuals, as leaders of society, in order to provide them with a distinctive cultural matrix within which to interpret the Church's profound rethinking of her contemporary role and to provide an established model for their own critical rethinking in quest of intellectual and cultural renewal.

16. Since *Pacem in Terris* provided a religio-social hermeneutic of contemporary reality and, consequently, correlates with the "Church in the Modern World" among the conciliar documents, it is quite clear that the Council in its *doctrinal* constitutions intended to go beyond the demonstration-model provided by the encyclical. For some preliminary details on this matter see Gremillion [1976], pp. 537–538, 561–562. Once we appreciate the complexity of the larger communication process under development, we begin to understand the unfortunate circumstances at the Council which led to the "Decree on the Instruments of Social Communication." See Abbott [1966], pp. 319–331 and Vorgrimler [1967–1969], Vol. 1, pp. 89–104. This is a case where a socially complex topic, more pertinent to the *ad extra* concerns of the "Church in the Modern World," got on the agenda while the bishops were intensely engrossed with developing a communication process adequate to the *ad intra* nature and pastoral needs of the Church. The Decree, as promulagated, is the result of some short-sighted expediency and the lack of parliamentary ingenuity.

17. Especially John XXIII's pastoral goal of revealing men to themselves, as formulated in *Humanae Salutis*. See Abbott [1966], p. 707.

18. The concept of *art* introduced here with all the implications of esthetics is perhaps one of the *most important* in this whole essay. Over the past twenty years this has been one of the most neglected dimensions of Vatican II. Among contemporary theologians only Hans Urs von Balthasar has taken the esthetic dimension of theology seriously as a conceptual concern. See O'Meara [1981] and von Balthasar [1982]. For an important correlation of esthetics with civilization and culture (a theme which we shall develop toward the end of this book) see Hall [1973], pp. 23–29, 81–84, 183–190. Reflection on the esthetic dimension of the documents promulgated by Vatican II has made me aware of two things. (1) In contemplating this literary work of art there must be a reduction, spontaneous or otherwise, consisting in a "willing suspension of disbelief." (2) When this literary work is viewed as a purely intentional object, it is – in Ingarden's words – perceived as a "multiply stratified creation," and its art is intuited in its "metanarrative text." Since this metanarrative content is dependent on a conditioned type of consciousness for its animation and concretion, it cannot be said to be totally heteronomous. See E.S. Casey in Dufrene [1973], pp. xviii, xx. The problem is much the same as watching a three-dimensional movie: you cannot

appreciate its photographic effects unless you are wearing the proper type of glasses. The esthetic vision, then, of Vatican II is not an autonomous work of art, but one available only to phenomenological intuition.

19. Under the unpretentious rubric of "sales-resistance" I wish to introduce the important topic of *prejudice*. Much of phenomenology is devoted to a recognition and explanation of prejudice, and the Council's use of phenomenology is an acknowledgment and acceptance of that fact. By way of introduction to this theme see the word, "Prejudice(s)," in the index of Carr [1974], p. 282.

20. As described, this is essentially the method used by John XXIII in *Pacem in Terris*. See Gremillion [1976], #134–135, pp. 558–559. In both Pope John's approach and that of the Council the focus on human *subjectivity*, whether individual or collective, is part of a *pastoral* plan rather than any speculative endorsement of a philosophical theory.

21. For one tentative interpretation, seriously in need of nuancing, see Rahner [1979]. Less cautious voices are: Greeley [1982], Martin [1981], Herr [1982], and Tracy, Küng, and Metz [1978]. Until some commonly acceptable paradigm of Vatican II is discovered, there is no great utility in speaking about its "failure" or the need for Vatican III.

22. This is not to say their influence has not been already felt in a few individualized instances; e.g., in theology Hamer [1964] and in philosophy Wallace [1977], [1983b].

23. The speculative problems regarding methodology and reductionism stem from the more fundamental issue of the relationship of faith and reason. For a concise statement of the issues see the "Critical Remarks" in Byrne and Marziarz [1967], esp. p. 810. The full panoply of issues involved in reductionism may be seen at a glance by asking the simple question: "Can an atheist be a theologian?" This question is judiciously handled, if not resolved, in Brian L. Hebblethwaite [1980], pp. 3–6 *et passim*. The preoccupation with methodology, however, must not be viewed as an exclusively academic or theoretical problem, but also as symptomatic of a cultural state of mind. See Voegelin [1978], p. 7. In our new moment of human history this essentially Enlightenment mindset has outlived much of its usefulness.

24. In the American Church the one development which just may reverse this whole trend is the hierarchy's shift to *global* problems such as in the national pastoral, "The Challenge of Peace," issued on May 3, 1983. See *Origins: NC documentary service* 13:1 (May 19, 1983) 1–32. This pastoral confronts, at least in part, issues raised by *Humanae Salutis* and *Pacem in Terris*.

25. See Crowe [1980].

26. See Merleau-Ponty in Natanson [1973b], Vol. 1, p. 102.

27. See Spiegelberg [1975], pp. 24–34. Spiegelberg's focus in this article is on the pedagogical benefits to be derived from this workshop approach. He does not significantly relate this group-technique to Husserl's view that intersubjective phenomenology is the final stage of his methodology, as ultimately leading to a universal transcendental philosophy. See Carr [1974], pp. 102–103. As a case-study for phenomenologists, Vatican II's procedures illustrate how phenomenologists (i.e., the Northern European bishops and theologians on the theological commissions) and non-phenomenologists (i.e., the average bishop at the Council) can work together in a "workshop approach" to produce a commonly accepted phenomenological analysis of something which they both share and desire to appreciate in an enriched way.

28. See Merleau-Ponty in Natanson [1973b], Vol. 1. p. 102.

29. This analogy, as applied to the United Nations, is used constructively in the context of "the present Promethean period of change" by Muller [1982], p. 17.

CHAPTER 6

PHENOMENOLOGY IN THE CONTEXT OF VATICAN II

In order to appreciate the role of phenomenology at the Council, we must remind ourselves that it was a pastoral Council. Unlike certain previous councils (e.g., Lateran V and Trent) there was — by definition, at least — no *ad intra* "crisis" in either Catholic theology or morality. Pope John XXIII presented a worldwide summation of Church life in *Humanae Salutis*, and there he judged it as "in great part transformed and renewed." There was, however, a serious world crisis *ad extra* which in the context of European intellectual history I have chosen to call the "crisis in human beings." This "crisis" at the socio-cultural level reflects the *ad intra* psychoethical confusion stemming from a good century of intellectual and moral subjectivism, and this is further compounded by the *ad extra* collapse of global social and economic structures which can no longer handle the explosive growth of new global interdependencies.[1] As Gerald and Patricia Mische have wisely perceived, this is a Crisis of Growth related to structural lag.[2] This structural lag, however, presents not so much a technological or political challenge as it does a *moral* one.[3] In such a dislocated situation Pope John saw the need for a pastoral Council intent on moral renewal.

Phenomenology as the new via media

The mere mention of the word, "renewal," would have recalled to European bishops and theologians the writings of Husserl who had advocated an intimate connection between personal, social, and scientific renewal through the use of his methodology.[4] But John XXIII's *Pacem in Terris* was a decisive influence for them to move in the direction of phenomenology. In his encyclical John's thought was not cast merely as the product of his *subjective* religious ideas nor as the result of some *objective* scientific study reducing both men and reality to neatly packaged "things." Rather, in a quite non-formal way he had constructed a phenomenological *via media* between the transcendent world of religion and the empirical world of everyday living.[5] With such a powerful demonstration-model of phenomenology dealing with the natural life-world of global society the European bishops and theologians were inspired to follow something of the same course at the Council.[6]

However, the bishops and theologians sensitive to this potential latent in the Council viewed themselves, not as isolated phenomenologists, but as part of an intersubjective community.[7] Consequently, they employed their methodology in a way subordinate and auxiliary to the Council's larger pastoral purposes. This purpose was not to "reconstruct" the Church's religious or theological consciousness, but to affect the concrete Catholic way of life. This sensitivity did not prevent them from acting like serious-minded and professional phenomenologists.[8] Although the life-world of this religious community was ordered by a religious ontology, these thinkers were not adverse to subjecting it to the stresses and strains of free variation in the imagination. (Paul VI's reemphasis of the axiom of doctrinal integralism in *Ecclesiam Suam* was not done in a vacuum.) The pastoral intent of the Council did not prevent the bishops from occasionally resorting to some very technical shadings of doctrinal points, although more of this was due from pressure brought to bear by historical studies than by phenomenology itself. As a final result, however, the Council displays an innovative application of the phenomenological method which opens avenues to anthropological enrichment not available to a merely scholastic interpretation of the Council.[9]

The six steps or phases of the phenomenological method

Spiegelberg lists six steps or phases in the use of the phenomenological method.[10] Each step may be used separately to constitute a small phenomenology in itself, and not all professional phenomenologists employ all six steps in their work. Spiegelberg's treatment of these steps, although deriving from a phenomenology based on individual subjectivity, opens up a comprehensive sense of the methodology as a whole and correlates well with my own purposes here.[11] I intend to limit my own reflections to how these steps are discernible in the conciliar reflective processes and procedures. Only one slight addition will be made. I shall supplement Spiegelberg's treatment with some prefatory remarks on dialogue.[12] This type of communication is an essential ingredient of any corporate use of phenomenology, which necessarily involves the participants in an ongoing, empathetic analysis of the vicarious experience of their partners in the conversation.

Dialogue

Dialogue at the Council was the process whereby phenomena were gathered and sorted out. The formal dialogue conducted on the floor of the Council and in the working committees has been printed, in large part, in the *Acta Synodalia* of Vatican II, and for scholars this would provide the most direct access to the phenomenological aspects of the Council.[13] Inasmuch as the Second Vatican Council was a "workshop" of about twenty-five hundred bishops, a great deal of parliamentary procedure and committee work was necessary to keep this dialogical traffic flowing freely and constructively. At the beginning of the Council an attempt was made to control this dialogue by restricting it to the documents submitted by the Preparatory Commission. That attempt failed, and the dialogue thereafter was virtually unhindered.[14] As a pastoral Council Vatican II's dialogue had a built-in bipolar quality about it.[15] Local bishops, for example, when addressing a theological issue, would naturally be prone to voice it as the people back home appreciated it. The same thing may be said, *mutatis mutandis*, for the many specialized professionals at the Council, e.g., canonists, administrators, historians, etc. The focus of analysis and reflection, then, see-sawed between abstract truth and its multiple empirical expressions throughout the world at all levels of life.

Descriptive phenomenology

Unlike the *Acta Synodalia* where phenomenological description would be more overtly perceived, the Council documents in their finalized form are a mixture of scholastic and phenomenological descriptive styles.[16] Hence, these documents are in need of a good deal of textual criticism (or "metaphenomenology") to separate out these two elements. My brief remarks here can only hope to point out those avenues whereby phenomenology somewhat naturally found its way into the conciliar reflective process. When the bishops returned "to the things themselves" as individualized in each one's concrete experience, they each entered their personalized realm of the *mysterium fascinans*[17] as the ultimate ground of religious and human *meaning for them*. Since their scholasticism already provided each of them with a functional comprehension of the act/content of their subjective consciousness, they were not, like philosophical phenomenologists, in pursuit of any theoretical understanding of the workings of their own consciousness. Rather, each one centered his focus on a preliminary description of the religious, human, or socio-cultural phenomena under consideration in order to express their authentic *intentionality for him*. All this, however, was simply the necessary groundwork for a later corporate discernment of *intentionality for the bishops as a whole*. This descriptive process, while comprehensive and meticulous, was not totally presuppositionless.[18] As we noticed with John XXIII in *Pacem in Terris*, the subconscious focus was christocentric, even when viewing phenomena typically catalogued as human or secular.[19] Although the religious ontology at the heart of Catholicism allows for a great deal of reification or objectification, its practical, pastoral paradigm is the "Whole Christ."[20] The bishop's descriptive undertaking has, then, a strong emotive tonality both as deriving from a theandric conception of religious truth and as conducted predominantly on the basis of connatural knowledge.[21]

This emotionality permeating the conciliar descriptive process is really an index not only of its religious authenticity and pastoral potential for enrichment, but also of the intensity of its phenomenological focus. Unlike the scientifically neutral analysis of most professional phenomenologists, the analytical intensity of Vatican II is symptomatic of life-and-death commitment to the phenomena under consideration. Within the limits set by some topic there would be an intense and conscientious inventory of the pertinent phenomena as experienced by the bishops, and this would be especially true in matters dealing with meaning and values. *Abstract* meaning and values, however, often had to play an auxiliary role to the practical, *pastoral* meanings and values which the bishops were trying to orchestrate to remedy the "crisis in human beings." So, the descriptive process went through many phases and recastings, as the various versions of the conciliar documents under development attest.[22] One of the inevitable side-effects of this extended, collaborative process would have been, for the vast majority of the bishops, an enriched sense of the corporate self of the Church. For someone, however, like Archbishop Marcel Lefebvre, who had not been able to relate to this complex process, there would be a resulting sense of deep betrayal and intense rage. Such strong emotional displays at the Council are important indications of the profound serious-mindedness with which the bishops went about describing the *mysterium tremendum* at the heart of their corporate life-world.

Phenomenology of essences (i.e., essential or eidetic phenomenology)

This step is the place where scholasticism and phenomenology so naturally overlap that their definitions are sometimes hard to distinguish from one another.[23] Both systems of thought are extremely sensitive to the importance of intentionality and essences, but it takes an acute observer to distinguish how the two systems differ about these basic notions.[24] As a world meeting, the Council would have been faced quickly enough with the need to distinguish between the essential and the accidental, the necessary and the contingent.[25] Consequently, the bishops were reasonably well-prepared to grasp the essential structures of any phenomena presented to them and to perceive the essential relationships both within and among them.[26] In extraordinarily complex matters there were, of course, theological specialists on hand to offer any help needed. The bipolar reflective style of the local bishops would also have kept such abstract essences in touch with their empirical foundations. (Consider for a moment the problem of defining the "essence" of marriage which would be acceptable in both Western democracies and Oriental or African cultures!) That the process of "free variation in the imagination"[27] was operative at the Council in an extraordinarily creative way will become strikingly apparent later when we reflect on the new image of the Church as the People of God. (Had the pastoral purpose of the bishops been to enhance the state of mon-ogamous marriage or to emphasize the sponsal relationship of the individual soul to Christ, they could just as easily have described the Church as the Bride of Christ.) While the theological commissions provided the professional ex-pertise in this analytical discernment of "essences" (i.e., noemata), the voting procedure used at the Council was the judgmental mechanism to confirm that all such essences and their interrelationships were the product of a corporate intuition.[28]

Phenomenology of appearances

This phase in the method would represent merely a shift from the *what* to the *how*. The focus here would be on the multiple aspects or modalities under which the same object can present itself to our consciousness. As a striking example of such sensitivity to visual appearances, Spiegelberg offers "Monet's eighteen versions of one slanted view of the facade of the Cathedral of Rouen, as seen at different times of day."[29] Attention to such detail would not only characterize an artist of any type but also someone judging on the basis of connatural know-ledge. The Church has had, however, such a long history with the principle of "saving the appearances"[30] and arguments of theological fittingness that her sensitivity to this type of phenomenology need not be emphasized. In all likeli-hood, this type of sensitivity had a great deal to do with the positioning of the role of the Virgin Mary in the Council documents.[31] At such a world meeting as Vatican II the bishops were also inundated by the cultural diversity of the one Church with its one truth. This experience enabled them to re-see the Whole Christ as reflected in the rich diversity of human beings living in diverse cultures. This is evident in the bishops' hearty endorsement of the principle of accultural-ization for Catholic life and practice.

Constitutive (or genetic) phenomenology

Of all the methodological steps we have discussed so far, this is undoubtedly the most important for understanding the pastoral nature of Vatican II. Its reflection on the religious and empirical world of today is quite similar to that of John XXIII in *Pacem in Terris*, except that the techniques and imagery have been greatly refined. The constitutive phase calls for an awareness of how the phenomena take *shape* in our consciousness. (Here connatural knowledge is important for the "feel" that the shape is taking place "right.") When we visit a strange city, for example, we can feel somewhat helpless and passive in the face of the geographical details overwhelming our consciousness.[32] But with time we start to get control of the situation and in an active way begin to piece together the layout of the city in our minds. Two things are going on simultaneously here: the on-going *act* (noesis) whereby we piece together our mental map of the city, and the map itself as a developing *object* (noema) in our mind. A phenomenological theorist, such as Husserl, would be primarily fascinated by the workings of the noesis; a practitioner of applied phenomenology, such as the bishops and theologians, would be more interested in the way the noemata themselves are taking shape in the ecclesial consciousness.

This functional map (or image, theory, Gestalt) is something gradually created in our minds on the basis of our everyday experience, and we correct or add to the details of this map as we go along. What we sometimes forget, however, is that it is this functional image, theory, or Gestalt which determines *what we can see*![33] In the sixteenth century, for example, everybody "saw" a geocentric universe until Copernicus fabricated a new heliocentric model.[34] Although the universe remained unchanged in appearance, the new model required on the part of people a shift of the visual Gestalt which involved no little psychological shock[35] and, with time, enormous problems regarding the physics of celestial mechanics. Somewhat in the same fashion, John XXIII viewed the empirical data of a disjointed humanity and perceived a radically new Gestalt under development: that of the peacemaker. The bishops at Vatican II viewed the same data, approved John's fundamental insights, and formulated them as the corporate, ecclesial concept of the People of God. While the Council has presented us with this new *theoretical* model of our religious universe, we have yet to figure out the operating principles of its "celestial mechanics."

Reductive phenomenology: Two pertinent types

There are two types of reductive phenomenology found in the work of Husserl which are pertinent to our reflections here. The first type is in the service of science, and the second is in the service of human beings.[36] What is uniquely peculiar to the first type of reduction is that Husserl (after the manner of Descartes) practiced a methodical suspension of belief (epoché) in the existence of the natural world.[37] This "bracketing" of one's natural attitude towards existence is really what any natural scientist has to do in order to put on a totally objectivistic and neutral attitude toward the data of his research. Mathematicians also bracket a portion of a complex problem in order to put it "on hold" while they work on a separate, more accessible part of the problem. The phenomenologist practices this type of epoché in order to pursue his eidetic analysis of the phenomena as they exist in his consciousness.[38] To the extent that he arrives at their *apodictic meaning for him* he also intuits their universal essence(s). This process, as mentioned previously, is somewhat comparable to "abstraction" in scholasticism, and to the extent both processes aim at the distillation of universal essences, both are in the service of abstract, theoretical science. Unfortunately, Husserl got so involved with the constitution of his own consciousness that he seems to have lost contact with the "bracketed" portion of reality and to have lapsed into a variety of Kantianism.[39] To the extent this type of reduction/abstraction was used at the Council in the pursuit of eidetic essences, it would have been used in the larger context of scholasticism which favors realism rather than idealism. (That, at least, is what Paul VI reminded us of in *Ecclesiam Suam.*)

The second type of reduction, however, is far more important for understanding the nature of Vatican II. This type of reduction works somewhat the *opposite* of the first type and consists in a *methodical suspension of belief* (epoché) *in all the sciences*, natural or otherwise. This type of reduction — quite disconcerting for most modern men — is a precondition for entering the life-world which is the prephilosophical, precultural, and prescientific world given to each man in his immediate experience.[40] In the *Crisis* Husserl thus describes this unfamiliar reductive process:

> Clearly required before everything else is the epoché in respect to all objective sciences. This means not merely an abstraction from them, such as an imaginary transformation, in thought, of present human existence, such that no science appeared in the picture. What is meant is rather an epoché of all participation in the cognitions of the objective sciences, an epoché of any critical position-taking which is interested in their truth or falsity, even any position on their guiding idea of an objective knowledge of the world. In short, we carry out an epoché in regard to all objective theoretical interests, all aims and activities belonging to us as objective scientists or even as [ordinary] people desirous of [this kind of] knowledge.[41]

Once the philosopher has returned to this life-world he may then use the first type of reduction to "understand how it is given and how it is constituted in human consciousness so as to have meaning and ontic validity."[42] What would be the nature of any such life-world, and what would phenomenological analysis of it ultimately be aiming at? David Bidney answers such questions for us thus:

> The *Lebenswelt* may be understood as the human world *posited as existing by man* and *constituting the intentional field of his action.* It is the world *relative to man*, the kind of world he shares with other human beings. It is the world *as naturally selected by man* in virtue of his interests in a given ecological environment. The *Lebenswelt* comprises not only the naturally selected environment but also the social and cultural world of human society. The *sociocultural* life-world is a *historic* achievement of man in a given ecological environment and *varies with time and place for different societies.* Husserl is explicit on this point: "Among the objects of the life-world we also find human beings, with all their human action and concern, works and suffering, living in the world-horizon in their particular social interrelations and knowing themselves to be such." [. . .]
>
> The *new science* of the *Lebenswelt* which Husserl now envisages involves the description and intentional analysis of the human life-world *as a phenomenon of human consciousness.* The *task* of a scientific phenomenological philosophy is ultimately the *construction of a meta-anthropology* to investigate the genesis of the life-world in human consciousness, how it is constituted, and its a priori structures in the human subject.[43]

All of the above is, of course, a description of the *natural* life-world, of which there are many: e.g., the Chinese, Hindu, European, etc.[44] Ultimately Husserl hoped to build the superstructure of science on the ground common to all these human life-worlds. In this respect he hoped to solve both the "crisis in the sciences" and the "crisis in human beings." By their suspension of the sciences at the Council, however, the bishops were intent on returning to their *religious* life-world. Although in Catholic religious belief the natural and religious life-worlds are correlated and complementary to one another, it is not legitimate to interpret the religious life-world exclusively in terms of the natural life-world. That would be a form of reductionism and would imply that in its doctrinal constitutions (i.e., *Lumen Gentium* and *Dei verbum*) Vatican II was simply elaborating a sociology of knowledge. Rather, as John XXIII intended, it was formulating a new "split-level" type of *pastoral* theology previously unknown.

Although the bishops came from various nations and cultures, they formulated their contemporary, corporate consciousness as Catholics living in a world transcending their natural confines. They investigated the genesis of this religious life-world, explained how it is given, demonstrated its constitution in the human consciousness, and catalogued in great part the *a priori* structures of this corporate subject. All of this creative reflection was done to achieve an enriched comprehension of the moral meaning and ontic validity of the corporate life-world of the Church. This ecclesial reflection on a really "transglobal" religious life-world also formulated a blueprint for a meta-anthropology in the first two chapters of *Lumen Gentium*.[45] But in order to "incarnate" this blueprint in the diverse *natural* life-worlds around the globe today, the Council endorsed the principle of acculturalization discussed previously. The religious meta-anthropology formulated at Vatican II leads naturally into our final topic, hermeneutic phenomenology.

Hermeneutic phenomenology

Anyone who has had an introductory course in the bible knows that hermeneutics is a set of reasonable guidelines for the intelligent interpretation of the scriptures. These guidelines are based, for the most part, on sound historical and theological studies. Martin Heidegger, preoccupied throughout much of his life with the problem of man's existence in a puzzling universe, became convinced that phenomena had additional, hidden meanings beyond those immediately available to our intuitions. (Quantum physicists had been insisting on that point since the early part of this century.)[46] Whatever the merits of the five steps previously discussed, Heidegger saw the need for a new hermeneutic phenomenology to interpret such hidden meanings. His own technical analysis of human being resulted in an interpretation of man's existence as being-toward-death.[47] Via Bultmann and other scripture scholars this type of hermeneutics — in one form or another — has made its way into Catholic religious reflection.[48] The Council's analysis of human being not merely resulted in but consciously created a pastoral interpretation of man's existence as being-toward-Christ. Inasmuch as Jesus proclaimed himself the Way, the Truth, and the Life (cf. Jn. 14:6), this is a quite understandable, and even expected, paradigm for religious human existence. In fact, the theological doctrine of man made in the image of God, when correlated with the scholastic notion of "obediential potency," virtually rules out any other Catholic paradigm for human existence. As formulated by the Council, however, this new Christian hermeneutics is developed for a turning point in human history and is tied in with the very survival of mankind.[49]

A preliminary overview on the use of these techniques

The over-all conceptual thrust of Vatican II may be summed up in the phrase, *fides quaerens intellectum* (i.e., faith in search of understanding).[50] The distinctive feature of today's search is, however, its *unique, pastoral context*: the modern crisis in human beings. At a turning point in human history, then, the Council's work recapitulates in a corporate, if abbreviated, way not only the creative religious undertaking of the first apostolic community awaiting the parousia, but also the work of Husserl, particularly as his concerns came to focus in the *Crisis*. There are, however, some significant differences.

In the first few centuries of the Christian era the Councils were preoccupied with clarifying certain *theoretical* points of Catholic doctrine (e.g., the divinity of Christ, the nature of the Holy Spirit, Mary as the Mother of God). As a pastoral Council, Vatican II did not deal with such problems. In regard to phenomenology the Council was not interested in theoretical, but *applied* phenomenology.[51] As theorists, the bishops and theologians may have belonged to different schools of phenomenology, but they were united in the practice of a commonly understood *method* established in its fundamentals by Husserl. Hence, phenomenological "theory" is taken for granted or by-passed, and the analytical method is applied to religious, not mundane phenomena as in the case of Husserl or others. Furthermore, the Council is not focused on the object's genetic relationship to its *ad intra* act (noesis),[52] but on new and creative *acts ad extra* (praxis). The intentional isomorphism, however, between act-essence-act, as considered by the Council, is of the same *theoretical* quality achieved by Husserl in his mature phenomenological reflection. The raw data of the phenomena to be analysed was presented by the oral and written interventions from all the bishops on the floor of the Council. The phenomenological redaction of this data was done by the commissions charged with developing the finalized documents. These commissions were effectively dominated by Northern European bishops, theologians, or their sympathizers who were favorable to the phenomenological descriptive handling of religious ideas.[53]

The use of phenomenology at the Council was meant to be a conciousness-raising process aimed at a realistic, but flexible, sense of the Church in the modern world. This larger aim was achieved only by attending to two more immediate purposes: first, by authentically reflecting the corporate ideas and judgments of the bishops so as to contribute to the Council's own consensus-building process; and secondly, by synthesizing these corporate intuitions in such a way that they would become the intentional ground for the new attitudes, values, and acts appropriate to Christians in today's turbulent world.

The above genetic reflective process needed three phases of development in order to come to maturity. *First*, there was the elementary eidetic analysis of the raw data as deriving from the bishops on the floor of the Council. This would have necessitated the use of the epochē, if only to break out of stereotypical scholastic thought-patterns. The dominant techniques of this early stage of reflection would have involved dialogue, descriptive phenomenology, and the phenomenology of appearances and of essences.[54] This formulation of "essences" may better be called the "eidetic thematization" of doctrinal and moral truths, in order to distinguish it from the "essences" formulated in the objectivist manner of scholasticism.[55] *Secondly*, as the pastoral sensitivity of the Council became more finely attuned, the "turn to the life-world" became more consciously accepted and necessitated the suspension of *all* the sciences. By this time, however, the bishops — like Husserl — were working out of a completely teleological conception of their corporate consciousness. Up to this point the raw data of the phenomena had been emanating from the individual religious life-worlds as verbalized by the various bishops from around the globe. Now the quest was on for the common ontology at the heart of all these individualized religious life-worlds: i.e., for the intentional ground of the corporate religious life-world of the Church. *Lastly*, after this intentional core had been discerned as the Glorified Christ, the vitally alive God-Man (i.e., a *concrete* universal), there came into play an active constitutive phenomenology which formulated a hermeneutical construct called the People of God. This phenomenological interpretation is an eidetic thematization of empirical *a priori* data (i.e., religious experiences) and correlates the Council's notion of the contemporary Church at the level of *theoretical praxis*. Perhaps it would be clearer if we said the People of God is simply religious terminology for a *theoretical anthropology*.

The above presentation is merely a preliminary sketch of a quite complex process. The ideas involved and their genetic development can only become clear within the further discussions of this essay. Now is the time to begin laying the foundation for that fuller comprehension by studying the adjusting consciousness of the Church in its own conciliar quest for a new self-understanding.

Summary

This chapter, intended for an audience with at least some generic awareness of phenomenology, has been quite technical and is more in need of some high-lighting rather than any attempted summary. The main purpose of the chapter as a whole has been to introduce the reader in a general way to how the participants at Vatican II adapted the method and techniques of phenomenology to the pastoral purposes of the Council.

Three observations made in the chapter deserve a parting emphasis. (1) The introductory paragraph formulated in a finalized way the religio-social setting within which I view the work of the Council. The really important point made there is that the critical challenge facing mankind is essentially a *moral* one. In discussing these global issues I was also able, for the first time, to use the *ad intra/ad extra* distinction in a slightly more complex way typical of the real complexity of this distinction. (2) Perhaps the most important point reemphasized in this chapter is that the eidetic statements generated by phenomenology are really a *via media* between subjective and objective concepts, as we typically use that terminology. (3) Of the six steps of the phenomenological method, discussed in this chapter, it is essential to grasp that the second type of reduction really involves the suspension of *all* the sciences! In Husserl's conception of phenomenology this is a necessary precondition for re-entering the natural life-world with renewed vision; it presumes, of course, that this renewed vision is shaped by a totally teleological consciousness. In the context of the Council that teleology is orchestrated by the Glorified Christ functioning as a concrete universal throughout all levels of the corporate Catholic consciousness.

This chapter ended with a brief summary of how the phenomenological method was technically employed at the Council. From this point on, however, much of our discussion will hinge on a developing awareness of constitutive and hermeneutic phenomenology. To foster this developing awareness the next chapter will discuss the dynamics of the ecclesial consciousness as it adjusts to get its final pastoral focus.

NOTES

1. It should be quite apparent that I have slipped into a slightly modified usage of the *ad intra/ad extra* distinction to indicate a dialectical relationship between human beings and their external world. From this point on the reader should be alert to the changing uses of this distinction.

2. See Mische [1977], p. 5.

3. Throughout this essay I emphasize the moral challenge. There are those, of course, who suggest a solution almost exclusively on the basis of technological optimism. The best example would be Fuller [1981]. Since the problems under consideration are so complex, however, the intent of this essay is to suggest that both schools of thought ought to be working *together*.

4. A concise but quite substantial resume of Husserl's ideas may be found in Aron Gurwitsch's "The Last Work of Edmund Husserl." See Gurwitsch [1966], pp. 397–447.

5. It is a well-known fact that Msgr. Pietro Pavan of the Lateran University composed the encyclical on the basis of Pope John's ideas. Others later consulted were Fr. Luigi Ciappi, O.P., the pope's official theologian; Fr. Goerge Jarlot, S.J., sociology professor

at the Gregorian University; and very likely Msgr. Loris Capovilla, the pope's secretary. See Zizola [1978], pp. 12, 19–20.

6. Within the context of the *Crisis* Merleau-Ponty recalls Husserl's concept of the philosopher which applies equally well to John XXIII as a theologian in the context of *Pacem in Terris*: "The philosopher is, he says, 'working in the service of humanity,' meaning that the philosopher is professionally bound to the task of defining and clarifying the conditions which make humanity possible – that is, the participation of all men in a common truth." See Natanson [1973b], Vol. 1, p. 49.

7. Methodologically speaking, the *individual* practice of philosophical phenomenology does have a complex problem when it confronts the matter of intersubjectivity. See Spiegelberg [1982], pp. 138–141; Gurwitsch [1966], pp. 432–436; and F.A. Elliston in Elliston and McCormick [1977], pp. 213–215. In spite of the fact that the theoretical undergirding for the notion of intersubjectivity has not always been tidily in place, this has not prevented phenomenologists from reflecting on the idea. This would especially be the case for the Catholic philosopher, G. Marcel. See Spiegelberg [1982], pp. 452–453. However, once the *fact* of intersubjectivity is accepted and there is the intent to reflect on man in his "natural attitude," then the logical assumptions or consequences are those listed in Schutz and Luckmann [1973], p. 5, and these provide the working-principles for reflecting on the life-world.

8. In order to concentrate on phenomenological theory and method, I have carefully avoided discussing how individual Catholic theologians employed this type of analysis prior to the Council. The simple listing of these theologians as provided by Farley [1975], pp. 244–255 and John [1966], pp. 130–134, 167–168, 186, 189 are adequate for my purposes here. However, all of these theologians were working out of a historical background in which phenomenology was a precondition for academic respectibility outside the narrow confines of scholasticism. On this larger background see Pelikan [1969–1970], Vol. 2, pp. 245–309.

9. Before beginning any technical discussion I suppose I should lay out my "Phenomenological Creed," which is essentially that formulated by Natanson [1973a], p. 190:

Underlying this study has been the conviction that Husserl's thought constitutes a unity which has unfolded in a complex but essentially continuous fashion. For all its inadequacies, the psychological position of *Philosophie der Arithmetik* contained the seed of the position advanced in the *Logical Investigations*, whose critique of psychologism prepared the way for the phenomenology of the *Ideas*. In turn, the methodology developed there went far beyond the propounding of technique and evolved instead into a transcendental logic on the one hand, as developed in *Formal and Transcendental Logic*, and a transcendental monadology on the other hand, as portrayed in *Cartesian Meditations*. And with the full expression of transcendental phenomenology, Husserl turned to his most profound theme, the search for a philosophy of the life-world which could revitalize the meaning of history through a new critique of reason.

10. See Spiegelberg [1975], pp. 54–71. For a somewhat more detailed treatment of the same matter see Spiegelberg [1982], pp. 681–715. Perhaps one of the best compact introductions to most of the ideas treated in this chapter would be Peter Koestenbaum's "Introductory Essay" in Husserl [1975], pp. IX–LXXVII. Good collateral reading would also be provided by the article, "Toward a phenomenology of experience," in Spiegelberg [1975], pp. 175–179.

11. See Excursus V on Anthropology under the subheading, "Vatican II's consequent openness to phenomenological method."

12. See Excursus VI on Dialogue under the subheading, "From cautious endorsement to real sensitivity."

13. See Latin Texts [1970–1980]. In the polemicized theological environment of the postconciliar period there has been the beginning of some scholarly research into these important documents. On occasion, however, such research seems to shade into something resembling apologetics. An example of this would be O'Connor [1984], pp. 10–21, where he provides a technical analysis of that disputed phrase, "subsists in," as found in *Lumen Gentium.* See Abbott [1966], #8, p. 25. Worthy, and even necessary, as such a technical analysis may be for pedagogical purposes, its aura of defensive objectivism lends itself to projecting Vatican II within the confines of an ill-fitting scholastic straight-jacket. However, once the Council is appreciated within its phenomenological and pastoral context, such problems are at least placed in their proper perspective, if not solved.

14. See Excursus VI on Dialogue under the subheading, "The popes as monitors of group dynamics."

15. The more technical aspect of this bipolar quality of the full ecclesial consciousness will be reserved for Chapter Ten, dealing with Revelation (*Dei verbum*).

16. Even if we grant that the phenomenological descriptive style is the dominant methodology used at the Council, scholasticism is a looming presence throughout the documents: e.g., in terminology ("subsists in"), in ideas (natural law), and in ontology (the coherence in all orders of being and at all levels). It is too simple a solution to say that such conceptual realities should, therefore, be understood within the preconceptions of Transcendental Thomism. It is a fundamental axiom of Catholic belief that authentic reason *cannot* contradict authentic faith. With the employment of the phenomenological method as the *via media* descriptive vehicle, the future challenge for any critical approach to the Council's documents will be to discover how faith, phenomenology, and scholastic realism are used in correlation for *anthropocentric* purposes.

17. Our use of terminology associated with the important work of Otto [1923] is meant to place the Council's reflective process within an historical context concerned with the religious life-world rather than that of objective science. By which I mean that the concept of "mystery," emphasized in the Council documents, shares a history since the turn of the century not only with "scientific" biblical or sacramental theology, but also with the phenomenology of religion. Another pioneer in this style of reflection would also be G. van der Leeuw. For his notion of "The Phenomenology of Religion," see Leeuw [1963], Vol. 2, pp. 683–689. The seminal work of Otto and van der Leeuw has been continued and developed in America by the academic work of M. Eliade. (We shall return to this topic more extensively in Chapter Ten.) The type of religious reflection and analysis demonstrated at Vatican II is comparable in quality to the above-mentioned scholarship, but it differs in two important ways. (1) The goal of the Council's reflection is ultimately oriented to practical, pastoral human needs. (2) Its religious contemplation must be judged within the tradition of Christian mysticism and spirituality, rather than by the Post-Kantian and Lutheran presuppositions of Otto or by the academic neutrality implied by Eliade's comparative objectives. For the larger European context of such a development see T. Steinmann's "Modern Mysticism," in Pelikan [1969–1970], Vol. 2, pp. 392–406.

18. No one has appreciated this point better than Natanson [1973a], p. 12. who writes:

> Phenomenology purports to be a "presuppositionless" philosophy. What is meant is simply the principle that nothing can be accepted by the inquirer unless he has scrutinized its character and implications and also recognized that it is a feature of experience. Strictly speaking, a presuppositionless philosophy is not a philosophy without assumptions; *it is a philosophy in which assumptions are candidly admitted, examined, and accounted for.* The obligation of the phenomenologist is to be fastidious in the inventory and analysis he makes of what is taken for granted by both common-sense men and theoreticians as well. Major examples of philosophical presuppositions include what Husserl calls *the "general thesis" of the natural attitude:* the tacit faith ordinary men have in the reality of their world, the assumption that the shared world of everyday life is indeed the same for all normal individuals, that whatever exists in our world has a natural history — a causal basis — that we can reasonably expect the world to continue in the future in much the same way it has in the past, and that *value, symbolic significance, aesthetic worth, and religious commitment are elements of or associated with the mundane world they transcend. Such cardinal presuppositions of experience are not denied or cancelled out.* How could they be? Rather, the phenomenologist attempts *to discern their character and to locate their limits. Once "under control," assumptions may be appropriated for philosophical use.* [Emphasis added.]

The phenomenological method at Vatican II, as used to explicate the "general thesis" of the natural *religious* attitude, discerns the character and locates the limits of the assumptions (or "prejudices," if you will) at the heart of Catholicism. These assumptions, now conciously "under control," are then turned not merely to theological use, but to the far more practical purpose of human renewal.

19. See Excursus VII, Obediential Potency, especially under the subheading, "The implications of obediential potency at the Council."

20. The term, "Whole Christ," derives from Mersch [1951], pp. 51–53: "The Idea of the Whole Christ." An earlier edition of this work was Mersch [1938], which may profitably be compared with Vonier [1937]. Both books represent divergent trends in ecclesiology on the verge of World War II. At Vatican II both views are reconciled within a new eschatological framework in order to achieve the pastoral and humanistic goals of the Council. (This topic will be treated in Chapter Eight.)

21. If one grants the suspension of the sciences in Vatican II's use of the phenomenological method, the *only* remaining basis for a cognitive type of religious discernment is the connatural knowledge of the bishops. By reason of the fact that this type of knowledge is grounded in an *affective* grasp of truths and values, it can have a highly charged emotional quality if the occasion warrants it. At the Council journalists were quick to report any indications of emotional display, particularly on the part of the Roman Curia. See Wiltgen [1978], pp. 28–29, 134. It is to be regretted that no comprehensive psychological studies of any worth have appeared in the postconciliar period dealing with the emotional trauma associated with the shift of the religious Gestalt endorsed by the Council. Only the occasional sociological article alerts us to these larger problems. See Anthony and Robbins [1982] and Douglas [1982].

22. For the developmental stages of the major documents which have been the focus of this essay see Vorgrimler [1967–1969], Vol. 1, pp. 4–7 (Liturgy); Vol. 1, pp. 106–137 (*Lumen Gentium*); Vol. 3, pp. 159–166 (*Dei verbum*); and Vol. 5, pp. 1–76

(*Gaudium et Spes*). The primary source to track the details of these stages of development would be Latin Texts [1970–1980].

23. Scholasticism and phenomenology *do* differ in appreciable ways. For a concise introduction to these differences see Spiegelberg [1982], p. 37 and footnote 19 on pp. 47–48 (i.e., how Brentano's concept of intentionality differs from Aquinas'); pp. 97–103 (on Husserl's conception of intentionality); pp. 95–97 (on Husserl's doctrine of universals/essences). Spiegelberg [1981], pp. 3–26 contains an extended technical article entitled: "'Intention' and 'Intentionality' in the Scholastics, Brentano and Husserl (with Supplement 1979)."

24. The descriptive phenomonelogy, discussed previously, quite often represents the preliminary phase leading to an intuition of *essences*. It is a more profound type of analysis than the phenomenology of appearances, to be discussed shortly. As long as Husserl remained clearly focused on his original aim of reestablishing the epistemological foundations of science, the type of essence which he was dealing with was reasonably clear. Such empirically grounded (i.e., concrete) essences/universals are exemplified in mathematics, logic, and the natural sciences, and they are manifested by strong apodictic evidence. The equivalent notions in scholasticism are nuanced as "abstract" essences/universals and provide the ground for a higher metaphysical order of being understood analogously. The nearest Husserl would come to such an order would be in his "transcendental logic." See Husserl [1978] or Bachelard [1968].

Husserl's non-metaphysical, concrete essences are all understood univocally, and as empirically grounded have an ontic orientation to matter. Hence, he never speaks of "abstracting" from *matter*, as a scholastic would, but in a somewhat Cartesian manner resorts to a "reduction," which is a methodical doubt about the extra-mental *existence* of such essences. The practical end-product in the area of technical science is, however, pretty much the same, whether one is a scholastic or a phenomenologist. Any differences between the two systems could easily be handled by some nuancing of the meaning of the essences being discussed.

However, as Husserl expanded his research beyond the natural sciences into the larger "regions of reality," there seems to be a certain "softening" both of his notion of essence and the rigor required for apodictic evidence. Furthermore, these essences as "unities of meaning" are *not* eternally fixed in some Platonic way, a fact seemingly confirmed by the modern shift from a Euclidian to a non-Euclidian universe. This *theoretical* problem has been extensively discussed by Levin [1970]. Whatever may be the theoretical resolution of this difficulty, the fact remains that it had a loosening-up effect on the phenomenological movement in its outlook on essences, their temporality, and the sort of intuition whereby they are grasped. The popular writings of Merleau-Ponty would provide a reputable example of such post-Husserlian developments, particularly on the eve of the Council. See T.J. Kisiel, "Merleau-Ponty on Philosophy and Science," in Kockelmans and Kisiel [1970], pp. 251–272.

This range of interpretation relative to the meaning of essences, their temporality, and their constitution in consciousness may be found among the phenomenologically inclined bishops and theologians at the Council. In many cases this trend was welcomed as closer to the *biblical* outlook on reality. Certainly, this factual situation leant itself to the methodological flexibility encouraged by John XXIII in his opening speech at the Council. It also, however, leant itself to the Council's descriptive handling of religious essences being equated with a merely *functional* ontology, not one construed according to classical scholastic theory or that of the later phenomenologists.

See Excursus I on the Life-world under the subheading, "'World' vs. life-world." (We shall return to this topic in Chapter Eight.)

25. On the eve of the Council there appeared in 1959 B. Häring's extensive reflections on moral theology entitled, *Das Gesetz Christi.* See Häring [1961–1966]. In the *Catholic Book Reporter* (Fall, 1961) pp. 17–18, R.F. Smith, S.J., said this treatise was "one of the five or six most important books of theology produced in this century." The book was immensely popular in Europe and presented moral theology in a new and positive way; it breathed a certain biblical kerygma in peaceful possession of itself and avoided the arid juridicism and casuistry of the older manuals. This book, however, should be read in conjunction with Bourdeau and Danet [1966], esp. pp. 226–228, where we read: "So 'The Law of Christ' owes much, and its author makes no secret of it, to the *phenomenological current*, especially as found in Germany." (Emphasis in text.) Häring's style of reflection represents a type of thinking which had a strong influence on the Council. Firstly, it exemplified a constructive phenomenological description of religious essences (e.g., virtues); secondly, it provided a popularly received example of the methodological flexibility encouraged by Pope John; and lastly, it projected a tone of irenicism and basic evangelical values within the Catholic traditional heritage, such as the Council hoped to achieve.

26. According to phenomenological theory consciousness involves two correlated elements: the *noema* (i.e., the object, eidos, essence) and the *noesis* (i.e., the act, the intentional experience referring to the object). Both the noema and the noesis can be analysed by phenomenological reflection. See F.A. Olafson in Elliston and McCormick [1977], esp. pp. 162–163. As an example of phenomenology applied in a pastoral way the focus of the bishops at Vatican II was almost exclusively *noematic* (i.e., object-oriented), as a precondition for further pastoral acts *ad extra* in the Church's mission to the world. Husserl's theoretical concern with noetic acts *ad intra* is not manifest at the Council, but Vatican II's choice of the phenomenological method itself displays that the bishops were pastorally concerned about this dimension of consciousness-formation.

27. On "free imaginative variation" see Spiegelberg [1982], pp. 700–701. Merleau-Ponty points out that Husserl's turn to the life-world convinced him that *facts* go beyond what the phenomenologist can imagine. See Natanson [1973b], Vol. 1, p. 102. A new precedent in phenomenological theorizing was set by Sartre who made a radical distinction between perception and imagination; this partially accounts for some of the non-cognitive features associated with the movement. See Spiegelberg [1982], pp. 517–519.

28. For collateral reading on this point see "A phenomenological analysis of approval," in Spiegelberg [1975], pp. 190–214. What may be even more pertinent is that a Gestalt interpretation of noemata (Gurwitsch) and a judgmental theory (Føllesdal) may be discerned in the Council's procedures. See R.C. Solomon, "Husserl's Concept of the Noema," in Elliston and McCormick [1977], pp. 168–181.

29. See Spiegelberg [1975], p. 65. This process, which may at first appear rather unimportant, is described more significantly in Spiegelberg [1982], pp. 703–705.

30. This principle may be traced back to the era of Plato and, as endorsed by Pope Urban VIII, became notorious as applied in the Galileo Case. See Cantore [1977], p. 195.

31. On the controversy over the place of Mary in the Council documents see Vorgrimler [1967–1969], Vol. 1, pp. 125–126, 133–135, 137.

32. This comparison is used in Spiegelberg [1975], p. 67. The parallel development in Spiegelberg [1982], #5, pp. 706–708 should also be considered. This analogy used

by Spiegelberg is a good one inasmuch as it indicates there are *active* and *passive* aspects to constitutive phenomenology and the analogy may be applied to the discernment of any "essence," even if viewed only as relational being. The analogy also implies a certain inherent temporality to consciousness inasmuch as the full discernment takes place only over a period of time, but this "historicity" of consciousness has its own ordered grounding in intentionality, i.e., successive events in time ultimately reveal an ordered pattern of some sort. What Spiegelberg's brief description does not attend to is the possibility of a radical shift of Gestalt: this is why we allude to Copernicus in this discussion. A shift in the Gestalt may be simply *visual* as in the case of Copernicus, or it may also involve the very *dynamics* of the object under consideration, e.g., the formulation of a new theory of gravity as suggested by Kepler and Newton.

33. See Einstein's remarks on this topic in Heisenberg [1971], pp. 63–64. Recall also Paul VI's insistence in *Ecclesiam Suam* that the Mystical Body remain the intentional ground of any new description of the Church.

34. See Kuhn [1957], pp. 134–184. For a post-factum phenomenological analysis of the geocentric data see Spiegelberg [1975], pp. 104–105.

35. A shift of the visual Gestalt has been characterized by psychologist, Richard Gregory, as "really quite frightening." See Miller [1983], p. 50. See also Kuhn [1962], pp. 62–65. For some of the disturbing psychological effects on experimental subjects who were not able to assimilate such shifts adequately, see Bruner and Postman [1949], pp. 206–223. Maritain [1968] represents, it seems to me, an example of "theological shock" grounded in the shift from objectivity (meaning *in se*) to subjectivity (meaning *for me*) in the postconciliar period.

36. Reduction, as developed by Husserl, is far more complex than my brief presentation. Koestenbaum in Husserl [1975], pp. LVIII–LIX lists five different types. Lauer [1978], pp. 51–57 prefers to speak of the six levels of reduction. Carr [1974], pp. 110–120 speaks of a historical reduction. For practical working-purposes I prefer the opinion of Natanson [1973a], p. 65 that the full range of phenomenological method can be expressed by two species of reduction: i.e., eidetic and phenomenological reduction. The *eidetic* type includes the two diverse forms of reduction discussed in this essay (plus a third type "via an analysis of intentional psychology," not discussed in this essay).

Notable by its absence in this essay is any reference to the transcendental reduction. In any discussion of *pure* phenomenology this is a key-teaching of Husserl. See Van Breda in Elliston and McCormick [1977], pp. 124–125. Only after the eidetic reduction has achieved the intentional sense of the phenomena under consideration does the transcendental reduction further reduce these meanings to subjectivity as their "origin." However, the meaning and application of transcendental reduction is still under some discussion and clarification even today. See Spiegelberg [1982], pp. 118–123, 144–145, 709–712. In this essay I deal with reductive phenomenology only to the extent it has some pertinence to Vatican II's style of reflection. Inasmuch as the Council represented a *religious* application of phenomenology, its "transcendental turn" attempting to confront *analogous* levels of consciousness might conceivably differ in important details from Husserl's notion which viewed consciousness as *univocal*. When the eidetic reduction is being employed at the Council, the ecclesial transcendental ego is *presumed* as operative, but the "transcendental turn" does not take place until the constitution, *Dei verbum* (discussed in Chapter Ten). All I would mention at this point is that the corporate contemplative focus of the Church, as found in *Dei verbum*, effectively — albeit obliquely — achieved what Husserl viewed as the intended purpose of the transcendental reduction: i.e., a glimpse of the transcendental ego or self. At the present moment, however, this is all quite theoretical. As a working-principle, I believe we may accept the opinion voiced by David Bidney in Natanson [1973b], Vol. 1, p. 135, that the transcendental reduction is not required for reflection on the life-world.

37. A good number of phenomenologists speak of the *epochē* as a technique distinct from the reduction. Lauer [1978], pp. 49–50, does this in a satisfactory way where the reduction is seen as the ongoing application of the epochē in order to achieve subjectivity in all its purity. In the *Cartesian Meditations* Husserl speaks of a transcendental epochē, rather than reduction. See Husserl [1982], #44, p. 93.

38. This should clarify, if such is needed, Husserl's "principle of principles," mentioned early in the first chapter of this essay. Husserl opposed his radical experience derived from the phenomenological intuition of essences to the positivistic empiricism of Hume and Comte which was grounded on the immediate experience of sense data. See David Bidney's observations in Natanson [1973b], Vol. 1, pp. 123–125; also Spiegelberg [1982], pp. 106, 109.

39. See Spiegelberg [1982], pp. 126–128, 139–141.

40. "Each life-world shows certain pervading structures or 'styles', and these invite study by what Husserl calls an 'ontology of the life worlds.'" See Spiegelberg [1982], p. 145. This is an extremely important idea since *Lumen Gentium* has provided a corporate expression of the ecclesial ontology unifying the concrete life-worlds of the various local churches around the world. The comparative religious studies of M. Eliade, which culminate in an ontology of many religious life-worlds, illustrate this methodological objective of Husserl: e.g., Eliade [1954].

41. See Husserl [1970], p. 135. Also Natanson [1973a], p. 128. On the vital importance of this suspension see Excursus V on Anthropology under the subheading, "The radical nature of Vatican II's reflection."

42. See D. Bidney in Natanson [1973b], Vol. 1, p. 129.

43. See D. Bidney in Natanson [1973b], Vol. 1, pp. 128–129. Emphasis added.

44. See Excursus I on the Life-world under the subheading: "Husserl's inspiration for the life-world."

45. The meta-anthropology of Vatican II is one of the topics of Chapter Eight.

46. See Bohr's remarks on this in Heisenberg [1971], pp. 39–41.

47. See Spiegelberg [1975], p. 69, and Spiegelberg [1982], #7, pp. 392–393. Heidegger's thought is not, it seems, compatible with classical ontology, and is only intelligible as a "new ontology." See Landgrebe [1966], pp. 118–119, 160–161. This is not to say that his thinking has not had a profound impact on Catholic theologians. See Hurd [1984], pp. 105–137.

48. For one recent comment on this point see Sandra M. Schneiders, IHM, "Freedom: Response and Responsibility: The Vocation of the Biblical Scholar in the Church," in Eigo [1981], pp. 25–52.

49. The pastoral hermeneutics of Vatican II is *not* necessarily identical with any biblical hermeneutics which has a "scientific" basis in historical criticism.

50. *Fides quaerens intellectum* derives from St. Anselm and by reason of its centrality in Thomism has shaped most theological thinking in the Church since the thirteenth century. See Conley [1963], pp. 59–72. As theoretical issues in Thomism, the intentional range of both "faith" and "understanding" is quite wide-ranging. See Deferrari,

Barry, and McGuiness [1948], pp. 419–420 (*fides*) and pp. 576–580 (*intellectus*). The ultimate purpose of this type of speculative theology is *contemplation*. See Conley [1963], pp. 81–103. Vatican II's doctrinal penetration and kerygma, however, added a new tonality to this long-established tradition of contemplation, which now became oriented to the needs of the modern world and *praxis*. See next note.

51. Although the Council's use of phenomenological method remains compatible with Husserl's standard theory, particularly in its analysis of religious phenomena, its genetic phenomenology and hermeneutics are oriented to a new type of *praxis* tailored to meet the pastoral challenge formulated by John XXIII in *Humanae Salutis* for our dislocated world. Thus, while remaining faithful to the contemplative tradition of speculative theology, the pastoral thought of Vatican II suffuses this contemplative tradition with a new *humanistic* gravity-shift. The theological synthesis resulting from the Council's reflections thus lends a more realistic and down-to-earth dimension to the contemplative tradition of theology in the modern world. See Van Ackeren [1967], pp. 44–45.

52. Theological research (e.g., Häring [1961–1966]) would have already provided extensive examples of the intentional relationship between the virtues (noema) and their constitutive acts (noesis).

53. At the Council there were two major theological blocs: Roman School Theology and a loosely federated "Central and Northern European" group (sometimes called the "European Alliance") united in opposition to the first bloc. See Rynne [1963] and Wiltgen [1978], who both recognize this phenomenon, but from opposite ends of the theological spectrum. Neither author, however, recognizes the historical context nor the intellectual implications of this profound cultural cleavage at the Council; their view of the Council is that of journalists, rather than theologians, historians, and philosophers. The actual list of names elected to the conciliar commissions by the bishops in the first session may be found in Anderson [1962], Vol. 1, pp. 42–44; the supplemental members added by John XXIII are also found in Anderson [1962], Vol. 1, pp. 53–55. Once this essentially cultural grouping had occurred, it fell under the intellectual leadership dominant in each group. For the Central and Northern European group the accepted academic methodology was that of phenomenology.

54. It must also be presumed that these techniques must have been applied to the schemata prepared for the first session of the Council in order to retrieve from them whatever was of value.

55. On "thematization" in theology see Van Ackeren [1967], p. 43. On "thematization" in phenomenology see Husserl [1978], pp. 33 sq.

CHAPTER 7

THE DYNAMICS OF AN ADJUSTING ECCLESIAL CONSCIOUSNESS

Paul VI vis-à-vis mankind

Toward the end of *Ecclesiam Suam* (#96–115) Paul VI appropriated a vision of mankind that would soon appear in the second chapter of *Lumen Gentium* to describe the Church as the People of God.[1] By somewhat anticipating this imagery in his first encyclical the pope implicitly affirmed that his papal vision and concerns were coextensive with those of the Council. In order to assure such complementarity of outlook the pope, we must assume, used this imagery *consistently*, if not identically, with the doctrinal intent of the bishops. This observation should cause no difficulty since the Holy Father only juxtaposed two different "inertial systems" (i.e., religion and humanity). They are correlated only to the extent his spiritual principle of discernment projects an *ad hoc* organization of religious priorities and proximities onto the concrete, empirical data of mankind. His vision, consequently, is more a formal statement of the papal mission and its sense of responsibility than any observation about humanity itself. Why, then, do we dwell on this image at all? (1) For scholars it offers a clear insight into one rather prosaic use of spiritual principles in correlation with empirical data: mere extrinsicism. (2) But later, out of the ashes of the same religious principles and the same data the phoenix of a new hermeneutical phenomenology will arise in the Council's creative formulation of the People of God.

The vision of mankind which Paul VI offers in *Ecclesiam Suam* is one totally fabricated by his adjusting religious psychology. The view, however, is so remote and spiritualized that it seems to be drifting off into a personal mystique, rather than being any realistic reflection on empirical data.[2] One axiom of the Holy Father's religious convictions is that no one may be excluded from the maternal concern of the Church.[3] On this basis, the papal view of mankind, as gathered in imagination about the Chair of Peter, sees it as falling into four concentric groupings.[4] This demographic arrangement is purely formal and a good example of an obvious religious projection. The outermost circle embraces all those undifferentiated by any religious commitment. Nearer to the center are gathered monotheists like the Jews and Moslems, and followers of the Afro-Asian religions. Nearer still are Christians of every type, and immediately about the papal throne are Catholics themselves. With all these groups the Church must enter into respectful and constructive dialogue. She must teach men about truth, justice, freedom, progress, concord, civilization, and peace. The whole reflection is dominated by the pope's overriding desire "to increase the holiness and vitality of the Mystical Body of Christ."[5] All this is somewhat remote from the quest for Christian efficacy expressed by John XXIII in *Humanae Salutis*.

Mystical Body vs. People of God

Paul VI resorted to such an intellectualist presentation in *Ecclesium Suam* for three reasons. (1) He did not want to steal the thunder from the new insights in *Lumen Gentium* about to be promulgated within four months' time. (2) While the fundamental thrust of his encyclical was to outline his pastoral priorities, it also allowed him to alert people to the theological workings of his own mind. (3) Finally, the letter permitted him to highlight the centrality of the Mystical Body of Christ as it existed in his own religious consciousness.[6] Although the Council was about to present a new, or at least generally unfamiliar, image of the Church as the People of God, Paul knew that the two images were meant to complement one another. Rather than displacing the Mystical Body from its centrality in the mystery of the Church, the Council desired to add to it a startlingly new and unappreciated dimension. In the first chapter of *Lumen Gentium* the bishops formulated their principle of spiritual discernment, not according to the extrinsicism of Paul VI, but according to the intrinsic nature of the life of the Church:

> As all the members of the human body, though they are many, form one body, so also are the faithful in Christ (cf. I Cor. 12:12). [. . .][7]
> All the members ought to be molded into Christ's image until He is formed in them (cf. Gal. 4:19).[8] For this reason we who have been made like unto Him, who have died with Him and been raised up with Him, are taken up into the mysteries of His life, until we reign together with him (cf. Phil. 3:21; 2 Tim. 2:11; Eph. 2:6; Col. 2:12; etc.).[9]

Spiritual discernment, christocentric intentionality, and moral renewal

When someone states a principle of spiritual discernment, we should also realize he is making at least an indirect statement about intentionality. He is, in fact, stating some facet of the ontological presuppositions or derivatives inherent in the functional image, theory, or Gestalt which decides *what he can see!* In this instance we are, of course, dealing with a religious intentionality. A high percentage of the bishops — had they so desired — could have stated things on the basis of a strictly philosophical intentionality. The point is, however, that at the Council the bishops were not functioning as philosophers, but as religious leaders and teachers. Consequently, their vision, functional image, theory, or Gestalt was totally christocentric. This means that in the religious dimension they *cannot* see anything unless it possesses (in scholastic terminology) at least an "obediential potency" to be conformed to Christ.[10] The ontological basis of this potency exists in all men inasmuch as human beings have been created in God's image (cf. Gen. 1:26). Consequently, in all the discussion which follows two things must always be kept in mind. (1) The God-given paradigm for integrated humanity can only be Christ as the New Adam. (2) Human dynamisms, whether viewed individually or corporately, can make religious sense only when seen in correlation with Christ as the revealed model of perfected humanity.

In this religious sense, then, the Council's documents are truly the corporate *Journal of a Soul* for the Catholic Church.[11] Unlike John XXIII's spiritual diary these reflections of Vatican II were not written in a chronological and individualistic fashion, but in a collaborative way which grouped communal meanings, values, and experiences thematically. This observation in no way implies that the conciliar documents are a compilation of mere pietistic moralisms. In many instances there are authentic clarifications of doctrinal issues.[12] However, these insights are so subsumed under the overwhelming pastoral purposes of the Council and so entwined with descriptive phenomenology that careful professional analysis by theologians is needed to bring out their technical meanings.[13] In this quest essentially focused on moral renewal the Church asked herself basically the same questions which any Catholic on retreat would put to himself: "Who am I, really? What is the meaning of my existence? What are my true values? Do these actually shape my attitudes and conduct in everyday life? How do I intend to act for the future in order to be more genuinely my true self? *Church, what do you say of yourself?*"[14] While any responsible adult may profitably reflect on such questions, especially in our turbulent times, the reflective process for the Church is inevitably much more complex. Not only is she an international organization embracing many rites other than the Latin one, but she has an intellectual and cultural history spanning almost two thousand years. Yet, in spite of such difficulties she has pioneered in a process of self-confrontation which faces every nation or organization in the world today.

Easing into the operative ecclesial consciousness

When Cardinal Suenens introduced the *ad intra/ad extra* distinction on December 4, 1962, he did so far two eminently practical reasons: first, to recall the pastoral concerns voiced by John XXIII in his radio broadcast of September 11, 1962, and secondly, to suggest two broad categories for organizing the crush of materials being proposed to the Council. As things worked out, the bishops eventually promulgated two documents on the Church: its *internal* nature was described by the dogmatic constitution, *Lumen Gentium*, and its *external* relationships with the modern world were described by the pastoral constitution, *Gaudium et Spes*. In order to head off unproductive academic controversies the Cardinal also submitted a written intervention which suggested that, when any class of people was viewed in relationship to the Church, they should be viewed concretely: i.e., in their ordinary existence as human beings and not according to some abstract formula.[15] This accorded well with the sentiments of the vast majority of the bishops. As pastoral leaders, they were down-to-earth men, and this was particularly true for the missionary bishops who constituted almost fifty percent of the bishops at the Council. They wanted theological reflection to have some practical relevance and benefit to the real world in which their people lived. It was this very focus on "mundanity" which was about to make these bishops "transcendental meditators," whether they realized it or not.

With the negative reaction in the first session to the preparatory documents and the scholasticism which they embodied, there simply was no group of theologians – other than the phenomenologists – who could cope with the flood of concrete, religious experiences (*Erlebnisse*) flooding into the conciliar commissions from the pastorally minded bishops from all over the world. For at least a generation such theologians had been pioneering theology "in a new key" according to phenomenological thought-categories. Now, with the older scholasticism in a minority position and, at most, only able to exercise a moderating influence (especially in the person of Paul VI), these theologians were suddenly being given a comparatively free hand. They knew that on the basis of his *individual* subjectivity Husserl had formulated an academically respected theory of the *world as mine*. They also knew that reflection on the ego's consciousness of its being an incarnate body-subject had enabled Husserl to lay the foundations for a transcendental intersubjectivity, a communion with human beings as *alter ego*.[16] Their challenge, then, both as phenomenologists and as Catholic theologians, was could they formulate an expression of their religious *world as ours*? And could this *religious world as ours* evoke a vision and hope for a new *secular world as ours*?

The challenge to build a new consensus

It has been mentioned previously that the interventions of the popes at the Council were shaped by their desire to build consensus: they wanted no "winners" or "losers," but only a renewed ecclesial community.[17] Such efforts would have been fruitless, however, if there had not been a much more profound and ongoing effort at consensus-building permeating the work of the commissions throughout the Council. The phenomenologically-inclined bishops and theologians were faced with an enormous challenge. On the one hand, there were about twenty-five hundred bishops feeding in their concrete experiences rising out of the facticity of their own religious life-worlds. How to get some *meaning* out of this welter of subjective input? On the other hand, there was the minority party looking at things "objectively" from the viewpoint of the Roman School of theology: custodians of time-honored formulae if not contemporary communication. Although phenomenology had been elaborated by Husserl to be just such a *via media* between subjectivism and objectivism, the theologians intent on a reconceptualization of religious communication knew they had to honor the epistemological values of the perennial philosophy in order to get their ideas approved. Paul VI had said as much in *Ecclesiam Suam*.[18] When one imagines the span of possibilities in the use of phenomenology, its usage at the Council is quite judicious and in the "classical" mode pioneered by Husserl. Furthermore, such theologians had to authentically express the bishops' corporate ideas and sentiments, since it was the bishops on the floor of the Council who would express the final judgment by the voting procedures used to approve or reject such documents.

Among the bishops and theologians dominant at the Council there was one group particularly equipped to correlate scholasticism and phenomenology in a constructive way: the Transcendental Thomists.[19] Although their beginnings had a Kantian orientation, with time most of them had made an easy accommodation to the phenomenological method. Certain individual bishops like K. Wojtyla, not particularly identified as Transcendental Thomists, had professional degrees in both classical Thomism and phenomenology. Consequently, so simple a thing as the *ad intra/ad extra* distinction could easily be read either in terms of scholasticism's formal and material causality or phenomenology's noesis and noema (or, to get a bit more complex, the isomorphism between transcendental subjectivity and the natural attitude).[20] The scholastic concept of *being* could quickly be transposed into the phenomenological focus on *meaning*. The modality between abstraction and the various types of reduction, although significant, was quite well understood. In all such transactions, however, the common preoccupation with intentionality would have been the liason between both schools of thought. Thus, the bishops and theologians on the various commissions were enabled to transcend the barrage of facticity being presented by the bishops from the floor of the Council and to reenter the world of *meaning*, the world of *intentional consciousness*, and even a *new* world empirically derived from and correlated with the Council's corporate transcendental intersubjectivity. Their quest, somewhat like Husserl's, had been for a new theology grounded in the empirical a priori of human experience, with a view to shaping new attitudes toward religious and human reality.

An overview of phenomenology at work at the Council

As we move into what may be one of the more complex portions of this essay, we must realize that we are entering the realm of *pure consciousness*: i.e., the living mind at work searching for meaning in mundane facticity. Here it might be well for us to assume the role of outside observers, much as Alfred Schutz does when he studies some social entity. The point of the inquiry is *not* what sense this field of consciousness makes to us as observers, but what sense it makes to the people participating in this corporate process. "The axis of inquiry is turned to the egological realm, where the meaning is defined by how the individual interprets his own motives, plans, projects, and ultimately his own situation. *The task of the observer is to reconstruct the actor's intentions in terms of what the actor means by his act.*"[21] It must also be understood that the theses of philosophical phenomenology, as broadly developed by Husserl on the basis of *individual* subjectivity, are taken for granted.[22] The methodology is now simply being applied *corporately* to religious phenomena. Any such human reflection is permeated by a strong sense of temporality: i.e., it functions within a framework textured by its sense of inner time-consciousness.[23] It is, then, the peculiar sense of ecclesial time which structures the "spatial," or visual, horizon formulated in the major Council documents.

Possibly you may recall from Chapter Three the rather extensive remarks, in a liturgical context, made about the bidimensional sense of time at the heart of Catholicism. The *vertical* dimension represents the "eternal now" (i.e., a synchronic view of events), and may be called "sacramental time." In a liturgical context this "eternal now" functions in a *cyclical* timeframe. The *linear* (or diachonic) dimension is the teleological-historical unfolding of God's Plan, or the divine intentionality, in mundane human events. This may be called "eschatological time."[24] The "spatial" horizon of the Church as the People of God in *Lumen Gentium* is structured according to linear, eschatological time. The general purpose of this document is to discern the ontological core at the heart of the Catholic life-world which unites the individualized religious life-worlds of the local churches throughout the world.[25] By implication this ontological core sets the intentional parameters for the acculturalization process endorsed by the Council.

In *Dei verbum*, however, the document on revelation, there is what might usefully be called a "transcendental turn." This allows the corporate consciousness of the Church to escape from a certain "ecclesial monadology;"[26] here the eidetic focus turns to the vertical dimension of the "eternal now" and contemplates the unchanging realities grounding the concrete intentionalities (*noemata*) existing in the ecclesial consciousness. This contemplative process is *not* a left-handed form of Platonism, but a heightened effort at the phenomenological apperception of religious realities. By its very nature the apperceptive process implies that the empirical data being contemplated become "transfigured" with intelligibility, and the Council's use of the phenomenological procedures leading up to such an "intuition" simply means that the *noemata* existing in the ecclesial consciousness are open to on-going levels of increasing refinement and intelligibility.

The *integral* intentional ground of the ecclesial consciousness is the intersection-point at which the vertical and linear horizons meet and on which these two systems of internal time-consciousness pivot. The traditional formula of this intentionality is established in the first chapter of *Lumen Gentium* where the Mystical Body is endorsed as the ontological paradigm of the *ad intra* spiritual nature of the Church.[27] We can now appreciate Paul VI's emphasis on this doctrine in his encyclical, *Ecclesiam Suam*.

The *ad intra/ad extra* distinction and dialectical isomorphism

In this world of pure consciousness the use of the *ad intra/ad extra* distinction becomes a fascinating study in an interlinked, dialectical isomorphism. "The root of this consonance," as Natanson says, "is hidden in the phenomenological attitude, for when one is engaged in a philosophical interrogation in Husserl's sense, he is at the same time attending to the world which men inhabit as creatures."[28] As mentioned previously, the most overt use of this distinction is the correlation between *Lumen Gentium* and *Gaudium et Spes*: i.e., the internal nature of the Church and its external relationships with the modern world. However, *within Lumen Gentium itself* the ontological intentional ground *ad intra* is provided by the Mystical Body, whereas the *external* characteristics of the Church as a visible society are made manifest by the People of God. It might be well to mention here that this is simply a recasting of the functional ontology expressed by St. Augustine's imagery of the City of God. Consequently, in the confrontation with mundanity the People of God are the *ad intra* ecclesial component involved with the *external* secular relationships formulated in *Gaudium et Spes*. Lastly, the *ad intra* intentional ground of the Church as Mystical Body (or as the "listening" People of God) is correlated with its *ad extra* eternal truths in *Dei verbum*.

This brief reflection on dialectical interrelationships (isomorphism) is presented in terms of the three major documents which this essay focuses upon. However, once the principle is understood, it may be applied to the other documents of the Council. By a sense of the interconnectedness of the conciliar style of thought one may get a good sense of the living consciousness of the Church. These notions will become clearer as they are applied in more detail in the following chapters.

Summary

This chapter portrayed the historical consciousness of the Church on the brink of making a serious transition in its style of thinking and expression i.e., from the abstract, intellectualist view typified by Paul VI's scholastic objectivism to the phenomenological focus on concrete experiences in the service of the pastoral aims of the Council. Both views, it must be emphasized, were presented as complementary to one another, and not set in any significant antagonism. This mutuality of intention, if not of methodology, was a practical necessity at the Council since Vatican II was not an academic "think-tank" but an enterprise in building ecclesial community. In such a delicate process we began to appreciate the utility of Husserl's "classical" phenomenology in comparison with other possible types, and we became more aware that there were both scholastics and phenomenologists at the Council who could facilitate this transition in a collaborative way.

Toward the end of Chapter Six we presented, in a quite gingerly way, a preliminary overview of the use of phenomenological techniques at the Council. In this chapter we again presented an overview of these techniques but as applied in some of their complexity. Particularly important was the ecclesial awareness of inner time-consciousness for establishing the Church's horizons both in *Lumen Gentium* and *Dei verbum*. We also began to appreciate the *ad intra/ad extra* distinction as a display of dialectical isomorphism within diverse levels of consciousness.

Having laid these foundations, we are now ready to reflect on the first two chapters of *Lumen Gentium*. Although this brief sample of the constitution may only be a case study in metaphenomenology, the investigation will help us to understand how the use of phenomenological techniques at the Council resulted in a new ecclesial hermeneutics for the needs of the modern world.

NOTES

1. See Carlen [1981], Vol. 5, pp. 154–159.
2. The Holy Father's anxieties seem to be dominated by a concern for preserving doctrinal and moral integralism while coming to the aid of an alien and sinful world. John XXIII's implied model of the Good Samaritan acquires a cautionary tonality at the hands of Paul VI: "A physician who realizes the danger of disease, protects himself and others from it, but at the same time he strives to cure those who have contracted it." See Carlen [1981], Vol. 5, #63, p. 149.
3. See Carlen [1981], Vol. 5, #94, p. 154.
4. See Carlen [1981], Vol. 5, #96–115, pp. 154–159. The Latin phrase is: "quasi *orbes* circum centrum ductos." *Acta Apostolicae Sedis* 56:10 (Aug. 20, 1964) 650. See Carlen [1981], Vol. 5, #96, p. 154. This accounts for the cautionary and prosaic nature of Paul's imagery: it remains a psychological projection. Had the Holy Father said: "quasi *orbes finientes* circum centrum ductos," then he would have been speaking explicitly about concentric "horizons." This would have moved the pope's imagery from the realm of the psychological into that of phenomenology. Inasmuch as *Ecclesiam Suam* is primarily a *policy* statement regarding his pontificate, Paul VI felt it more appropriate to leave such *doctrinal* nuancing to the dogmatic constitution, *Lumen Gentium*, about to be promulgated by the Council. Consequently, the "circles of dialogue," mentioned in the encyclical, reflect at most Paul VI's religious attitudes and his readiness to engage in the exacting task of dialogue required by the modern global situation. See Wojtyla [1979], p. 29. Had the Holy Father explicitly chosen to use the word, "horizon," rather than "circle," a whole new tonality would then have permeated his reflection on mankind:

> [. . .] the horizon cuts across the distinctions of inside–outside – belonging to man, exterior to man. In the horizon, exteriority merges with interiority; man merges with the world . . . . The horizon is the translation of man into the world.

> [. . .] it is his world, the human world, the inhabited world. It is not in the division of scientific concepts that man becomes aware of his participation in the image of the world but in the unity of lived experience. Man lives in the horizon, the horizon is himself, the horizon is the world, the horizon reflects back to him the human world, namely the world as visible in the beam of human reflection.

See Van Peursen in Elliston and McCormick [1977], p. 185. In *Lumen Gentium* the transition has been made to the religious *horizon*, the religious *life-world*. By Paul VI's very delicate handling of this whole matter the Holy Father is allowing the Council to introduce to the world its own innovative style of phenomenological reflection. In the course of our reflections Paul VI's insistence on the centrality of the Mystical Body will be integrated into the Council's over-all methodology.

5. See Carlen [1981], Vol. 5, #116, p. 159. This is the same objective which Paul VI associated with the renewal program as a whole. See Carlen [1981], Vol. 5, #44, p. 144: "... with a view to infusing fresh spiritual vigor into Christ's Mystical Body considered as a visible society."

6. Inasmuch as the pattern of papal intervention at the Council was strongly influenced by the desire to build consensus (cf. Chapter Six, note 14), it would have been totally out of character and contrary to his pastoral role for Paul VI's first encyclical to have emphasized the Mystical Body if the Council's formulary of the People of God, soon to be promulgated in *Lumen Gentium*, were somehow at variance with this time-honored doctrine. As the voice of the Catholic consciousness, Paul VI seems to be equating Mystical Body with ontology, and thus leaves the way open for People of God to suggest "visible society." In scholastic terminology this is the form/matter relationship. In phenomenological terms, however, this is an ontic statement of the intentional ground of the ecclesial consciousness (ego) about to reflect on itself as an incarnate body-subject (*Leib*). See F.A. Elliston in Elliston and McCormick [1977], p. 219.

7. See Abbott [1966], #7, p. 120.

8. This totally christocentric axiom expresses the teleology and hierarchial ontology inherent in the faith-relationship, both at the level of individual consciousness and at the corporate level of the Church as a spiritual society. It is this type of axiom, inaccessible by way of any scientific method, which is the bedrock of the conciliar style of reflection. From this point on, consequently, *this essay will accept as a working-principle* that the phenomenological suspension of the sciences has taken place at the Council and that the bishops are working within the ambit of their religious life-world. In the course of this essay, however, we will point out additional instances where the suspension of the sciences is operative, but our argument can only be cumulative and not demonstrative. See also Excursus I on the Life-World under the sub-heading, "The practical character of the religious life-world."

9. See Abbott [1966], #7, p. 21.

10. See Excursus VII on Obediential Potency.

11. This reference to John XXIII's *Journal*, while useful to get the personalistic, spiritual "flavor" of the Council's style of reflection is really not adequate to the religio-cultural scope of its renewal program. A more apt comparison would be to see it in relationship to the type of theological recasting which took place during the Deuteronomic Reform in the Old Testament. See Anderson [1966] in his Subject Index under the listings for "Deuteronomic," p. 581. Another comparison, more apt to convey the cultural implications of this adaptation, would be early Christianity's recasting of the narrowly Jewish framework of the Good News to meet the needs of the Graeco-Roman world. Such analogies, drawn from the past, are useful – provided that we appreciate the renewal program of Vatican II as oriented to the *future* at a *unique* moment in human history.

12. Two of the more obvious instances of doctrinal development would be in the area of collegiality and religious freedom. The Council's formulation of these two issues, while authentic, is non-formal and non-technical. This point becomes particularly clear if we recall that the vehicle for expressing integral doctrine since the Council of Trent, at least, has been the objectivist and realistic thought-categories of scholasticism. Just before the final vote on *Lumen Gentium* formal and technical issues were interjected into the Council in an extrinsic way by certain "Announcements" by the

Secretary General. See Abbott [1966], pp. 97–101, and J. Ratzinger, "Announcements and Prefatory Notes of Explanation," in Vorgrimler [1967–1969], Vol. 1, pp. 297–305. In the case of religious freedom, furthermore, it remains to the theologians to work out the technical details of the development from the *Syllabus of Errors* (1864) to *Dignitatis Humanae Personae* (1965). See J.C. Murray in Abbott [1966], p. 673. By "development" I mean a teleological-historical comprehension of change, as Husserl employed that terminology. Wojtyla [1979], p. 23, makes an interesting use of the *ad intra/ad extra* dialectical reading of the Council's documents on this very point of religious freedom.

13. See Excursus IX on Interpretation under the subheading, "The interpretation of Council documents."

14. "Rogamus ergo ab Ecclesia: Quid dicis de teipsa?" Cardinal Suenens, December 4, 1962, in Latin Texts [1970–1980], Vol. 1, pars iv, p. 223. This question plays a key-role in Wojtyla [1979], p. 35 sq. on "The Consciousness of the Church as the main foundation of Conciliar initiation." In the phenomenological context of Vatican II Cardinal Suenen's question may be rephrased: "Ecclesia, quid *cogitas* de teipsa?" The Council's documents are meant, of course, to provide us with an insight into this corporate, living thought-process. We shall return to this question again in Chapters Nine and Ten.

15. For the exact quotation see Excursus III, "Concrete Human Relationships and Cardinal Suenens."

16. See Natanson [1973a], pp. 99–101. Carr [1974], pp. 82–109 devotes a whole chapter to Husserl's concept of intersubjectivity. Its discussion of the social dimension of the individual consciousness, as transcendental subjectivity, makes fine background reading for the work of Vatican II. For an intentional analysis of Alter Ego see F.A. Elliston in Elliston and McCormick [1977], pp. 215–217.

17. See Excursus VI on Dialogue under the subheading, "The popes as monitors of group dynamics."

18. See Carlen [1981], Vol. 5, #28, p. 140 and #47–49, pp. 145–146.

19. See Muck [1968] for a comprehensive study of Transcendental Thomism.

20. See Natanson [1973a], p. 185.

21. See Natanson 1973a], p. 112.

22. If a person knows what the phenomenological method is, he need not agree with some theoretical interpretation of it in order to use it responsibly. This was very much the case with Alfred Schutz. See Schutz [1962–1976], Vol. 3, esp. pp. 82–84. This was very much the case of the Northern European bishops/theologians at the Council. Such men tend to be high-level theoreticians whose reflection is grounded in Kant, Hegel, Husserl, Heidegger, Merleau-Ponty, or some such philosophical theorist. I suspect such thinkers would be uncomfortable with Schutz's orientation to the life-world and would be exercising a counter-force to set such ideas into a larger *theoretical* context, which really militates against the *pastoral* nature of Vatican II. Hence, my own solicitude to try to stay anchored in Husserl's common-ground methodology while discussing the Council's phenomenological style of reflection.

23. On inner time-consciousness in phenomenological reflection see Natanson [1973a], pp. 96, 116 and esp. pp. 137–138. See also J.B. Brough, "The Emergence of an Absolute Consciousness in Husserl's Early Writings on Time-Consciousness," in Elliston and McCormick [1977], pp. 83–100, but esp. pp. 96–97, where Husserl's use of the "vertical" and "horizontal" intentionalities of consciousness are discussed. These ideas may be usefully compared with our Excursus II on Sacramental Time.

24. For the connection between eschatology and modern revolutionary movements, see Excursus VI on Dialogue under the subheading, "Dialogue in the context of eschatology."

25. On the "ontological core" (or general structures) of the life-world see Husserl [1970], p. 139. See also D. Carr in Elliston and McCormick [1977], p. 208. The recovery of this core common to all life-worlds is, in principle, the presupposition for the philosophical renewal of the natural sciences. See D. Carr in Elliston and McCormick [1977], pp. 206–209. Presumably the work of Vatican II regarding the religious life-world had much the same goal in mind for the "science" of theology. But more is implied. In the life-world, which this book views as the multi-layered workings of a bipolar consciousness, all the sciences – natural, human, philosophical, and theological – have their originary matrix. In this enlarged view of the life-world, both religious and natural, we have the "ecumenical" common-ground for humanity's dialogue.

26. It is well-known that Husserl's doctrine of the transcendental ego seems to involve a certain type of monadology. This topic is discussed by Ludwig Landgrebe's "Phenomenology as Transcendental Theory of History," in Elliston and McCormick [1977], esp. pp. 104–105, 109–110. The ahistorical type of phenomenological reflection found in *Lumen Gentium* represents the Church as transcendental (corporate) Ego in its living self-presence contemplating itself as incarnate body-subject. The intersubjectivity involved is totally *internal* to the Church itself. This expression of corporate monadology means the Church is focused on her own "eidetic essence" to the exclusion of all other religions. The "transcendental turn" involved in *Dei verbum,* the document on revelation, has the utility of drawing the Church out of such "self-centeredness" and placing her immediately before God and His message to mankind. This is the common-ground which the Church shares with all Christians and, to a lesser degree, with Jews and Moslems. At any event, the Church's eidetic analysis at this level lays out for all men to see the ontological core of the revealed essences as they exist in her contemporary consciousness. If you prefer, you can also say this is a public statement of her "prejudices," but I am using the term within the context provided by Carr [1974], p. 282 under "Prejudice(s)." Unlike the ontological end-product achieved, for example, by an Eliade whose eidetic analysis of an individual religion is an external, individual application of phenomenological method, the ontology produced by the ecclesial analysis is the result of an internal, corporate application of the methodology. (We shall return to the topic of ecclesial monadology under the rubric of "ecclesio-monism" in Chapter Ten dealing with *Dei verbum.*)

27. See Abbott [1966], #7–8, pp. 20–24.

28. See Natanson [1973a], p. 119.

PART III

THE FINAL ACHIEVEMENT

CHAPTER 8

THE NEW ECCLESIAL HERMENEUTICS

The Mystical Body and the consciousness of Vatican II

The first thing we must realize is that the *religious* life-world presented by *Lumen Gentium* could not have surfaced without an adroit use of reductive phenomenology: a double epochē at first, and ultimately a third one.[1] As mentioned previously, in *Lumen Gentium* the *ad intra* view of the contemporary ecclesial consciousness (which totally transcends mundane temporality) "brackets" or completely abstracts from the concrete details of human existence *ad extra*, as treated in *Gaudium et Spes* (i.e., "The Church in the Modern World"). The first epochē, then, is a suspension of belief in the existence or reality of the secular, social world. The second epochē is a bit more complex. After positing the Mystical Body as the intentional ground of the ecclesial consciousness in the first chapter of *Lumen Gentium*, the bishops "turn their backs" to this source of spiritual illumination in order to reflect on concrete, religious human experiences in today's world.[2] Although they never return to this religious conceptualization in any extended way, *it remains the intentional, objective focal-point around which all the doctrinal reflections of the Council pivot.* To illustrate this assertion in a rapid but summary way, we may say that *Dei verbum* displays the "mystical" dimensions of the ecclesial consciousness whereas the People of God in *Lumen Gentium* display the Church's concrete "body-awareness."[3]

It is important at this point to nuance what we mean by the *ecclesial consciousness.* Normally when the above epochē is performed, it is but a preliminary step toward the *technical* eidetic analysis of the phenomena thus reduced and, ultimately, toward Husserl's transcendental reduction. This type of analysis *never* took place at Vatican II since it was a pastoral, not a dogmatic council like Vatican I. While such a technical, phenomenological enterprise remains a theoretical possibility for some future council, it did not take place at Vatican II. Rather, both of the above-mentioned epochēs, especially that allowing the bishops to suspend their technical christocentric focus, faciliated an "anthropocentric turn" whereby the bishops and their theological assistants could reflect on *their own concrete human experiences* in the Catholic way of life.[4] Such experiences remained the concrete a priori ground throughout all the conciliar reflections; consequently the resulting doctrinal formulas of Vatican

II are *non-formal* thematizations derived from the *meaningful thought-patterns* of the living ecclesial consciousness. This entry, however, into what can only be the Catholic life-world necessitated that third use of reductive phenomenology, *the suspension of all the sciences.* Even in *Dei verbum* (which gives a first impression of a new "theocentric turn" implying a different basis for the eidetic analysis being conducted) the empirical a priori still remains concrete human and religious experiences as manifesting the contemporary thought-patterns of the Catholic life-world.

The Mystical Body and the phenomenology of the natural attitude

The result of all this on the *religious* plane is an approach to intersubjective phenomena comparable to Alfred Schutz's at the *natural* level: i.e., a phenomenology of the natural attitude.[5] For *sociological* purposes Schutz analysed the "taken for granted" routines and the "typifications" of daily life because these contained the meaning-structures for the whole range of membership in any society: i.e., from ordinary men to philosophers and scientists. For *pastoral* purposes the bishops at Vatican II employed a phenomenology of their own "natural" (religious) attitudes to discover the meaning-structures which reflect the moral values of Christ and unite Catholics in their own quest for authentic religious and human values. To interpret such procedures as a "sociology of religious knowledge"[6] or possibly some variation of a "psychology of religion" would be to fall into a crass form of scientific reductionism. In their practice of the phenomenology of the natural attitude the bishops obviously employed descriptive and eidetic phenomenology, as well as the phenomenology of appearances, in order to analyse their experiences. More importantly, however, the thematization of these experiences in the corporate ecclesial consciousness (e.g., as the People of God, collegiality, religious freedom, etc.) is the product of a constitutive phenomenology.[7] Lastly, the use of hermeneutical phenomenology will become apparent when we explain the humanistic dimensions of the People of God towards the end of this chapter.

In such a radically different mode of theologizing what guarantees the intentional consistency of the new formulas with the doctrine of the past? This problem, as you may recall, was latent in John XXIII's opening speech at the Council. There he insisted on doctrinal integralism, but largely ignored the fact that for at least six hundred years such doctrines had been understood and developed according to the objectivism of scholasticism. This problem is answered in the first chapter of *Lumen Gentium* where the bishops posit the doctrine of the Mystical Body *as then-understood* (i.e., within the scholastic tradition) and as the quasi-metaphysical and formal ground of their reflection.[8] This makes clear why Paul VI insisted on the centrality of the Mystical Body in his encyclical, *Ecclesiam Suam*, just a few months before the Council was about to project a new image of the Church as the People of God. In Husserlian terms, however, the Mystical Body would be functioning here as the equivalent of a general essence (universal) apodictically known in the abstract terms of pure phenomenology; however, as something approximating a formula of theoretical mathematics, it need not be seen as having any great orientation to the world of praxis.[9] This observation should become clearer as this chapter developes.

In undertaking this new approach to religious truth, then, the bishops were, in effect, saying that their anticipated development of doctrine would be, if not identical, at least consistent with this previously established heritage. From a *religious* point of view the supreme integrating factor, or "vital balance," in such a delicate reflective process dealing with serious religious matters would be the guidance of the Holy Spirit. From a *phenomenological* point of view the onto-logical consistency would be found in the to-be-expected isomorphism between the transcendentally reduced world (speculative order) and the world of the natural attitude (practical order) and, furthermore, the teleological-historical consciousness of an intersubjective community reflecting on its own life and heritage. However, any thematization of experiential reality, which attempts to correlate with a highly abstract, quasi-metaphysical and formal ontology, must content itself to be categorized as a *functional* ontology.[10]

Functional ontology and the theoretical order

The idea of a functional ontology has application in both the speculative and practical orders, although in the context of the religio-cultural issues we are ultimately concerned with, the practical order is by far the more important. We are familiar with the idea, if not terminology, of a functional ontology in the speculative order today largely from the theoretical studies having to do with gravity, the all-pervasive materialistic force governing bodies above the atomic level. Currently the workings of gravity are interpreted within two diverse systems of meanings (i.e., ontologies): Newton's Laws based on an absolute space and time, and Einstein's General Relativity Theory based on a relativity of space and time. Even though Einstein acknowledges a certain isomorphism between the two systems by his "principle of equivalence," we know that these two systems of interpretive meaning, while *functionally* equivalent in most cases of ordinary observation, have profound speculative differences shaping men's approaches and attitudes toward reality. Perhaps the following statement by **Nobel Prize-winner**, Charles H. Townes, will assist us to see the implications of this purely speculative problem in a fuller light:

> Galileo espoused the cause of Copernicus' theory of the solar system, and at great personal cost because of the Church's opposition. We know today that the question on which Galileo took his stand, the correctness of the idea that the earth rotates around the sun rather than the sun around the earth, is largely an unnecessary question. The two descriptions are equivalent, according to general relativity, although the first is simpler.[11]

If in the first chapter of *Lumen Gentium* the Council posits as its intentional ground the Mystical Body substantially as understood within the heritage of scholastic objectivism but immediately goes on to a phenomenology of the natural attitude which analyses human experiences and thereby develops a great meta-anthropology commensurate with the needs of modern men, then the *speculative* being, (or coherence of meaning) of this unexpected and radical about-face is in the *relation*, i.e., in the correlation of the intentional ground with the system of religious meanings derived from the individual experiences of the bishops participating in the Council. (Such a relation would approximate what Thomists call an "analogy of proportionality.") Vatican II, then, is a religious affirmation of Husserl's own belief in a comprehensive isomorphism permeating all levels of reality, from the most speculative to the everyday existence of the life-world. This belief in ordered meaning is the mainspring activating the pursuit of modern science. In this sense the religious reflection of the Church, like the philosophical work of Husserl, intends to be a positive and constructive force in this common enterprise of mankind. As this speculative pursuit of truth in science calls for the contributions of our finest theoretical minds, so also does the modern theological reflection of the Church.

Functional ontology and praxis

The faith-affirmation of a profound isomorphism pervading all levels of existence has profound practical implications since John XXIII set the *unity of mankind* as one of the major pastoral goals of the Council.[12] The normal development of the empirical sciences today goes from concrete experiences to abstract theory, and the modern tendency to theologize on the basis of a concrete situation relates to this pattern. If such theologizing is not done with competence, then the whole affirmation of an undergirding theoretical isomorphism is thrown in jeopardy along with John's pastoral goal of working for the unity of mankind. In order to understand more clearly what is involved here, let us postulate by way of example that our total experience of reality is shaped by the inertial system of a Newtonian universe. We can further simplify this universe by saying that its total ontology is summed up by Newton's Second Law of Motion (f = ma). This law formulates the necessary and ordered inter-working of the three abstract, but empirically derived "essences" (i.e., force, mass, and acceleration) discerned in the changes of our universe. But it becomes extremely difficult to recognize this law as it actually functions in specific and concrete instances of physics. As Thomas S. Kuhn remarks:

> [...] For the case of free fall, f = ma becomes $mg = m(d^2s/dt^2)$; for the simple pendulum it is transformed to $mg \sin \theta = ml(d^2\theta/dt^2)$; for a pair of interacting harmonic oscillators it becomes two equations, the first of which may be written $m_1(d^2 s_1/dt^2) + k_1 s_1 = k_2(s_2 - s_1 + d)$; and for more complex situations, such as the gyroscope, it takes still other forms, the family resemblance of which to f = ma is still harder to discover.[13]

In no way is it important to comprehend the mathematical complexities of these formulae; their mere visual presentation conveys a sense of the general law's intricate applications under normal (i.e., controlled) circumstances. (The theorem for free fall does not, for example, illustrate a person's "free fall" down a long flight of stairs!) Only a reasonably well-trained mind can possibly recognize the isomorphism between all these theorems and their general law. In any adaptation to a totally new mode of conceptualization, such as the General Theory of Relativity, the task of reinterpreting these theorems would, of necessity, have to be entrusted to competently trained specialists. The theorems, which we have been discussing, may serve as broad analogues for the pastoral process as intended by Vatican II. In this case the formula, f = ma, could be transposed roughly into the religious and human needs of a given populace correlated with its size and the rate of social change. Presumably, the application of any such hypothetical formula for a Third World nation would be somewhat "simpler" than that for a highly complex First World nation.

The point of the above analogy, however, is that the mind of Vatican II requires that in their pastoral adaptations all the individual units of whatever place or culture actively seek that common isomorphism uniting them both as human beings and as Catholics. That *active* pursuit of religious and human commonality in the midst of everyday existence was *demonstrated* at the Council by the bishops when they "gestated" out of their own individual ex-periences the notion of the People of God. With time the pastoral adaptations of the local churches are expected to become, even in their global diversity, intelligible exemplifications of the christocentric ontology grounded in the

Mystical Body and thereby contribute to the unity of mankind. Any particularized involution into an isolated or centrifugal type of pastoral development would be a serious departure from the authentic program of renewal endorsed by the Council. In the analysis and evaluation of such complex changes, particularly those occasioned by the new phenomenological style of reflection, the role — and I would emphasize the *corporate* role — of the theological specialist is apparent.

Functional ontology as dialectical isomorphism

Although the Mystical Body is posited in the first chapter of *Lumen Gentium* as the ontological ground of the Church, the term itself labors under the fact that it is the product of the tradition of scholastic objectivism. This term, "Mystical Body" — somewhat like "paschal mystery" — represents the mind's tendency to reify what is really rooted in the living and the human. Actually, the primary analogue for both of the above terms is the Glorified Christ. Ratzinger has well summed up the most elemental "Catholic prejudice" by expressing the *meaning for us* of the Glorified Christ to be the Logos-Shepherd.[14] If you can tolerate another mechanistic analogy, the Logos-Shepherd represents the primordial paradigm for divinity and humanity functioning as "a pair of interacting harmonic oscillators." This dual dimension of the Glorified Christ, much like Newton's Second Law used in the discussion previously, provides the ultimate ontological rationale for any man-made formulas in the Catholic religion and any dynamic relationships which these formulas are intended to symbolize. Once we recognize these points the complex analogical relationships within the dogmatic constitution on the Church may be expressed in a quasi-mathematical formula based on the *ad intra/ad extra* distinction:

$$\frac{\text{(ad intra)}\ \ \text{LOGOS}}{\text{(ad extra) SHEPHERD}} = \frac{\text{Mystical Body:Lumen:soul:form}}{\text{People of God:Gentium:body:matter}}$$

The scholastic connection

Having dwelt at some length on the phenomenological context of the above formula, perhaps some time may be given to its correlation with scholasticism. The first chapter of *Lumen Gentium* on "The Mystery of the Church" is a speculative overview of the *ad intra* functional ontology of the Church viewed primarily as the Mystical Body of Christ. A scholastic theologian would say this chapter presents the *formal* principles constituting the Church. The second chapter on "The People of God" is a speculative presentation of the *ad extra* functional ontology of the Church as a visible, empirical entity. A scholastic theologian would say this chapter presents the *material* principles constituting the Church. We can inject a little "life" into the scholastic terminology above by expressing the same relationships by the soul/body correlation, which is more expressive of the phenomenological sense.[15] Here the People of God would be appreciated as the *becoming* of the ecclesial world in its transcendental consciousness.

Although the above two chapters provide a conveniently separate description of the *ad intra/ad extra* dimensions of the Church, this disjunction is unnatural for two reasons. (1) The ontological analogy on which the whole reflection of *Lumen Gentium* is based is the Incarnation of Christ, not as the Christ of mundane temporality, but the Risen Christ everlastingly present to his members as the Logos-Shepherd.[16] (2) Like the human soul and body in their normal state the formal and material principles of the Church cannot exist in isolation from one another. When they are unified, then the operative scholastic principle is: *causae sunt causae ad invicem sed in diverso ordine.* This may be rendered somewhat freely as: "When any set of compatible causes is joined in a dynamic interrelationship, they function as 'interacting harmonic oscillators' according to the principles proper to their respective causalities."

Blueprint for the new servant leaders of mankind

Although the first two chapters of *Lumen Gentium* present an ahistorical, transcendent, and theoretical view of the Church, a scholastic theoretician would be inclined to evaluate this new ecclesial paradigm as a rather low-level type of theologizing. It hardly represents the much more sublime and comprehensive theology deriving from the centrality of the Holy Trinity in Catholic thought.[17] The primary religious analogue for *communio* itself is to be found in the family-life of God, the relationship of mutual love between Father, Son, and Holy Spirit.[18] The fundamentals of such a theology are, of course, present in the documents of the Council, but they are so oriented to the pastoral objectives of the Council that theology seems to be playing "second fiddle" to social utility. This criticism has some academic merit to it, until one realizes that the Church is not theologizing during some High Renaissance of Christian civilization but on the brink of a New Dark Ages.

For important historical and pastoral reasons, therefore, the bishops embarked on this down-to-earth style of theologizing. They had a crucial design-project in mind: to reinvent the business of the Church, to reinvent evangelization.[19] No modern corporation engages in such a complex undertaking unless its very survival is at stake or enormous pressures are being brought to bear for change. Jonathan Schell, however, has pointed out that today's global problems are so massive that we must reinvent politics, reinvent the world.[20] John XXIII endorsed substantially the same view in *Humanae Salutis*, his radio broadcast of September 11, 1962, and his encyclical, *Pacem in Terris*. Remedying the "crisis in human beings" was for John XXIII the ultimate practical goal of the Council. In reinventing the business of the Church the bishops were simply responding to this larger global challenge. By formulating their notion of the People of God the bishops were providing us with a blueprint of the moral qualities men and women would have to cultivate if they were to measure up to these global challenges and become the new servant leaders of mankind.[21] The only way we can begin to appreciate what is involved here is to recall the historical circumstances giving rise to this new religious idea.

Vonier and the People of God

The concept of the People of God was introduced to American readers in 1937 by Dom Anscar Vonier, O.S.B., an eminently respected writer on things spiritual and theological.[22] At that time, as you may recall, vitalistic thinking on the nature of the Church was on the increase, at least in Northern Europe. Some of this was due to the revival of historical studies inspired by German Romanticism, and some of it was due to an anti-scientific, non-cognitive outlook which had developed out of the disillusionment following World War I. In 1943 Pius XII rather discriminatingly chose the best fruits of this type of religious speculation and incorporated them into his great encyclical on the Mystical Body.[23] Although the pope hoped in this way to bring some of the more romanticized tendencies of this vitalistic mindstyle under control, he was not totally successful. In less than a decade he had to return to some new aspects of vitalism in his encyclical, *Humani Generis.*[24]

Although Vonier appreciated the validity of this vitalistic trend in ecclesiology, his pragmatic British sensibilities made him uncomfortable with it. One gets the distinct impression that, in spite of the vaunted biblical, liturgical, and kerygmatic renewal then taking place in Europe. Vonier felt a large area of religious dynamics was being left untapped.[25] In his ominous era he saw the Mystical Body as a highly spiritualized image of the Church which offered Christians an easy refuge from pressing tasks at hand. All the militant historical forces of that day — Nazism, Fascism, Communism — were intent on shaping a *people* and the solidarity associated with corporate, communal action. Laicism and secularism were also intent on blocking Christians from exercising any effective social influence. In such an environment Vonier recognized in the rich biblical notion of the People of God a theological concept which, as a paradigm of the Church, would assist in eliciting the *psycho-social* implications of the moral values portrayed by the Mystical Body of Christ. In this way he hoped to develop an ecclesial countercultural force which, with time, would begin to mitigate the dominant secular and political trends of that day.[26] At the Second Vatican Council the bishops appropriated Vonier's theological paradigm of the Church to describe in a theoretical, yet applied way the *ad extra*, material, corporate, and empirical aspects of the Church.

The bishops' use of the People of God

Vonier's discomfort with an over-spiritualized understanding of the Mystical Body can, of course, have its parallel today with an "over-liturgized" understanding of the People of God. At Vatican II, however, the bishops were quite faithful to Vonier's original purpose for this imagery when they turned to reflect on the "flesh and blood" dimensions of the Church: i.e., the meaning for them of concrete humanity's ordering to God. This "sense" of their religious life-world began to take the form of three ecclesiocentric "horizons" correlating Catholics, Christians, and all the unbaptized.[27] (Paul VI, as you may recall, used a somewhat comparable imagery in *Ecclesiam Suam.*)[28] Now, however, the bishops' principle of spiritual discernment (or eidetic analysis) is quite different. Although verbalized in an extrinsic way as God's universal call to salvation,[29] their new vision of humanity is really grounded on mankind's *intrinsic* ontological ordering, as created in God's image, to be one with the People of God.[30] With Christ, as mankind's God-given Redeemer and Head of the Mystical Body, providing their functional image, theory, or gestalt the bishops can *only* see all the *wholesome human dynamisms* which have an obediential potency to be conformed to Christ. This fusion of the formal and material elements found in the first two chapters of *Lumen Gentium* results in a vision of the *corporate* New Adam fresh from the hands of his Creator and made in the image and likeness of God.[31]

The new religio-social hierophany

What is really being projected here is a flowering of mysticism and phenomenology. It is a NEW VISION ON MOUNT TABOR (cf. Lk. 9:28–35): *humanity* transfigured in the image of Christ and hearing God say, "This is my Son, my Beloved."[32] (Cf. Mt. 3:17) Here are all the wholesome human dynamisms of the twentieth century resplendent with divinity! In a sense, this is mankind's NEW PENTECOST. Every man can hear this Word of God *in his own laguage*, and the message of the Good News *reveals mèn to themselves*. If the cosmo-theandric scale of the People of God constitutes the measure of the human phenomenon under consideration, then we are being presented here with a "total and creative hermeneutics" for a NEW HUMANITY! The Gothic cathedral has been superseded as the metaphysical expression of man's upward striving for God. Pope John's awareness of a new humanistic anthropogony being under development in our era has been appropriated by the Church and clarified. As a product of religious contemplation this is a synchronic vision of man in the "eternal now;" as a product of phenomenology related to diachronic temporality it is an eschatological vision. On the basis of this new hermeneutics of the Spiritual Man, who once created that civilization known as Christendom, the Church is now intent on constructing the Cathedral of the New Humanity — working not with stained glass and hewn stone, but now devising those fabulous plans whereby the dwelling-place of God may be shored up and beautified by the flying-buttresses and living stones of modern humanity's wholesome dynamisms.

The esthetic impact of this vision

This is a very compelling esthetic experience for any religiously-minded person placed in immediate intuitive relationship with this innovative vision. As St. Augustine once remarked about a comparable experience: "Thou didst breathe fragrance upon me, and I drew in my breath and do now pant for Thee."[33] Such an experience, in one or another degree, is generally available to religious people seriously reflecting on the Council's teachings since this is the very area where connatural knowledge most properly functions. By this sort of affective intuition, then, the notion of the People of God may be almost instantaneously "comprehended" by religiously sensitive souls, and in an obscure but powerful way its further humanistic implications can be appropriated by the felt-experience of their whole being. For those not familiar with the phenomenological basis of such an experience the subliminal impact of the humanistic dimensions of the religious message may be little understood, just as we seldom really appreciate the strong emotional overlay certain colors convey to us.[34] Since, however, it is our feelings here, rather than our reason, which becomes the dominant vehicle of intentionality or affective apperception and "insight," in such an esthetic experience *we become the real communicators* and tell ourselves what is being communicated. In such essentially esthetic judgments there is often a wide divergence of opinion between the viewer and the original artist who created the object under consideration. Whatever the judgment on either side, you can be sure it "reveals men to themselves," if only they would reflect on it.

The two texts of Vatican II

The above reflection, then, indicates there are two texts involved in the documents of Vatican II: a printed text and a metanarrative text. The *printed* text provides the Church's contemporary reflection on her own life-world, the being of which is a complex correlation of divine and human phenomena. The sophisticated pastoral theology developed in principle by the Council indicates the earnestness with which the bishops grappled with the communication-problem involved in conveying such complicated truths and values to the world community. By using in a complementary way both the scholastic and phenomenological methods the Church has devised a twentieth-century split-level kerygma, or proclamation of the Good News. This is the flowering of the split-level pastoral theology inspired by John XXIII both in *Humanae Salutis* and *Pacem in Terris*. Such a pastoral theology provides the seminal principles of interpretation for the whole range of other ideas developed by Vatican II. The intent of this new style of communication is to affect man from the inside-out by influencing the whole man in his mind, attitudes, and affections. At the Council, then, the bishops tried to set the consciousness of humanity in resonance with that of the Church so that they would begin to function as "a pair of interacting harmonic oscillators." The key to understanding the Council's sophisticated thought-processes and authentic idea of renewal is — as Wojtyla points out — the *consciousness* of the Church.[35]

Nowhere is this more apparent than in the *metanarrative* text where, interwoven with the religious vision of the People of God, there is a compelling esthetic vision of the New Humanity. From the viewpoint of sheer artistry the pursuit of religious enrichment exemplified by Vatican II surpasses the achievement of Michaelangelo, who strove to re-present the story of salvation on the walls of the Sistine Chapel in artforms appropriate to the tastes and achievements of the Renaissance. Perhaps it would be better to say that the same religious spirit, which set Michaelangelo to his great creative challenge, has prompted the bishops to formulate a new vision of man compatible with the challenges of our promising but perilous age.

In conclusion, we may say the *telos* of Vatican II's phenomenological style of religious reflection captures the aims previously set for the Council by John XXIII and Paul VI: first, that its *pastoral* reflection serve to glorify the doctrine of the Mystical Body and, secondly, that the *doctrinal* deposit of the Church more effectively serve the pastoral and human needs of mankind, and somehow begin to communicate with men from within.

Summary

This chapter began with a discussion of the phenomenological techniques employed in the construction of *Lumen Gentium*. After explaining the three-fold use of the epochē it was insisted upon that the Mystical Body, as posited in the first chapter of this dogmatic constitution, is the ontological ground of this document and the intentional focal point around which *all* the doctrinal reflections of Vatican II pivot. The next major point considered was the phenomenology of the natural attitude used in the process of Vatican II's reflections on its own concrete religious experiences. We then tried to correlate such ideas with the notion of a functional ontology at both the theoretical and practical levels. The discussion made us aware of the need for competent theological specialists to coordinate and illumine the complex transition which the ecclesial community is now engaged in. Lastly, in a somewhat schematic way we were able to correlate the doctrinal reflections of *Lumen Gentium* with the ontological paradigm provided by the Glorified Christ as Logos-Shepherd.

The second part of this chapter consisted mainly in a discussion of the hermeneutics involved in the notion of the People of God. This paradigm was perceived as a moral blueprint for the new servant leaders of mankind (i.e., the twentieth-century version of the Good Samaritan). Further insight into the religio-social implications of this paradigm was provided by reflecting on Vonier's original aims in developing this theological notion. When the two dimensions of the Church as Mystical Body and People of God are viewed in conjunction, a new religio-social hierophany manifests itself, and this may aptly be called the Vision of a New Humanity. This hermeneutics of the Church, simultaneously involving a religious anthropology, derives from the phenomenological processes involved. It has a compelling esthetic impact on religiously-minded people, but it can also be easily misunderstood. There are, then, two texts involved in the documents of Vatican II: the published *printed* text and a *metanarrative* text, and it is the latter which is the esthetic vehicle of the new religio-social hierophany, mentioned above. This innovative style of phenomenological reflection emphasizes the care which the bishops took with the problem of pastoral communication in order to bring to maturity the aims formulated for the Council by both John XXIII and Paul VI.

NOTES

1. This chapter requires a fairly good grasp of the matters discussed previously in Chapter Six: "Phenomenology in the context of Vatican II."
2. Peter Koestenbaum in Husserl [1975], p. lvii uses the image of "backing into" the light as a graphic analogy for the reduction. On the Mystical Body as "the source of light for Catholic theology" see Vonier's remarks in Excursus VIII under the subheading, "The Mystical Body in *Lumen Gentium.*"
3. There are two broad frameworks within which a phenomenological noema may be interpreted: a *judgmental* paradigm (Føllesdal) and a *perceptional* one (Gurwitsch). See R.C. Solomon, "Husserl's Concept of the Noema," in Elliston and McCormick [1977], esp. pp. 172–173. The interpretation of any noemata connected with the Catholic life-world (e.g., the People of God) easily lends itself to the "snapshot" paradigm whereby the understanding of a noema derives from "a perceptual *Gestalt*, a *percept*, and a *theme.*" See Elliston and McCormick [1977], esp. p. 170. However, the *judgmental* paradigm of noemata is also effectively operative at the Council through the intentional ground provided by the doctrine of the Mystical Body. Consequently the noematic core or nucleus for the somewhat plastic "empirical essence" of the People of God is to be found in its correlate, the Mystical Body. "The analogy with biology – the cell with its changing protoplasm and its unchanging nucleus – is not inappropriate here." See Elliston and McCormick [1977], esp. p. 177. Suggested technical reading in this area would be Sokolowski [1974], p. 58 sq.
4. By "anthropocentric turn" I mean simply the same type of refocusing on experiences which Husserl had to make in the *Crisis* when he returned from the theoretical world distilled by philosophical phenomenology in order to investigate the life-world. This is a quite unfamiliar style of theologizing in most Catholic circles. Even Transcendental Thomists, who are quite competent in the use of phenomenological techniques, tend to pattern themselves after Husserl, the theorist, in their theologizing, rather than the Husserl of the *Crisis.*
5. It is with some hesitancy that I introduce Schutz since he disagreed with Husserl on important theoretical issues. See Schutz [1962–1976], Vol. 1, pp. 140–149: "Husserl's Importance for the Social Sciences," and Vol. 3, pp. 51–91: "The Problem of Transcendental Intersubjectivity in Husserl." In a critical but respectful way, however, he always remained a student of Husserl. In America Schutz is one of the better-known authors both for *applied* phenomenology and for his reflections on the *natural* life-world. See Natanson [1973a], p. 106 ff. The reflections of Vatican II, unlike those of Schutz, are focused on a *religious* life-world and are in quest of an ontology, not a sociology. It is, however, only in Chapter Ten when we discuss revelation (*Dei verbum*), that the full scope of this ontology and the nature of the Council's style of phenomenological analysis will become clear. Due to the horizontal and vertical dimensions of this religious life-world we shall resort to insights provided both by Schutz and Eliade to understand it. The horizontal (linear) structuring of *Lumen Gentium* lends itself to Schutz's insights, and by employing them we are entering the religious life-world from the "ground up," so to speak.
6. The thirtieth annual convention (1975) of the Catholic Theological Society of America devoted itself to "Catholic Theology in Social and Political Context." The leadoff article was Gregory Baum's "The Impact of Sociology on Catholic Thought." See Salm [1975], pp. 1–29. As far as I could determine, there were no references to

Schutz in the proceedings, although a few phenomenologists such as Heidegger and Ricoeur did come in for passing mention.

7. This statement should be read in the context of Carr [1974], pp. 68–81: "Genetic Phenomenology."

8. See Abbott [1966], esp. #8, pp. 22–23 and the sources listed in footnotes 17–21. See also Excursus VIII on the Mystical Body under the subheading, "The Mystical Body in *Lumen Gentium.*"

9. In effect, the Mystical Body is being posited as an *abstract*, universal ontology of the Church. Later in this chapter the People of God will be appreciated as the *concrete*, universal ontology (materially speaking) of the Church. Finally, in Chapter Ten dealing with revelation (*Dei verbum*) the Glorified Christ will be recognized as the *concrete*, universal ontology (formally speaking) permeating the entire ecclesial conscioussness.

10. One of the problems associated with any discussion of ontology is that modern philosophy – if it uses the concept at all – generally has a *univocal* understanding of this term, whereas Catholic theology and philosophy, by reason of their supernatural theism, have traditionally espoused an *analogical* understanding of it. In a univocal system of thought a concept either is or is not normative for ontology: there are no other options possible. Husserl attributed such quasi-metaphysical value to logical and mathematical noemata, and thus came to his unique appreciation of the human consciousness. See Carr [1974], p. 69. A philosopher of a more empirical bent, such as Polanyi [1958], pp. 69–77, 399, might be content to interpret such evidence within a totally biological and psychological framework. In an analogical system a concept may be normative *at its own level of reality*, but become functional when viewed *in relationship to a higher order* of things. Hence, when discussing intelligence, "reason," or consciousness as they exist in God, we may extrapolate from how these function in human beings. Such a procedure, however, presumes a belief in an isomorphism permeating all levels of existence and thus justifying an analogical interpretation of being and meaning.

11. See Townes [1966], p. 7.

12. See Abbott [1966], pp. 717–718.

13. See Kuhn [1962], pp. 188–189. Also see Carr [1974], p. 36, for "the image of falling, of a gravitational pull on consciousness" in relationship to the natural attitude. From a theological point of view, also, the need to hold the mind "in a state of continual suspense" makes for some interesting complications.

14. See Vorgrimler [1967–1969], Vol. 1, p. 299. The full passage was cited previously in Chapter 3, note 40.

15. For example, in *Lumen Gentium* we read of the spiritual influence of Christ's Spirit in the Church: "This He does in such a way that His work could be compared by the Holy Fathers with the function which the soul fulfills in the human body, whose principle of life the soul is." See Abbott [1966], #7, p. 22. As regards the mission *ad extra* of the Church, John XXIII in his first encyclical quotes with approval the Epistle to Diognetus: "To express the matter simply: what the soul is to the body, Christians are to the world." See Carlen [1981], Vol. 5, #146, p. 19.

16. See Abbott [1966], #7, pp. 20–22. It might be well to mention here that the numerous biblical references cited in this paragraph represent "the Scriptures" *as they exist in the contemporary ecclesial consciousness.* If the Church at Vatican II is reflecting out of the natural attitude of her own life-world, the methodology used for this procedure liberates her from the academic strictures of the biblical sciences. Her primary

concern with the Scriptures here is their *meaning for her*. Whether professional scripture scholars concur with the interpretations given these texts is another matter entirely.

17. I have in mind here particularly the rich tradition of the Greek Church. Charles Moeller has handled this point sensitively in his article, "History of Lumen Gentium's Structure and Ideas." See Miller [1966] esp. pp. 125–126. Another sympathetic reflection on these issues would be John Meyendorff's "Vatican II and Orthodox Theology in America." See Miller [1966], pp. 611–618. These differences are expressed more in depth by Michael Schmaus' article, "The Concept of Trinity and of Christology in the Eastern Liturgy." See Shook [1968], Vol. 1, pp. 130–152.

18. See Wojtyla [1980], pp. 61–62; the references in his index under "Trinity, Holy," highlight Vatican II's teachings in relation to this doctrine. For complementary considerations see Kress [1967], pp. 121–124.

19. The most important postconciliar development of this theme may be found in Paul VI's apostolic Exhortation, "Evangelization in the Modern World," (Dec. 8, 1975). See Paul VI [1975]. This extremely important document, which represents a straight-line development from the ideas of John XXIII in *Humanae Salutis*, is part of a three-tier doctrinal synthesis of Paul VI correlating evangelization, catechesis, and human development. See Hater [1981] and Gremillion [1976], pp. 387–415.

20. See Schell [1982], p. 226.

21. By the "new servant leaders of mankind" I mean twentieth-century Good Samaritans in the same sense Paul VI applied this term to the work of Vatican II at its close. See Paul VI [1966], p. 61. In America, however, the term "servant leadership," which has developed out of the field of management in the light of Christian reflection, conveys more of a sense of practical reality and a context of modern organizational procedures. See Greenleaf [1977].

22. See Vonier [1937].

23. See Carlen [1981], Vol. 4, pp. 37–63.

24. See Carlen [1981], Vol. 4, pp. 175–184. This encyclical is dealing with trends which are contemporary but have a long intellectual history: i.e., cosmological renewal ideas and vitalistic renewal ideas. See Ladner [1959], pp. 10–26. To stereotype the encyclical as simply a tissue of epistemological observations is to distort its pastoral intent.

25. See Vonier [1937], esp. pp. v–vi, xi–xiii, 6–7, 74–86, 167–176. Also see Excursus I on the Life-World under the subheading, "The religious life-world and its modern 'ecumene.'"

26. Vonier's pragmatic focus differs quite markedly from the narrowly technical and theoretical focus typical of continental theologians, especially those grappling with the scriptural or patristic origins of this idea. This academic mindset is typical of preconciliar thinking and the endorsement of *status quo antea* intellectual and cultural trends which have been outmoded by the "new moment" of human history. Two articles representative of this outlook are Y. Congar's "The Church: The People of God" and R. Schnackenburg and J. Dupont's "The Church: The Church as the People of God," in Schillebeeckx [1965], pp. 11–37 and 117–129 respectively. Both articles recognize that the Mystical Body and the People of God are notions which complement one another.

27. See Abbott [1966], #14–16, pp. 32–35. Van Peursen in Elliston and McCormick [1977], p. 185, remarks: ". . . the horizon cuts across the distinction of inside-outside – belonging to man, exterior to man. In the horizon, exteriority merges with interiority;

man merges with the world. The horizon is the translation of man into the world." This essentially phenomenological appreciation of the horizon provided by the life-world is facilitated by the *religious* horizon provided by Vatican II. Its horizon, both in *Lumen Gentium* and *Dei verbum*, is populated only by human (or spiritual) beings. The phenomenological ground of this fact is that the Council's eidetic analysis is focused on empirical human experiences. The translation of man into such a world is facilitated by the fact that it is a completely *hominized* world ultimately radicated in the Glorified Humanity of Christ. The exigencies of such a world are shaped by intersubjectivity, empathy, and *communio*. To the extent "things" (e.g., words, symbols, events, traditions, etc.) appear in this religious horizon, they have no coherence apart from Christ who provides the ontology and teleological-historical sense permeating this field of corporate consciousness.

28. See Carlen [1981], Vol. 5, #96–113, pp. 154–158. It must be emphasized that Paul VI's "circles" of humanity are the result of a psychological projection, whereas the "horizons" in *Lumen Gentium* are a result of phenomenological analysis of the life-world. This is another instance of the Holy Father's delicate sense of propriety and his desire not to steal any thunder from the new ideas being developed by the Council.

29. "All men are called to belong to the new People of God." See Abbott [1966], #13, p. 30.

30. The *moral* goals and presuppositions of the People of God are detailed in #9–12 of *Lumen Gentium.* See Abbott [1966], pp. 24–30. The term, "obediential potency," simply refers to man's *intrinsic* capacity, under God's power, to achieve such moral goals.

31. This is obviously an eschatological vision of the Church and not precisely a presentation of the "sinful, pilgrim Church." This will be taken up more fully in the next chapter.

32. One of the really perceptive journalistic reflections on the Roman Catholic Church today has been written by Peter Nichols, Rome-correspondent for *The Times* of London. On the basis of his experience while writing the book he writes: "I find the Transfiguration a recurring image, but never before as a moment for a whole divine strategy to be changed." See Nichols [1981], p. 357. As explained below, the Transfiguration as interpreted by this book is a *subliminal* message being projected by Vatican II and hence easily subject to misinterpretation.

33. See Sheed [1943], #XXVII, p. 236.

34. The really traumatic aspect of this subliminal vision is the fact that it contains a *radical shift of the visual Gestalt* no less dramatic than Copernicus' conception of a heliocentric universe which resulted in a need to re-think the whole dynamics of the system. For religiously sensitive people this is a quite traumatic experience. For the resolution of this problem see Excursus V on Anthropology under the subheading, "The shift of the visual Gestalt and its dialectical resolution."

35. See Wojtyla [1980], p. 35 ff.: "The consciousness of the Church as the main foundation of Conciliar initiation."

CHAPTER 9

THE CHURCH IN THE MODERN WORLD

Once we comprehend that the first two chapters of *Lumen Gentium* correlate the traditionally received doctrine of the Mystical Body (objectivity) with its experiential counterpart, the People of God (subjectivity), the remainder of this constitution as a product of phenomenological reflection quickly becomes intelligible. It is essentially a *teleological* reflection on the "horizon" (i.e., its membership, actual and potential) of the People of God as meaningful to themselves. The teleology involved, however, is shaped by the linear, eschatological timeframe of the Catholic consciousness.[1] (The vertical timeframe of the People of God will be taken up in the next chapter which deals with Revelation.)

Lumen Gentium from the perspective of Husserl's *"Crisis"*

From a phenomenological point of view *Lumen Gentium* displays several interesting parallels to the reflections of Husserl in the *Crisis*. (1) Husserl started there from the *cultural* fact of his experience of the mathematization of the natural sciences; *Lumen Gentium* starts from the *revealed* fact of ecclesial experience of the hominization (in Christ) of the really real. (2) Just as Husserl provided us with a teleological-historical reflection on the corporate consciousness of modern natural scientists, so also *Lumen Gentium* is a teleological-historical reflection on the corporate consciousness of the Church. The only difference here is that Husserl's view was oriented to the past, whereas *Lumen Gentium's* view is oriented to the future. (3) The context of "crisis" within which Husserl conducted his reflections was the European world of 1937, whereas the context of "crisis" within which *Lumen Gentium* meditates is the modern global scene first sketched by John XXIII and finally discussed at the Council in *Gaudium et Spes*, "The Church in the Modern World." (4) As Husserl's teleological-historical reflections manifest his notion of the natural "historicity" of the human consciousness, so also *Lumen Gentium* manifests the Church's notion of the religious "historicity" of the corporate ecclesial consciousness.

Historicity in phenomenology and Catholic reflection

The core-problem involved in the notion of historicity dates back to Parmenides and Heraclitus in the fifth century, B.C., and is the "Problem of the One and the Many." Heraclitus, as we know, was the champion of "facticity:" all things were in a flux. Parmenides was the champion of Being: things were known only to the extent they participated in the eternally intelligible and immutable One. The essentials of this controversy have contoured all of intellectual history: empiricism vs. idealism, subjectivism vs. objectivism, Dilthey vs. Husserl. However, it was Husserl's aim to transcend this polarization by discovering a "new empiricism." This search ultimately led him to the phenomenological method which provided *concrete universals* (noemata) serving a liason-purpose between the human need for meaning and the overwhelming experience that the phenomena under consideration were in a state of flux. Historicity for Husserl, then, was one of those *via media* conceptualizations which best made sense only when "the One and the Many" were viewed *simultaneously and in bipolar tension* within the gaze of phenemonological contemplation. Although the noemata (and their constitution) are derived from, involved with, and even progressive with temporality (durational flux), nonetheless they are repositories of *meaning* and hence imply a structured "sense" to the flux of experience.

Admittedly, there are still unresolved problems associated with Husserl's view of historicity, as David Carr has pointed out.[2] However, as we move into the Church's awareness of its own inner time-consciousness, structured both vertically and horizontally on the basis of a comprehensive christocentric paradigm, the technical problems associated with historicity in philosophical phenomenology no longer fit the new perspective. This is clear when Pope John II, using phenomenological reflection, speaks of the *pattern of meaning* which religious historicity necessarily involves:

> God gives himself to man created in his own image, and this "image" and "likeness" alone can make this communication [of God with man in history] possible. This communication creates the innermost, transcendent, final thread in the history of each man and of humanity as a whole. It is also a "trans-historical" thread, since, while taking account of the transitory character of man inscribed in time together with the whole visible world, it also reveals in him the element that does not pass away, that resists time, destruction and death. As we have just said, this is the *historicity* of man — this arrest, this hold on what passes away to extract from it *what does not pass away*, what serves to immortalize the most essentially human element, the element through which man is the image and likeness of God

and surpasses all the creatures subject to an ephemeral existence. *Historicity* is also the existence of *some one* who, while "passing away," retains his identity.[3]

The "becoming" of what does not pass away: Eschatology

It is within this understanding of religious historicity that we would now like to return to *Lumen Gentium*, which deals with the eschatological, linear dimension of ecclesial inner time-consciousness. Eschatology is simply the religiously coherent unfolding in mundane time of the full mysteries revealed in the "eternal now" (i.e., the vertical dimension) of the ecclesial inner time-consciousness. Therefore, we shall have to return again to the notion of historicity, as nuanced by Revelation (the world of what does not pass away), when that topic is discussed in the next chapter. At the present moment we would simply alert the reader to two points. First, there is an isomorphism between our present discussion of *Lumen Gentium* and the forthcoming discussion of *Dei verbum* in Chapter Ten. Secondly, lurking on the "fringes" of the eschatological horizon of *Lumen Gentium* are topics like the scriptures, tradition, and the sacraments which, as revealed items, are more appropriate to the "eternal now," rather than the pilgrim-mission orientation emphasized by eschatology.

In *Lumen Gentium* the sacramental timeframe does insinuate itself into the discernment of the two basic categories of people in the Church: hierarchy and laity (Chapters 3 and 4); the intentional ground for this distinction is the degree to which their "obediential potency" has been actualized under God by the sacraments.[4] The foundational view here is one of a religious ontology, but as we know from the second chapter of *Lumen Gentium* on the People of God, this hominized type of ontology, as oriented to human needs (i.e., anthropocentric *service*), is replete with eschatology, a sense of mission.[5] This eschatological dimension asserts itself more obviously in Chapters Five through Eight, where the dynamic religious teleology of the People of God is introduced on gradually ascending levels. On the earthly plane the People of God, as a whole, experience an *ad intra* exigency to be united with God, and this is manifested by the corporate pursuit of holiness (Chapter 5).[6] However, within the Church a special class of people, the members of religious institutes, have been publically mandated to bear witness to this ideal *ad extra* in the service of the common spiritual good (Chapter 6). At the heavenly level this religious teleology finds its fulfillment in union with God and the communion of saints (Chapter 7).[7] Quite fittingly, the Virgin Mary, as a redeemed member of the People of God, is presented as the perfect disciple at the level of comprehensive symbolism epitomizing all the essential moral qualities which the corporate ecclesial consciousness on an experiential basis has come to esteem and strive for (Chapter 8).[8] This panoramic vision of Mary, as Mother of the Church, somewhat resembles Dante's view of the heavenly assembly at the close of the *Paradiso*; consequently, this es- chatological vision of the Church is starting to fuse with the events in the "eternal now."

The new ecclesial hermeneutics and the unbelievers

Attractive as all this may be for Catholics, and possibly some other Christians, I cannot see how this transhistorical christocentric paradigm of truth and morality can have any appeal to unbelievers. Indeed, many sincere Jews, Moslems, atheists, or others could rightly find this religious idealization triumphalistic, mystogogical, and maddeningly self-centered. They would have every right to complain, par- ticularly since Vatican II, as a pastoral Council, addressed itself to "all men of good will."[9] The more perceptive phenomenologist, however, might intervene here with a kind word for this religious enterprise. By reason of the methodology employed at the Council the Church's transposing of religious formulas into a "new key" is meant to reorientate the focus of Catholic thought to contemporary thought-patterns and to express a desire to collaborate in mankind's search for an authentic anthropology commensurate with today's global challenges.[10] The Church is not settling for any cheap solution to human problems by tenaciously holding onto her traditionalistic "objectivism" in philosophy. At the same time she is not compromising her previous heritage by settling for a solution to human problems by way of politics or social engineering. She is seriously in quest for a new type of humanity which the world has never known. For a start, that would mean fostering something like a global "ecumenical ethics" and constructive, collaborative efforts in the service of human progress and develop- ment. Everybody in our nuclear age has a vested interest in such a global human enterprise, regardless of his or her religious persuasion. The fact that Vatican II employed a christocentric paradigm to structure this enterprise simply means this is the only way which the Church had at its disposal to render the under- taking religiously intelligible to Catholics and to motivate them to undertake the enormous tasks which it implies. While I am grateful for such a benign interpre- tation of the humanitarian *telos* inherent in the Catholic *aggiornamento*, I must insist these insights are available only to professionally trained phenomenologists. Where, then, is the explicit institutional statement which gives an impetus to move in the direction suggested above?

The challenge to Christian efficiency

It is important to realize that no such clear and explicit statement about the anthropocentric orientation of Vatican II was made *during* the Council itself.[11] Such a statement was made both before the Council and immediately upon its closing, and these provide the practical, pastoral context in which the Council was conducted. The statement made prior to the Council appeared in *Humanae Salutis* and formulated John XXIII's goal to evangelize by constructive deeds, rather than by mere words:

> This *supernatural* order must, however, reflect its *efficiency* in that other order, the *temporal* one, which on so many occasions is, unfortunately, the *only* one that occupies and worries man.[12]

This pastoral, pragmatic norm was formulated in the specific context of today's dislocated world. Two global problems were the context, if not focus, of *Humanae Salutis*: the danger of nuclear war and the dehumanization of men by atheism, affluence, or abject poverty.[13] In effect, social problems comparable to Husserl's *Crisis* had outgrown the European scale to become global, and Pope John simply responded to this situation in a religiously intelligent way. Therefore, working toward the resolution of such worldwide human problems became the ultimate practical (and pastoral) goal of Vatican II. Even though the bishops may have given the popularly received impression that their focus was exclusively religious, their choice of the phenomenological method and their analysis of empirical human experiences inform us that they never lost sight of these practical problems. Consequently, in his closing speech at the Council on December 7, 1965, Paul VI could rightly say: "The old story of the Samaritan has been the model of the spirituality of the Council."[14]

Pragmatism and the religious life-world

It is the *pragmatic* dimension of the challenge to Christian efficiency which renders the Council's return to its own religious life-world intelligible. As Schutz and Luckmann remark: "We can say that our natural attitude of daily life is pervasively determined by a *pragmatic motive*."[15] What pragmative motive, other than Pope John's challenge in *Humanae Salutis*, prompted the Council Fathers to return to their religious life-world? They wanted to *renew their roots in an experiential way*. They already had a conceptual appreciation of this world in the doctrine of the Mystical Body, as summarized in the first chapter of

Lumen Gentium. Now, however, in the light of serious global needs they wanted to reach out to all men by way of dialogue and collaborative action for the good of mankind. In the Catholic Church it is a common practice for a priest to go on retreat in order to spiritually prepare himself for what he knows will be a very difficult assignment.[16] That is exactly what the bishops did. Before moving out into an unknown world wracked with complex problems, they returned to the spiritual certainties and familiar guideposts of their own religious life-world.

The need for a spiritual constant

Any life-world, and more especially a religious life-world structured by an "eternal now," derives from

> a stock of previous experience, my own immediate experiences as well as such experiences as are transmitted to me from my fellow-men and above all from my parents, teachers, and so on. All of these communicated and immediate experiences are included in a certain unity having the form of my stock of knowledge, which serves me as the reference schema for the actual step of my explication of the world. All of my experiences in the life-world are brought into relation to this schema, so that the objects and events in the life-world confront me from the outset in their typical character . . .[17]

Consequently, when the bishops entered into dialogue and shared their experiences about their individual life-worlds, they were searching for that "certain unity" which would serve as a common religious bond (*communio*) and spiritual support for them all. There is much more cohesiveness and tensile strength about the religious thematizations of the Council than first meets the eye.

The bishops entered their religious life-world not to find the unfamiliar, the innovative, or the progressive, but to reestablish experiential contact with the familiar, the foundational, and the everlasting. Again, as Schutz and Luckmann describe it:

> Every explication within the life-world goes on within the milieu of affairs which have already been explicated, within a reality that is fundamentally and typically familiar. I trust that the world as it has been known by me up until now will continue further and that consequently the stock of knowledge obtained from my fellow-men and formed from my own experiences will continue to preserve its fundamental validity. We should

like to designate this (in accord with Husserl) the "and so forth" idealization. From this assumption follows the further and fundamental one: that
I can repeat my past successful acts. So long as the structure of the world
can be taken to be constant, as long as my previous experience is valid, my
ability to operate upon the world in this and that manner remains in
principle preserved. As Husserl has shown, the further ideality of the "I
can always do it again" is developed correlative to the ideality of the "and
so forth." Both idealizations and the assumptions of the constancy of the
world's structure which are grounded on them — the validity of my previous experience and, on the other hand, my ability to operate upon the
world — are essential aspects of thinking within the natural attitude.[18]

The implications of these phenomenological ideas

In their corporate reflection on their diverse religious life-worlds the bishops
were trying to comprehend the unity experienced in all this multiplicity. Within
the purview of phenomenology this unity would consist in a network of a priori
structures (the "and so forth" idealization).[19] These structures of stable meanings
and human relationships provide the stock of experiential (or "connatural")
knowledge which is the topological scheme of reference rendering this religious
life-world intelligible.[20] Any carefully crafted thematization of this schema, such
as the People of God, would really portray an experiential constant (or religious
"strategic vision") against which the bishops could judge their capacity to act
effectively in genuinely religious ways.[21] This experiential assumption is called
the ideality of "I can always do it again," and without such commonly accepted
assumptions a life-world of any sort is impossible.

This phenomenological style of reflection, however, is much larger than a
mere quest for the meaningful and accepted ways of acting in a religious life-
world. The bishops are ultimately searching for their authentic corporate self as
twentieth-century Christians, a people alive and united in Christ. As they reflect
on what appears to be a flood of experiential data, the bishops begin to perceive
patterns of constant values and a meaningful style of interpersonal relationships.
As they recognize and endorse such patterns, the bishops appreciate that these
experiential constancies reflect the workings of the corporate ecclesial consciousness as an intersubjective *communio*, i.e., their own collective ego.[22]
Consequently, once they have finalized this religious analysis in a serious doctrinal way, such as in *Lumen Gentium*, they will never discover a new self-
identity, a "someone else." The only way this could possibly happen would be
through the virtual collapse of such a life-world and the need to totally rebuild

another. By reason of the fact that there is a consistent isomorphism between the Mystical Body and the People of God, I hardly think the Catholic Church would tolerate any serious tampering with the religious life-world as formulated by Vatican II.

Today's problems between the religious and natural life-worlds

If we appreciate that the doctrinal reflective process at the Council is a phenomenological thematization of a *religious* life-world, we may momentarily pause on it in its correlation with the multitude of *natural* life-worlds existent today. The first thing to notice about the People-of-God formulary, as promulgated by Vatican II, is that it is an ontology or paradigm of a *global* religious life-world, an experiential foundational theology of the Catholic *ecumene*. It has no secular counterpart today among the natural life-worlds of our planet. To produce such a study would require an assembly comparable to the United Nations, or possibly the World Communist Party, employing phenomenology in the same fashion as the Council. As a result, Vatican II represents an advanced stage of applied phenomenology. The second point to notice is that there is often an extreme disparity between the constancies or "typicalities" of this religious life-world and many of the natural life-worlds. Sexual mores, for example, provide a quite obvious instance, although other cultural preconceptions impinging on doctrine (e.g., the use of private property) could also be cited. In the estimation of some Catholic theologians these discrepancies have become so onerous that it has become morally impossible for Christians to abide by the doctrinal and/or moral constancies traditionally ascribed to the religious life-world propounded by the Council. The implication is, of course, that these religious constancies have to be modified in important, if not substantial, ways. What many of these theologians have in common with the Council Fathers is their use of the phenomenological method.

   I have no interest in passing judgment on this theological enterprise. Some of the theologians associated with this movement have pioneered in a speculative way notions discussed in this book as connected with the work of the Council: e.g., the communication problem, the turn to subjectivity, and theological anthropology.[23] For the most part, the better minds amongst these theologians practice phenomenology as pure theorists, much as Husserl did prior to the *Crisis*.[24] By reason of the nature of the phenomenological reduction the resultant theoretical attitude (i.e., a state of continual suspension of belief) must, indeed, constitute a most unnatural and artificial attitude for such theologians when it comes to matters revealed by God.[25] Furthermore, if the "new moment" of human history has impinged on them at all, it seems to have done so only within the parameters of their theoretical preconceptions. These are essentially the same as the Catholic mindset which we describe in the first chapter of this book for the period of 1930–1950.[26] In such a context, then, we can say that such theologians do *not* use phenomenology as Vatican II did. Hence, it is a highly dubious assertion to claim their phenomenological style of theological reflection is carrying on or completing the work of the Council.

A summary of Vatican II's use of phenomenology

In order to move on to a final overview of the Council's documents let us quickly recapitulate the genesis and development of Vatican II's use of the phenomenological method. John XXIII apparently started out in *Humanae Salutis* from the position of classical scholasticism, although his innovative formulation of the prospective Council's goals does suggest he was trying to combine the social efficiency of Leo XIII with the communication issues raised by Transcendental Thomists. By the time of *Pacem in Terris*, however, he was employing a sociological application of phenomenology (closer to Schutz than Husserl) in correlation with classical scholastic ideas. Cardinal Suenens' suggestion that the Council view people, not in their abstract relationships, but in their concrete life-situations was the opening-wedge for phenomenology at Vatican II. Paul VI, cognisant of the development underway, endorsed this methodological approach to doctrine in *Ecclesiam Suam*, but only with reservations and only after once again reasserting the centrality of the Mystical Body. The option for an empirical a priori grounded in experience posed a final methodological decision for the Council Fathers. In what direction should their analysis proceed: in the direction of pure theory or in the direction of the life-world? Since Vatican II was not intended to be a doctrinal, but a pastoral Council, the choice was made to move in the direction of the religious life-world. This choice ultimately involved a suspension of all sciences and even a philosophical reduction, once the bishops relinquished scholasticism in the first session. This philosophical reduction also has some point with regard to the Council's use of phenomenology: the bishops only took from Husserl the use of his methodology and its assumptions necessary for its proper employment, but not any of his philosophical preconceptions (e.g., the impossibility of a metaphysics).[27] Lastly, the use of phenomenology at the Council did have an *extrinsic* reference scheme: the doctrine of the Mystical Body found summarized in the first chapter of *Lumen Gentium*. In this sense, objectivity and subjectivity were used in tandem at the Council.

The ecclesial consciousness *ad intra* and *ad extra*

If we may be allowed to abstract from the first chapter of *Lumen Gentium* as an extrinsic, objective, and doctrinal statement normative for the *whole* Council, then we are in a position to reflect on the rest of the documents from a phenomenological point of view. In this context *Lumen Gentium* is a product of the intersubjective ecclesial consciousness in its natural attitude. This reflection thematizes the meanings derived from a phenomenological analysis of the Church's experience of its own corporate self-identity as the People of God. *Lumen Gentium*, therefore, is a quite precise response to the question: "Church, what do you say of *yourself*?"[28] In this narrowly construed sense the constitution presents an egology of the Church.[29] Whether the Church is viewed as an institution or a purely voluntary organization by social analysts, this careful thematization of attitudes, motives, values, and goals makes for a fine case-study in the use of phenomenology and offers an insight into the corporate "personhood" of the Church. Experience, of course, is much larger than a person's own awareness of self. So, the question, "Church, what do you say of yourself?" is raised again.

It must be clear by now that in the phenomenological context of the Council this question has taken on a phenomenological intentionality. That should be evident from the type of response given to it in *Lumen Gentium*. In this new "*ad extra*" phase of reflection, however, the technical sense of the question is: "Church, what is the meaning for you when you confront this or that 'region of reality'?"[30] Or, in ordinary language: "Church, what do you say of yourself when you confront the realities of today's world?" The egological stream of consciousness, portrayed in *Lumen Gentium*, now shifts its reflection from itself as incarnate body-subject in order to contemplate the objects (*noemata*) residing in its consciousness.[31] These objects derive from two different sources of experience: the first originates from God's revelation and the second from everyday life in society. It is evident we are talking about two different "regions of reality" and, in a religious context, two different levels of reality. God's revelation is analysed in *Dei verbum*, a discussion of which will be found in the next chapter.[32] At the present I would only say that the phenomenological style of reflection found in this dogmatic constitution is of the same high calibre as that in *Lumen Gentium*. Both documents handle their subject-matter within the purview of the religious life-world. The second set of objects contemplated by the ecclesial consciousness pertains to both the secular and religious segments of modern society.[33] For brevity's sake, our discussion will confine itself to "The Church in the Modern World" (*Gaudium et Spes*).[34] As might be expected, when the ecclesial consciousness moves into the historical becoming of the modern world, the phenomenological style of reflection begins to deteriorate due to pressures from many directions.[35]

Gaudium et Spes as applied pastoral theology

From our reflections on the Council up to this point it must be reasonably evident that the cumulative effect of its phenomenological style of reflection has been to produce a new *pastoral* theology.[36] The *theory* meant to undergird this style of pastoral theologizing has been provided by the two doctrinal constitutions, *Lumen Gentium* and *Dei verbum*. The pastoral constitution, "The Church in the Modern World," derives from the original practical global concerns for mankind first voiced by John XXIII in *Humanae Salutis*, in his radio broadcast of September 11, 1962, and finally in *Pacem in Terris*. Consequently, *Gaudium et Spes* is a first, tentative application on a global scale of the pastoral theory developed in the two dogmatic constitutions mentioned above. For example, as *Lumen Gentium* developed the religio-phenomenological theory for *communio*, *Gaudium et Spes* tries to apply this concept to modern social phenomena under the rubric of "socialization."[37] An even more massive parallelism exists. As the two dogmatic constitutions formulated a comprehensive insight into the Church's religious life-world, so now in *Gaudium et Spes* these insights are brought into a first correlation with the many natural life-worlds under the rubric of "culture."[38] Since modern problems, however, are so complex, the document is a "dress-rehearsal for dialogue" with today's world, a marshalling of theoretical principles in relationship to the mixed-up state of affairs in the world so that, ultimately, the constitution is a study in chiaroscuro. The problems also happen to be quite frightening for many people. Therefore, the bishops tried to develop their ideas within a context of hope; in this regard they obviously tried to imitate the model set by *Pacem in Terris*. Because of such complexities this application of pastoral theology (as correlated with a phenomenological analysis of the socio-cultural world) is a highly modulated one, according to the norms of art and prudence.[39] It would, therefore, be a mistake to view this document as making "a precious contribution to the work of *doctrinal development* carried forward in *Lumen Gentium*."[40] Such a statement has no meaning unless we are only talking about the application of theory.

By this time at the Council, as Bishop Mark G. McGrath has pointed out, the bishops were quite conscious of using the phenomenological method as a tool in their description and analysis of socio-cultural realities.[41] However, their primary focus — as in *Pacem in Terris* — is now on *man* and only secondarily on his artifacts (i.e., ideologies, sciences, social structures, etc.). This focus is a direct result of the hominized ontology permeating both *Lumen Gentium* and *Dei verbum*. Of all the documents issued by the Council *Gaudium et Spes* is the one most replete with discernible split-level religious concepts (e.g., communio/socialization).[42] "The Church (i.e., the People of God) in the Modern World" is best read as a left-handed commentary on "Man in the Modern World," i.e., an inchoative religious anthropology, as Cardinal Roy previously pointed out. Within this framework Christ is held up as the paradigm of the New Man. I would only insist at this point that the Council's integral objective is for a new *global* anthropology. When you consider the many technical problems we have discussed relative to the use of phenomenology, the nature of pastoral theology, the scope of acculturalization, and the complexities of the communication process, this anthropological goal of the Council abounds with serious problems. A few words should be said on this point.

Common pitfalls in interpreting *Gaudium et Spes*

By reason of the somewhat rambling and verbose style of this document, the ideas mentioned above and their implications do not come through in a concise and forceful way. The sapiential vision of hope has muted the prophetic sense of urgency needed in a turbulent world armed with nuclear weapons. Much of the real difficulty for Americans, however, centers on the fact that we have no real acquaintance with the phenomenological background of this document. Because *Gaudium et Spes* deals with psycho-social issues familiar to the educated public, it offers three pitfalls for the unwary. First, many people read this document through the eyes of scientific reductionism: i.e., interpreting it mainly, if not soley, within the popularly received social or psychological ideas of their milieu. Secondly, theologically uninformed people use this lower-level constitution to interpret the complex theological and pastoral issues discussed in *Lumen Gentium*, or even *Dei verbum* (e.g., the "revelatory" value of the signs of the times). Lastly, the metanarrative text present (albeit turgidly) in this document may be distorted beyond recognition by the overwhelming problems of social reconstruction and pastoral management which the constitution calls for. An anthropology of the peacemaker in such a turbulent context can easily metamorphose into an anthropology of the liberator.[43]

Themes developed and yet to be developed for a richer strategic vision

In my estimation one of the most insightful theologians at Vatican II was Canon Charles Moeller. His brief history of *Gaudium et Spes* concludes with the themes included and dropped from this pastoral constitution.[44] Because of their importance as guidelines for future reflection, I summarize them here briefly. *Themes included in the constitution*: (1) Christian anthropology, "the elaboration of which is perhaps the most urgent task of the 20th century." The fundamental model for such a projected anthropology was provided by the theological dialectic inherent in Christ's dual role as Logos and Shepherd. (2) The autonomy of secular activities in their own spheres. (3) The Church which "civilizes by evangelizing." (4) The ambivalence and paradox of the term, "world," which contributes further to the dialectical character of the religious reflection of this document. *Themes dropped from the constitution*: (1) The Holy Spirit acting in history both to re-create and renew man "in justice and holiness of truth." (2) The Church transforming the world through her liturgy. (3) The humanism of the Sermon on the Mount viewed as the "charter of the kingdom of God." (4) Christian cosmology: history and the universe viewed from the plan of salvation. Here I simply conclude with and endorse Canon Moeller's own observations:

> It will be noticed that the four themese that practically disappeared are closely related to Eastern theology. The tendency of the text, however rich it may be, remained too Western. What the Orthodox have to say about it should be very significant.[45]

Vatican II: Invitation to dialogue

There are many other omissions, shortcomings, or limitations which the uninvolved critic could call attention to in the Council's formulation of its thought. But that would be to fasten on miscellaneous details at the expense of comprehending the real significance of the Church's complete re-expression of her existence at this moment of history. As one of the world's oldest and most traditional institutions, she has resorted to an extremely contemporary mode of reflection in order to open a phenomenological access into the heart of her living religious consciousness. By reason of the methodology employed the noemata, essences, or meanings expressed by the Council documents need *not* be totally adequate to the objective reality toward which they are directed.[46] What is required is that *they authentically reflect the Church's experience of that reality and thus reveal her true self in her natural religious attitude.* In view of the critical nature of the times the Church felt compelled to make this totally honest assessment of herself, her values, and her commitments. Then, of course, the uninvolved critic could say: "I'm sorry, but my experience differs from yours." The Church can respond quite honestly: "Let us share our experiences in more detail so that we can get to know one another better. In these critical times we must not let our differences stand in the way of friendship and working together for peace. By honesty, empathy, patience, and the desire to know one another better we can secure our common future in brotherhood."

An invitation to dialogue: that is the most elemental meaning of Vatican II.

Summary

This chapter provided a final analysis of *Lumen Gentium*, both as regards its general contents and as the theoretical basis (along with *Dei verbum*) for a new type of pastoral theology. The essentially teleological reflection of this constitution was then situated within the challenge to efficiency and the pragmatic context characteristic of Vatican II as a pastoral Council. The key to understanding the life-world as an environment of familiar constancies and as the precondition for successful action was provided by the notion of pragmatism. We also saw that the path through the life-world is the path to self-identity. There still remain some serious problems, however, due to the differences between the religious life-world and the many natural life-worlds existent today. Some theologians believe these problems can be mitigated, or even eliminated, by making important changes in the religious life-world, but that line of thought was not viewed as a particularly productive suggestion. The fact that such theologians may use phenomenology in the construction of their theories need not be viewed as a continuation of the thought and work of Vatican II.

After categorizing *Lumen Gentium* as a study of the Church's own consciousness of itself (egology), our study moved on to the objects (noemata) residing in this ecclesial consciousness. Two different sets of data make up these objects: the first set derives from God's revelation and the second from everyday life in society. The revealed data will be discussed in the next chapter on *Dei verbum*, but this doctrinal constitution deals with the religious life-world in the same fashion as *Lumen Gentium*. "The Church in the Modern World" (*Gaudium et Spes*) was appreciated as an application of the pastoral theory developed by *Lumen Gentium* and *Dei verbum*. This lower-level pastoral constitution dealing with global, socio-cultural life has been strongly influenced by the hominized ontology developed by the two dogmatic constitutions mentioned above, and it provides the type of split-level pastoral concepts (e.g., *communio*/socialization) now characteristic of Vatican II's isomorphic type of pastoral theology. Since the use of phenomenology at the Council implies a methodological idealism, the essences ("concepts") developed by the Council need not be totally adequate to the objective reality which they intend. Such essences (noemata) are more expressive of the authentic experience of the Church and her true identity in her natural religious attitude. Hence, the most elemental meaning of Vatican II is an invitation to all men to dialogue and a sharing of their experiences as a way to the building of friendship and peace.

NOTES

1. See C. Moeller's "History of *Lumen Gentium*'s Structure and Ideas," in Miller [1966], p. 138.
2. See Carr [1974], esp. pp. 261–266.
3. See Frossard [1984], pp. 59–60.
4. Chapters 3–8 of *Lumen Gentium* may be found in Abbott [1966], pp. 37–96. Paragraphs 18, 26 and 27 center the bishop's role and authority in the "sacred power" which he derives from his ordination. See Abbott [1966], pp. 37, 50–51. However, since the whole context of *Lumen Gentium* is eschatological, such foundational ideas are also oriented to mission.
5. Eschatology has an *extrinsic*, intentional ground in God and His Plan of creation and redemption. *Intrinsically*, however, it manifests the cumulative, teleological exigency of man's obediential potency as it seeks its normal, ontological fulfillment in co-operation with God's grace. This latter distinction is quite important in relationship to the thought of Vatican II which is grounded in the empirical a priori of *experience*. This is also the area in which connatural knowledge most properly functions for religious insights and judgments.
6. As in Paragraph 13 of *Lumen Gentium*, so also in this fifth chapter the bishops describe the human drive to religious fulfillment from its *extrinsic* foundation: i.e., God's call for all to seek holiness. See Abbott [1966], pp. 30, 65. Once God's grace is operative, however, there is – in its own order – a *natural* exigency for holiness.
7. It is interesting to note that Chapter Seven was inserted at the insistence of John XXIII. See C. Moeller's remarks in Miller [1966], p. 139.
8. C. Moeller in Miller [1966], p. 142 calls attention to the role of Paul VI in reconciling the opposite positions toward the place of Mary in the Church.
9. See the "Message to Humanity" in Abbott [1966], pp. 3–7. J. Gremillion in Miller [1966], p. 541 poses much the same question: "Granting that non-Christians cannot accept our premises, rooted as these are in the Christian faith, are they able to form with us a working consensus embracing the consequences of our incarnational view?" In an otherwise very fine and practical article it is Gremillion's unnuanced espousal of this "incarnational view" which dates and weakens his argument. Prior to the Council in France there were two competing schools as regards the theology of history: the "Incarnational" (de Lubac and Teilhard de Chardin) and the "Eschatological" (Danielou and Bouyer). See Connolly [1961], p. 149. The Council synthesized and transcended both of these academic controversies and presented a practical problem in civilization-building which Gremillion, as a sociologist, does not really appreciate in its full scope.
10. Canon Moeller in Miller [1966], p. 144 says: "It [*Lumen Gentium*] implies an *anthropology*, a vision of Christian existence, especially in chapters two and seven." My

own development of this theme, I feel, has been consistent, if not identical, with seminal insights originally provided by Moeller.

11. I realize this statement is open to some dispute, particularly from a selective theological interpretation of *Gaudium et Spes*. For two such interpretations see J. Gremillion and F. Houtart in Miller [1966], pp. 521–544 and 545–552. My thesis is that the anthropocentric dimensions of Vatican II derive from the *way* the questions were posed at the Council (i.e., by the phenomenological method) and the *context* in which they were posed (i.e., the "new moment" in human history). On this basis it is no surprise that the Council developed an anthropocentric theology consistent with its traditional doctrines. It should be noted, if only in passing, that the concept of a meta-anthropology – such as the Council has, in principle, developed – makes no sense except in a phenomenological-existential context.

12. See Abbott [1966], p. 706.

13. See Abbott [1966], pp. 703–704. It is this concrete context which lends Vatican II its prophetic *urgency*. As a creative and sapiential display of Catholic theology, Vatican II certainly carried out the twofold goal set for it by John XXIII in his opening speech: ". . . that the sacred deposit of Christian doctrine should be *guarded* and *taught more efficaciously*." See Abbott [1966], p. 713; emphasis added. Without the context of a "new moment" in human history, however, Vatican II becomes only an admirable academic study of the *status quo antea* or an excuse for *ad hoc* social activism.

14. See Paul VI [1966], p. 61. Much of Paul VI's pontificate was an effort to exemplify this model of the Good Samaritan projected by the Council. His encyclical, *Populorum Progressio*, boldly laid out the blueprint for this ideal. See Gremillion [1976], pp. 387–415.

15. See Schutz and Luckmann [1973], p. 6. See also Paul VI [1966], p. 62: "The modern mind, accustomed to assess everything in terms of usefulness, will readily admit that the Council's value is great if only because *everything* has been referred to human usefulness." (Emphasis added.)

16. Paul VI [1966], p. 59 describes this process of the Church (i.e., the bishops) "on retreat":

Men will realize that the Council devoted its attention, not so much to divine truths, but rather, and principally, to the Church – her nature and composition, her ecumenical vocation, her apostolic and missionary activity. This secular religious society, which is the Church, has endeavoured to carry out an act of reflection about herself, to know herself better, to define herself better and, in consequence, to set aright what she feels and what she commands. So much is true. But this introspection has not been an end in itself, has not been simply an exercise of human understanding or of a merely worldly culture. The Church has gathered herself together in deep spiritual awareness, not to produce a learned analysis of religious psychology, or an account of her own experiences, not even to devote herself to reaffirming her rights and explaining her laws. Rather, it was to find in herself, active and alive, the Holy Spirit, the word of Christ; and to probe more deeply still, the mystery, the plan and the presence of God above and within herself, to revitalize in herself that faith that is the secret of her confidence and wisdom, and that love that impels her to sing, without ceasing, the praises of God. *Cantare amantis est* (Song is the expression of a lover), says St. Augustine.

17. See Schutz and Luckmann [1973], p. 7.
18. See Schutz and Luckmann [1973], pp. 7–8.
19. See Sokolowski [1974], #39, pp. 100–101.
20. As regards the development of the experientially derived topology organizing the objects (noemata) of the Council's analysis and the acts related to them, it may be well to recall our discussion in Chapter Six on constitutive (or genetic) phenomenology. This topic will be more extensively developed in Chapter Ten under the subheading, "Constituting a religious hermeneutics of revelation and history."
21. For collateral reading here see Schutz and Luckmann [1973], pp. 18–20: "Plans and Practicabilities."
22. See Schutz and Luckman [1973], pp. 17–18.
23. Perhaps the most prominent of these would be Karl Rahner, S.J. For a concise treatment of his later theology see Mann [1969].
24. For an extensive treatment of this style of theologizing see Muck [1968]. To situate this movement within the historical context of Catholic thought see Schoof [1970], pp. 188–194: "Re-orientation within Neo-Scholasticism."
25. See Carr [1974], p. 36. This theoretical stance derived from philosophical phenomenology poses a serious obex to entry into the life-world which requires a suspension of all the sciences and even a philosophical reduction if one is to recapture the natural attitude. As Schutz and Luckmann [1973], p. 27 describe it: ". . . the natural attitude of daily life has a special form of epoché. In the natural attitude a man surely does not suspend his beliefs in the existence of the outer world and its Objects. On the contrary, he suspends every doubt concerning their existence. What he brackets is the doubt whether the world and its Objects could be otherwise than just as they appear to him."
26. The essence of this mindset is that it represents the theoretical concerns of university-level intellectuals. This book has discussed the broad contours of this historical, intellectual development. In the postconciliar period its major symptom is an emphasis on radical "foundational thinking," originally inspired by Heidegger. See Landgrebe [1966], p. 173 sq. If there is one thing we can be certain about, this type of concern with abstract theory did *not* occupy the attention of Vatican II.
27. See Excursus V on Anthropology under the subheading, "The radical nature of Vatican II's reflection." By reason of its phenomenological methodology Vatican II appears to be a unique example of one type of *Religionswissenschaft* (q.v., in the index of Allen [1978], p. 263). We shall treat of this topic more extensively in the next chapter, dealing with Revelation (*Dei verbum*).
28. Donald R. Campion, SJ, in Abbott [1966], p. 184, is quite correct in saying that this question constitutes "an architectonic theme or central vision" for Vatican II. Our discussion here hopes to explain *how* this question functioned in that way.
29. For collateral reading on "egology," see Natanson [1973a], esp. pp. 71–72. It must be understood, however, that the egology of the life-world is not the same as that derived by the transcendental reduction.
30. See Carr [1974], p. 282 in Index under "Region(s)."
31. It should be emphasized that the objects in the ecclesial consciousness are *noemata*. This has important implications about the significance which one attributes to the statements of Vatican II in relationship to previous Councils. For a technical discussion see R.C. Solomon's "Husserl's Concept of Noema," in Elliston and McCormick [1977], pp. 168–181. Furthermore, do the noemata of Vatican II's religious life-world, as elements of a totally hominized ontology, differ in significant ways from

the noemata of Husserl's philosophical phenomenology and those of Schutz's natural life-world?

32. The text for *Dei verbum* ("The Dogmatic Constitution on Divine Revelation") may be found in Abbott [1966], pp. 111–129.

33. For an introduction to the classification of the Council's documents, see Excursus IX.

34. See Abbott [1966], pp. 199–308. In his introduction to this constitution Donald R. Campion, SJ, provides a good outline of it. See Abbott [1966], pp. 183–198.

35. This principle applies also to the decrees and declarations of the Council. In *Gaudium et Spes* scholastic terminology appears with reference to "natural law." In Excursus IX (under the subheading, "The interpretation of Council documents") we have provided an important application of this in the case of Karl Barth. This poses an academic question: "Is this introduction of a scholastic notion in a phenomenological context an indication that the phenomenological method is being used imperfectly or that the scholastic term is receiving a new interpretation?" For one possible interpretation, see Luijpen [1967].

Inasmuch as *Gaudium et Spes* deals with both religious and socio-cultural phenomena, there is — as might be expected — a certain potential for disagreement latent in the document due to the diverse "scientific" methodologies today used to interpret such data. See Allen [1978], pp. 38–39. On "The Priority of Paradigms," see Kuhn [1962], pp. 43–51.

36. By a *pastoral* theology I mean one achieved by a phenomenological analysis of human experience, as exemplified by Vatican II. In this sense it may be called an *anthropological* theology, at least by reason of its methodological Idealism. Both the data of revelation (as recapitulated in the Glorified Christ) and the phenomenological method tend to complement one another in achieving a totally hominized ontology of reality. Such an ontology would certainly characterize the religious life-world as I have employed that term.

37. "The concept [socialization] has two different meanings, one in social anthropology and educational theory [which *Gaudium et Spes* uses], the other in economics [as Marxists or socialists view such matters]." For further details see "Socialization," in Bottomore [1983], p. 447. Since 1978 and more especially with the new Code of Canon Law, a new link of canonical vocabulary has appeared in this theological-social concatenation of *communio*/socialization. We may sum up this complex of juridical relationships by the term, "mutual relations." Hence, in a descending order the fuller sequence would be: *communio*/mutual relations/socialization. See Sacred Congregation For Religious [1978] and Canon Law Society of America [1983], pp. XI–XXVIII.

38. See *Gaudium et Spes*, Chapter 2: "The Proper Development of Culture." Abbott [1966], #53–62, pp. 259–270. This should be read in connection with Pope John Paul II's address to UNESCO, June 2, 1980. This was published in the English edition of *L'Osservatore Romano*, June 23, 1980, pp. 9–12 under the title, "Man's entire humanity is expressed in culture." By introducing the concept of "culture" the Council finally reestablishes a linkage with all the modern sciences, especially anthropology, sociology, psychology, etc. The common ground of all such sciences is human behavior. Since intentional "experience" describes the "behavior" of the human consciousness, the Council's phenomenological style of reflection and these contemporary sciences share a common ground in cultural studies. However, phenomenology enjoys a certain philosophical priority and normativeness due to the teleological and isomorphic

nature of consciousness. External human behavior can, at most, only be symptomatic of these more profound, ontological realities inherent in man's nature. See D. Carr's remarks on the life-world (and culture) cited in Excursus I on the Life-World under the subheading, "The practical character of the religious life-world."

39. For some important observations on the place of the sciences in *Gaudium et Spes* see Excursus I on the Life-World under the subheading, "The natural attitude toward the sciences in the natural life-world."

40. See Abbott [1966], p. 186: Emphasis added. The work of doctrinal development is only carried forward by serious theological studies comparable to that of Walgrave [1972] or wholesome moral/devotional traditions in the Church. All of these, however, reach factual clarity by doctrinal definitions either in Council (e.g., Vatican I on the papal primacy) or papal promulgation (e.g., Pius XII on the Assumption). By reason of its phenomenological descriptive style Vatican II's doctrinal development needs a great deal of critical scholarly reflection to determine more clearly just what that development is.

41. See Miller [1966], p. 429: "And in setting up the problem [i.e., of describing today's world] every effort was insistently made that it be objective, phenomenological and as little interpretive as possible." In *Gaudium et Spes*, accordingly, there is a sociological application of phenomenology. The array of theological teachings are simply prudential selections drawn from the thematizations previously elaborated in the two dogmatic constitutions.

42. Rather than my attempting to catalogue such correlations, the better course would be for the reader to learn to read *Lumen Gentium* and *Gaudium et Spes* as interlinked by a religio-human isomorphism. As a start, we would recommend Charles Moeller's two articles: "History of Lumen Gentium's Structure and Ideas" and "Man, The Church and Society" in Miller [1966], pp. 123–152 and 413–421. In *Lumen Gentium* (and *Dei verbum*) the Council was intent on formulating an anthropological theology, the paradigm of which was the Glorified Christ as Logos-Shepherd. This new type of "hominized" theology contains, in principle, a theological anthropology. In *Gaudium et Spes* the Council makes its first attempt, in a speculative-practical way, to start implementing this theological anthropology as praxis.

43. In order to perceive "structural sin," as many religious thinkers do in modern social dislocations, one must really step outside the completely hominized theology developed by Vatican II. In this style of reflection only *men* sin, not structures.

44. See Vorgrimler [1967–1969], Vol. 5, pp. 71–72.

45. See Vorgrimler [1967–1969], Vol. 5, p. 72.

46. See Robert C. Solomon, "Husserl's Concept of Noema," in Elliston and McCormick [1977], esp. p. 177.

CHAPTER 10

THE VERTICAL DIMENSION OF THE NEW ECCLESIAL HERMENEUTICS

Introductory remarks

Upon beginning our reflections of this most complex doctrinal constitution, *Dei verbum*, I would only remind the reader that any observations previously made about the use of phenomenological method in *Lumen Gentium* apply equally well here. These two dogmatic constitutions complement one another not only doctrinally but also in the matter of applied phenomenology. Up to this point I have interpreted the use of phenomenology at the Council in the Husserlian tradition of *Dasein* (i.e., the *esse intentionale* inherent in human lived-experience), not in the theoretical sense deriving from philosophical phenomenology but its pragmatic counterpart, the life-world. This interpretation applies equally well to *Dei verbum*, even though Vatican II in this constitution seems to be engaged, by reason of its sublime subject-matter, in some sort of "transcendental turn." Here, in a preliminary way, I will outline some distinctive features implied in the Council's phenomenological reflection on Revelation.[1]

A phenomenological overview of *Dei verbum*

The revealed matters (*revelata*) reflected upon in *Dei verbum* constitute the religious world as *passively* received by the Church. As pregiven by God, this essentially synchronic religious world is the *ground* upon which all motion, change, or activity take place in diachronic (eschatological) time, such as we previously described these things in *Lumen Gentium*. This "world" neither moves nor is stationary since it presents God's Eternal *Plan* as manifested in *history*. Within the horizon of this world each object (noema) has its properly distinctive meaning, but since it is seen against and within a many-layered field of objects (noemata) with their proper meanings, these also contribute to the intelligibility of each noema, especially those of a lower order: e.g., symbols (sacramental or otherwise), the scriptures as materialized in given texts, and traditions as concretized in historical time. Consequently, in this constitution there is a very sophisticated application of Husserlian intentionality, apperception, and a concatenation of appresentations not only toward correlated objects on the same level of things but through ongoing higher orders of meaning.[2] The process culminates, finally, in the Glorified Christ, as *Logos*-Shepherd, who illuminates this whole system of consciousness throughout all its layers by his own divinely endowed intelligibility. Once again, this is Dasein as a totally hominized system of religious consciousness.

The pastoral centrality of the Church in these reflections

In this reflection on Revelation, however, we must not lose sight of the fact that Vatican II in its totality was a pastoral council with the Church as its dominant theme. This flows from the fact that the Mystical Body provided the *objective* archetectonic paradigm of the Council's reflection on the Church. The constitution, *Dei verbum*, on the basis of ecclesial subjectivity, reflects on the "mystical" dimension of the Church, whereas *Lumen Gentium* projects it as incarnate body-subject. As Paul VI said in his closing speech to the bishops at Vatican II: "Men will realize that the Council devoted its attention, *not so much to divine truths*, but rather, and *principally*, *to the Church* – her nature and composition, her ecumenical vocation, her apostolic and missionary activity."[3] Although the Church in the constitution, *Dei verbum*, is directly focused on revealed matters, by reason of her use of the phenomenological method (which reflects on noemata as they have *meaning for her*), this constitution is also a case-study of the acting ecclesial consciousness. (If we view both as studies in *ethical* reflection, this constitution has some interesting parallels, as does the whole of Vatican II, with Wojtyla's *The Acting Person*.[4]) This case-study is not, however, any theoretical reflection on divine truths, but a non-formal, pastoral reflection on these truths as they exist in the religious life-world of the Church. This reflection derives from the a priori religious experiences of the bishops in Council as they corporately pondered and responded to that *subjectively* architectonic question: "Church, what do you say of yourself?"

Phenomenology and the ecclesial self-analysis

From a pastoral point of view the above interpretation of Vatican II and the place of *Dei verbum* within its ecclesial focus seems consonant with all which we have previously said in this book about the use of phenomenology at the Council. (This would be doubly true if we add the current "crisis in human beings," but we shall return to that point later.) After all, the Council is simply the Church asking herself about her *moral* responsibilities in the complex situation of the modern world and what she intends to do about it. As if on retreat, the Church of today — in an overt way appreciated by everyone — engaged in a corporate process of self-analysis regarding her essential truths, values, and structures, her dignity and her destination. Since the world of positivism and empirical research into socio-cultural forms or history could not provide answers for the profound questions which she was putting to herself, she had recourse to another avenue to the transcendent respected by many scholars: i.e., the phenomenological method. What is not appreciated by most people is that recourse to this method was part of the Church's effort to measure up to her full *moral* responsibilities to communicate with *all* men. This point may become clearer if we reflect on phenomenology as a *via media* between two diverse sets of audiences *ad intra* and *ad extra* to the Church.

The first communication problem was *ad intra* to the Church. It was the need to reconcile the theoretical differences between Roman School theology (realism) and the Transcendental Thomists (idealism). (How this methodology also met the more practical problems posed by the historians, representing the interests of empiricism and psychologism, will become clearer later in this chapter.) The second major problem concerned communication *ad extra* with the secular philosophical world: i.e., the entrenched controversy between empiricism and idealism, such as Husserl and the more recent phenomenological tradition of Europe conceived it. By using such descriptive phenomenological techniques focused on her own experience of her own religious life-world the Church was enabled to return to the primordial ontology at the heart of her religious consciousness. Reflection on the Mystical Body as the Church's phenomenal body was thematized in a meaningful new way as the People of God. In doing all this the Church expected that this process would be replicated, in some practical way, in the lives of her members so that they would equip themselves to lead authentic, relevant Christian lives in the contemporary world. However profound, and even heroic, such a massive process of self-reflection may have been, it is only one side of the coin.

The problem of ecclesio-monism

The speculative roots of the pastoral problem, which we are about to discuss, are both religious and methodological. The religious difficulty (to be treated momentarily) largely indicates that in the minds of the bishops/theologians the pastoral concept never matured much beyond its doctrinal and kerygmatic dimensions.[5] We will start, however, with the *methodological* aspects of the problem since it highlights the bipolar dialectic at the heart of the Council's

phenomenological reflection. Here three dynamic elements make up the subjective field of consciousness or belief: (1) the ego: i.e., our own existence as
that of a believing being; (2) our acts (noesis): i.e., our acts of believing; and
(3) the object (noema): i.e., the thing believed insofar as it is believed and with
all the complexities of its mode of givenness.[6] As an expression of phenomenological reflection, all three elements — and *only* these elements — are present
in the Council's reflection on its own life-world. By reason of the Council's
use of the philosophical and scientific reduction Vatican II "suspended" any
endorsement of the *theoretical* assumptions underlying Husserl's philosophical
phenomenology. This point would also apply to any post-Husserlian influences
discerned in the Council's workings.

Pope John's call to practical, pastoral renewal laid a great burden on the
shoulders of the Church. Consequently, the bulk of conciliar reflection tends to
be manifestly ecclesiocentric. As part of clarifying her own role-expectations
for new and unfamiliar tasks, the Church constituted out of her own *ad intra*
experience of her own religious life-world her contemporary sense of her corporate self-identity. From a purely methodological point of view it was *fitting*,
though not absolutely necessary, that this factual, unrelieved emphasis on the
ecclesial ego be counter-balanced by an equally doctrinal treatment of the
object (noema) *ad extra* of her belief. The point at issue here is simply the sym-
metrical and balanced treatment of the ecclesial field of consciousness: i.e., the
isomorphic relationship between the ego and its noemata. Furthermore, if
Lumen Gentium displays the *active* noetic acts of the ecclesial consciousness
as it strives for eschatological fulfillment, *Dei verbum* portrays the Church
more *passively* as listening to the word of God. Since the days of Heidegger
and Bultmann most modern scripture scholars have employed phenomenological
techniques as part of their hermeneutical approach to scripture, so such procedures are not exactly unknown to them. Furthermore, while biblical scholars
represent vested interests in historical methodology, their theological sympathies
tend toward the Transcendental Thomists who have a well-known affinity with
the phenomenological method.

The decisive factor, however, for a positive move in this direction was a
religious one: i.e., to avoid the impression of ecclesio-monism.[7] That would
describe a situation where the Church's kerygma had somehow become self-
centered rather than God-centered. Instead of pointing beyond herself as any
good herald or prophet ought to do, the Church would seem to be moving
entirely within her own level of existence and making herself the central object
of her own proclamation. (Paul VI was not the only theological engineer at the
Council!) Hence, to balance off the doctrinal statement of ecclesial egology
found in *Lumen Gentium*, it was theologically fitting that an equally doctrinal

statement be made about the object of the Church's belief, the word of God. In this constitution the bishops were striving to present the Church as totally God-centered and Christ-centered: "... here the whole life of the Church is, as it were, opened upwards and its whole being gathered together in the attitude of listening, which can be the only source of what it has to say."[8] Perhaps the only point that should be emphasized at this moment is that the ego and the object are simply two poles of the same field of consciousness. In other words, the field of consciousness represented in *Dei verbum* and *Lumen Gentium* is the one ecclesial consciousness reflecting its multi-layered ontological structure. Ecclesial being, human being (Dasein), and God-given being are all welded here into an isomorphic dynamic unity.

Historical pressures shaping the situation

There were several historical factors pressuring for a formal (i.e., doctrinal) treatment of Revelation, and these — on the surface, at least — are connected with essentially *religious* issues. Since the problem of theological modernism at the turn of the century two groups of scholars within the Church had been polarized on the basis of their methodological approach to revealed data. These were the scholastics (realists), who represented the classical understanding of Thomism, and the historians (empiricists) among whom are the biblical scholars. Since about 1850 historical theory (with all of its connotations of historicism, psychologism, and the historicity of human understanding as evolving in time) has presented a growing epistemological and technical problem for the Church, particularly in the area of biblical interpretation.[9] As in the Galileo Case scripture scholars must be the advocates for the "profane facts" accessible to human reason and scientific research; the only difference is that Galileo represented the interests of the physical sciences, whereas the biblical scholars represent the interests of historical research. Part of the reason for the scholastic intransigence toward both methodologies is that each represents but the "nose of the camel." Behind Galileo's approach to physical facts, as Husserl pointed out, loomed the larger philosophical problem of the total mathematization of reality, and that includes human reality. Only after three hundred years is this problem beginning to be sorted out. Behind the up-front problem of the errancy of some of the profane facts found in the bible looms the larger religious problem of the historical value of the four gospels, and behind that the larger philosophical problem of the historicity of the human consciousness.[10] (We shall return to that problem later in this chapter.)

Furthermore, in view of the ecumenical purpose of the Council an explicit (if not exactly formal) treatment of Revelation seemed imperative to meet the interests of any group outside the Church concerned about the authentic interpretation of the bible. Preeminent among such groups would, of course, be members of the various Protestant denominations.[11] It goes without saying that such outstanding observers at the Council, as O. Cullmann, were predominantly oriented to the historical mindstyle. However, all three groups — the scholastics, the historians, and the Protestants — had one thing in common: their heavy reliance on some distinctive "scientific" method in their approach to revealed data. To the extent these groups resorted to a science or philosophy to grapple with the world of physical facts, they thereby came to be participants in the world of "positivism."[12] Behind these essentially religious groups loomed an even larger world of "positivism" shaped by an evolutionary mindstyle: Neo-Darwinism, the cosmology of the physical sciences, philosophical anthropology, humanistic psychology, and Marxism. At the heart of all these movements are various efforts to shape a new non-biblical narrative, or "myth," to guide man's evolving self-identity.

The methodological challenge faced by the bishops

The enormous methodological problem facing the bishops here is how to handle divine and human reality without being trapped into one of the pitfalls provided by the world of "positivism" catalogued above. This could be done only by shortcircuiting the whole "scientific" process by acceptable phenomenological techniques: i.e., by the suspension of the sciences and a philosophical reduction, as previously explained in the book.[13] Consequently, by returning to the life-world of the Church the document on Revelation transcends (or bypasses, if you will) the world of "positivism" and contemplates the word of God as it exists in the ecclesial consciousness. Only after clarifying that word of God by phenomenological reflection does the Church, in a quite generalized way, take up some selective issues impinging on historical data relative to the field of sacred scripture.[14] In this conciliar enterprise necessarily concerned with a review of "profane facts" connected with revealed data the Church manages to stay out of any *technical* involvement with the scientific and philosophical issues without compromising herself on any point of doctrine. The procedure is perfectly legitimate in view of the *pastoral* nature of the Council. Had a really important technical issue confronted the bishops in their discussions, in all likelihood it would have been removed from the agenda as Paul VI removed the birth control issue and entrusted it to a technical commission. Or, as he did before the final vote on *Lumen Gentium*, the Holy Father could have inserted a "Prefatory Note of Explanation" clarifying the "authentic sense" of the debated issues.

The ontological character of the constitution

From all we have said about the phenomenological style of reflection employed at the Council, there is little need to dwell on the ahistorical, transtemporal view of Revelation formulated by the constitution, *Dei verbum.* Its topic is Revelation *as experienced and meaningful in the contemporary consciousness* of the Church.[15] In His goodness and wisdom God has chosen to reveal Himself through His Word. This He has done in a twofold way: by creating through His Eternal Word and by redeeming through the same Word-made-flesh. Accordingly, God's plan of revelation — whether manifested by deeds or words — possesses an inner unity deriving from the Risen Christ, as the one Word of God, the fullness of revelation, and its Mediator.[16]

Several points are implied in the above affirmation of faith. (1) If God, motivated by goodness and wisdom, revealed Himself through His Word, presumably the same motivation would have prompted Him to preserve this Word in its integrity among men. (2) The Risen Christ is the linchpin of meaning harmonizing the first and second creations, neither of which can, in principle, contradict the other. (3) The humanity of the Risen Christ, now fully intelligible in terms of God's plan of revelation, possesses for us a twofold intentionality: as the divine value-system rendered comprehensible in human terms and as humanness fulfilled by being totally united with the ultimate source of life, wisdom, and love. In a doctrinal sense (though not in the pastoral sense intended by John XXIII) this is the primordial paradigm for the revelation of man to himself. (4) A presumptive Principle of Complementarity needs to be employed by men to discover the inner unity correlating event and truth at every level of being. This is a necessary derivative of the bipolar isomorphism between act and object in the phenomenological reflection on consciousness. (5) What is reified as "Revelation" in this document is really a multi-layered system of consciousness so interrelated as to be called an intersubjective communing (or "dialogue") between spiritual persons. In such a living compenetration of consciousness (i.e., *communio* as co-presence) with its primary analogue in the Blessed Trinity what the document reifies as scripture, tradition, and magisterium are really vitally balanced thought-patterns (thematizations) of this ecclesial consciousness as teleologically ordered by the Father, as guided by the Holy Spirit, and as forming a living unity with the Risen Christ.[17] Here any profane categories of time no longer apply. On the part of God and His Plan the timeframe is the "eternal now," but on the part of the contemporary believers the unfolding of this plan takes place either in cyclical sacramental time or in eschatological time. This is the bi- or tri-dimensional timeframe, as you recall, which constitutes the inner time-consciousness of the Church.[18]

Constituting a religious hermeneutics of revelation and history

In *Dei verbum* where the biblical word, historical traditions, and concrete symbols are transformed into a higher unitary intelligibility we begin to appreciate, in an applied way, the working relationships between apperception and constitutive phenomenology. Here it would help if we recalled the example, given in Chapter Six, of how the map of an unfamiliar city gradually takes shape in our mind. Experiences of unfamiliar signs, unclear directions received, and the confusing flow of traffic gradually start to make sense until suddenly we see the whole pattern of things, not simply as a map, but as an epiphany of a living, organic unity: i.e., a *life-world*. If this applies to our getting acquainted with any city of man, it applies equally well to our getting about in the City of God. What I have described on the basis of Husserl's methodology should not be viewed as taking place in a religious vacuum. These phenomenological processes oriented to human being (Dasein) and its experiential meanings (noemata) are redolent with the sense of words traditionally associated with the idea of Christian renewal: e.g., transfiguration, metamorphosis, transformation.[19] If this dogmatic constitution, accordingly, is appreciated within a phenomenological context as portraying the dialectical interrelationships between an ascending order of spiritual realities, then it is also appreciated as reflecting in the ecclesial consciousness the Pauline recapitulation of the Divine Plan (Eph. 1:10): *instaurare omnia in Christo*, "to restore all things in Christ."

Early in the last chapter we broached the problem of historicity in the context of *Lumen Gentium*. In the light of the observations made there and the observations just made about apperception and constitutive phenomenology in the traditional sense of renewal shared by the Churches of East and West, it is time to return to the notion of historicity formulated in *Dei verbum*. No one has reflected on the religious sense of this notion better than Pope John Paul II:

> [. . .] the historicity of the events reported in the Gospels [i.e., the Gospels "faithfully relate what Jesus did and taught," *Dei verbum*, #19] enables me to add a remark on the subject of the knowledge or "knowability" of God [. . .]. This God in whom as Christians we believe is not only the *invisible creator* that our intelligence can attain through the

world and the creatures in it. He is a God who *comes* towards man and as a result *enters* history [which is our natural abode] . . .

Man is a being involved in history and therefore subject to passing time, but he is conscious of the passage of time, which he must fill by fulfilling himself. He has to establish himself in time and employ it to make himself into a unique being who will never be repeated. Historicity differs essentially from limitation by time, for all the beings in the world around us pass away with time. Man alone has a history and he alone creates it. It is true that he creates it while enmeshed in impermanence, but at the same time he creates it through that element in him which resists and overcomes the fleeting character of his existence. When I speak of "historicity," I am not thinking of the creation of history as culture or knowledge; I am thinking of the very mode of existence of man as man, of each man without exception.

So conceived, the historicity of man explains the appearance of God on the horizon and his entry into history. The Revelation reaches its zenith in the events forming the life of Christ which are recounted by the four Gospels and confirmed by the other writings of the New Testament, as the constitution *Dei verbum* [#17–20] says. The whole Revelation is historical in the sense that it refers to "historicity" as man's mode of existence in this world. It proclaims the "great works of God," namely the effects of his transcendent action – or rather of his gift to man. In history these works assume the concrete form of the history of salvation.[20]

In this reflection, which is a select cameopiece in a phenomenology of religion (i.e., the corporate Catholic consciousness) the Holy Father's stress on the subjective pole of Dasein fuses both religious experience and the modern humanistic concerns long associated with philosophical anthropology. What is perhaps more significant, however, is that his ideas would be readily endorsed by the "objectivistic" mindset of scholasticism, not so much on any theoretical basis but from a connatural knowledge, which has been the scholastic's tool for making sound judgments about concrete instances of God's Plan as being realized in history. Such judgments, of course, have been nourished in the rich loam of the patristic and contemplative literature of many centuries, so they are not without their commonly recognized patterns and trends. In both of the above religious outlooks there is at work a presumptive Principle of Complementarity contributing toward a consensus-building enterprise within the Church. What is distinctive, however, about John Paul II's remarks is that by identifying with contemporary thought-categories and humanistic concerns his words reach beyond the Church to all men.

A theoretical problem connected with philosophical phenomenology

Is it possible, in the manner of the later phenomenologists, to go beyond the
Dasein-radicated phenomenology of Husserl and its focus on Seinde (beings)
and still have an authentic, phenomenological interpretation of Vatican II? Is it
possible that through Dasein (i.e., *esse intentionale*) one could rise to Being
(Sein) which, as the supreme reality, would always have an interpretive priority,
and thus transfigure all lower-order realities? Would not such an advance in
theory enrich the pastoral insights of the Council? I have no doubt that such an
advance in philosophical phenomenology is theoretically possible.[21] I also have
no doubt that some of the theological experts at the Council interpreted
phenomenology in the manner of the later phenomenologists, such as Merleau-
Ponty or Heidegger.[22] The point is, however, that such a possible advance is a
theoretical philosophical problem and does not dovetail well with the *pastoral*
nature of Vatican II which employed both a philosophical and a scientific
reduction in order to return to its own religious life-world. Whether or not this
newer paradigm of phenomenological reflection might enrich the pastoral insights of the Council is something which will have to be settled by theoreticians
and acadamicians. One thing, however, is certain. If this type of theorizing is
not used in a consensus-building fashion, it could jeopardize the pastoral goals
of the Council. In a "worst possible scenario" Vatican II could suddenly metamorphose from being a pastoral council into a *doctrinal* one.

A larger pastoral problem of this constitution

In the faith-description of the sacral, transcendental consciousness of the Church,
as found in *Dei verbum*, we are confronted with a massive phenomenological
reduction.[23] The overarching ontology lending coherence to this document
abstracts from profane history (both present and past), from all "positivistic"
methodologies giving access to either revealed or natural data, and from all
cultural, psycho-social, or linguistic influences as these may have concretely
impinged on the development of contemporary Christianity (e.g., the problem
of Hellenization). I am not questioning the legitimacy of this type of reduction
within the context of a pastoral Council, but I am trying to comprehend its
pastoral intent *in relationship to that of Pope John XXIII*. The above formulation of revelation, taken in itself, has all the "over-spiritualized" connotations
which, prior to Vatican II, Vonier saw connected with the doctrine of the
Mystical Body. The ontology, however, is a predominantly hominized one both
as constituted by the ecclesial consciousness (ego) and as focused on the humanity

of the Risen Christ (object). Within this essentially contemplative matrix all things, spiritual and temporal, must find their ordered place and be judged.

Confronted with such a quasi-mystical vision of God's loving interrelationship with man, the bishops had no difficulty approving this as the substance of their religious experience and belief on the basis of their connatural knowledge. As a doctrinal and kerygmatic affirmation this is a statement for the ages. In a trans-temporal way it represents "a doctrinal penetration and a formation of con-sciousness in faithful and perfect conformity to the authentic doctrine . . . studied and expounded through the [phenomenological] methods of research and through the [phenomenological] literary forms of modern thought."[24] The document may, indeed, be a source of religious enrichment, as our several quotations from John Paul II have pointed out, but the pastoral gravity shift here seems heavily weighted in favor of very *intellectualized* religious and humanistic concerns. This is all a far cry from the more *down-to-earth* pastoral challenge formulated by John XXIII in *Humanae Salutis.*

The pastoral utility of this constitution

In a retrospective way we can, of course, read certain "pastoral" implications into this constitution, although these implications tend to be somewhat nar-rowly theological. (1) The document was formulated to counterbalance the strong ecclesiocentric tonality permeating the majority of the Council's state-ments. (2) It is, as one strand in the hermeneutics of the ecclesial consciousness, esthetically beautiful and complements the full significance of the People of God and the New Humanity projected by *Lumen Gentium.* (3) The document was also meant to be an internal reconciliation process healing the polarization over theological method which had divided Catholic scholars since the turn of the century. (This rebuilding of the we-phenomenon among scholars by way of consensus-formation at the Council was a quite arduous task, and one can get a sense of its complexity only by tracking this document through its successive stages of development.)[25] (4) This dogmatic constitution was also meant to be a gesture of high-level ecumenical outreach directed toward the intellectual leaders of the Protestant denominations and Orthodox Christians. (5) Lastly, this document is presumably an important counter-cultural faith-statement in opposition to any theories of man based on materialistic evolution (e.g., Marxism). We will reflect on this important topic in our Epilogue.

However, to appreciate the full complexity of the communication process involved in this document, one would have to approximate the intellectual attainments of a Rudolf Otto or a Mircea Eliade. By reason of the sophisticated handling of such complex theological issues, the great majority of the bishops relied in their ultimate decision-making, not on their professional expertise in such matters, but on their connatural knowledge. Given the pastoral nature of the Council and the method of analysis used, such connatural knowledge was perfectly adequate to the task set before it. That the bishops were intent on avoiding technical issues is apparent from the type of questions which they chose *not* to resolve: e.g., the material completeness of the scriptures, the scope of critical historical methods in biblical interpretation, the criticism of tradition, etc.[26] While connatural knowledge proved adequate for the discernment of the pastoral, religious issues set before it at the Council, we need not believe that it is any sort of prophetic tool in anticipating derivative problems in pastoral management flowing from the judgments made in such a discernment process.

The pastoral challenge in search of itself

The constitution, *Dei verbum*, in a way satisfactory to theological academicians, did achieve certain commendable purposes. The most important one was the formulation of a broad theological hermeneutics for the word of God as existing in the living consciousness of the Church. Within the context of that larger theological hermeneutics there was also an endorsement of an already growing scriptural movement and encouragement for the constructive use of the critical historical method.[27] This quest for a *theological* "penetration and a formation of consciousness" has, however, been accompanied by an unforeseen pastoral implosion far from the mind of John XXIII. The central issue seems to be a radical questioning and rethinking of Christianity, often enough under the pretext of returning to a certain "biblical simplicity." This quest can take many forms. In academic circles the theoretical discussion tends to pivot around a search for a "scientific" methodology (often enough derived from and applied to human "experience") or a quest for a radically new ontology.[28] In a rather ironic way the methodological idealism, which the Church employed at Vatican II for pastoral purposes, has been turned against her for philosophical or "scientific" purposes.[29] This type of rethinking, however, is not confined merely to the academic world. Quite often it is done in the name of serving certain concrete human or pastoral needs unrecognized or unattended by the Church in today's world.[30] This multi-faceted religious introversion has especially impacted on three areas: religious socio-political theorizing, traditional Christian moral values, and catechetics. Unless these problems are constructively resolved, the pastoral program of the Church will continue to drift erratically and spasmodically.

Towards a solution of this larger pastoral problem

The only reasonable way, it seems, of reconciling this tension between the phenomenological contemplative style of *Dei verbum* and the practical, pastoral goals of John XXIII is to repeat what I have said previously in the course of this book. (1) Vatican II was a pastoral council whose primary focus was on the Church. (2) Although the objective paradigm of the Council's documents is the Mystical Body, the phenomenological style of reflection used at the Council thematizes the subjectivistic dynamics of the corporate ecclesial *consciousness* (i.e., its *esse intentionale* or Dasein). (3) *Dei verbum* is a synchronic presentation of the vertical dimension of this consciousness, whereas *Lumen Gentium* is a diachronic presentation in linear, eschatological time. (4) The phenomenology of the ecclesial consciousness (as a life-world) found in these two dogmatic constitutions is brought into a first, tentative correlation with the global life-world(s) in the constitution, *Gaudium et Spes*. (5) Therefore, these three constitutions cannot be read intelligently unless they are read as *one* constitution with three *dialectically interrelated* parts and appropriately entitled: "The Church in the Modern World." It is this integral constitution which meets the full pastoral challenge as formulated by John XXIII and exemplifies the split-level type of pastoral theology which he projected as the fruit of Vatican II.

Concluding general remarks

This book has endorsed the thesis that there is a serious human crisis in the modern world. Consequently, in order to deal with such global problems Pope John XXIII called a pastoral council, not a doctrinal or reform one. Since this modern world-crisis is absolutely unique in human history, so Vatican II — as a *pastoral* council — became an absolutely unique type of council never before experienced in Church history. Both Pope John and the bishops had to grow into the full implications of this new pastoral undertaking, and that growth process is still going on in the Church today. Faced with such complex issues, the bishops in council put to themselves the corporate question: "Church, what do you say of yourself?" The purpose of this book has been to provide some coherent insights into what and how the bishops responded when answering that most important question.

The apochryphal literature of early Christianity records another important question posed at a decisive moment in Church history. As the story goes, St. Peter was fleeing from Rome to avoid a persecution, and on the road he met Christ headed for Rome. In some amazement Peter asked, *Domine, quo vadis?*

"Lord, where are you going?" Jesus responded, "I am going to Rome to be crucified." In the light of this answer Peter realized that fleeing from his moral responsibilities to his fellow Christians was not the path which Jesus wanted him to follow in those turbulent times. So, he returned to Rome. Catholics, and indeed all of mankind, today seem to be meeting the Church as it heads down the road in the "wrong" direction. The question rises naturally to our lips, *Ecclesia, quo vadis*? "Church, where are you going?"

It is in the spirit of that question that we offer the final reflections found in the Epilogue to this book.

NOTES

1. See Abbott [1966], pp. 111–128.
2. "Appresentation" is defined in Spiegelberg [1982], p. 739, as "the indirect perceptual presentation of an object mediated through the direct presentation of another, e.g., of the rear through the frontal aspect, or of other minds through their bodies." However, if one, for example, is analysing or describing the *backside* of a lock with a key in it, one can by appresentation "see" the key-hole and its *related* key. In the constitution, *Dei verbum*, the "keys" to the lower-order noemata are found on the higher levels until all "locks" (noemata) have one master-key in the concrete universal of the Glorified Christ as *Logos*-Shepherd. This section of the chapter should also be read in conjunction with Spiegelberg [1982], #3, pp. 699–702, "Apprehending Essential Relationships." In traditional theology the doctrine of the Immaculate Conception would be an example of appresentational apperception: in spite of the universality of Original Sin, it establishes an essential relationship between God's Plan and the doctrine of Mary as the Mother of God.
3. See Paul VI [1966], p. 59. Emphasis added.
4. See Wojtyla [1979a]. See also A.-T. Tymieniecka, "The Person and the Human Significance of Life," and T.P. Brinkman, "John Paul II's Theology of the Human Person and Technological Parenting," in Moraczewski [1983], pp. 213–257 and pp. 354–381 respectively.
5. Ratzinger has termed the pull between pastoral vs. doctrinal and kerygmatic vs. doctrinal "the dilemma of the Council itself." See Vorgrimler [1967–1969], Vol. 3, p. 169.
6. See "The Phenomenon of Reality and Reality," in Spiegelberg [1975], esp. p. 135.
7. See Ratzinger's remarks on this in Vorgrimler [1967–1969], Vol. 3, pp. 162, 167, 176. In this portion of our essay we are introducing the problem of ecclesio-monism in its simplest terms: i.e., the Church's responsibility, as a faithful herald, prophet, and teacher, to be a witness of the word received from God to the outside world. Within the phenomenological framework of this document the problem of ecclesio-monism is resolved in a twofold way: a parte cogitantis and a parte objecti. *A parte cogitantis*: in this constitution the ecclesial ego is presented as prayerfully listening to God's word *residing as an object* (*noema*) in the ecclesial field of consciousness and toward which the ego must, by the nature of things, direct its *ad extra* attention.

However, once the gnoseological (phenomenological) nature of *Dei verbum* is understood, then all of the *ad intra/ad extra* relationships involved between *Dei verbum* and *Lumen Gentium* may then be viewed afresh *a parte objecti*. In the comprehensive field of the ecclesial consciousness the role of the Glorified Christ, as the primordial *sacramentum*, provides the *ad intra* principle of intelligibility both for God's revelation (plan) and for the Church's function as a sacrament. See Abbott [1966], #1, p. 15. On this ground of total christocentrism the ontological relationship between the two doctrinal constitutions is: *Dei verbum* (*ad intra*) and *Lumen Gentium* (*ad extra*), but since the Mystical Body stands outside the phenomenological framework of these two documents, it stands as a conceptual and objectivistic norm implying both of their dimensions.

8. See Ratzinger in Vorgrimler [1967–1969], Vol. 3, p. 167.

9. In this regard see Harvey [1966], Henry [1979], and Smart [1979]. Two balanced treatments of this problem, as it impinges on Catholic doctrine, would be Connolly [1965] and Walgrave [1972]. It must be emphasized, however, that the pastoral concerns of Vatican II need not be identical with the theoretical concerns of a historical theologian.

10. Under the larger philosophical problem would also be included the Marxist conception of the historical dialectic, Darwinian evolutionary theories, and any radically materialistic psychoanalysis.

11. Religious groups are not the only ones who have an interest in matters of revelation. There is a whole group of modern "sciences" concerned with such matters, and in America they are generally grouped under the somewhat ambiguous title, "History of Religions." This important topic will be taken up again when we discuss Vatican II as a unique case-study in one type of *Religionswissenschaft*. (See note 18, *infra*.)

12. "Positivism" is employed by Ratzinger to express that modern spirit which tends to identify revelation (a *religious* fact) with its *historical* presentation, i.e., a form of scientific reductionism. This mindset, for the most part, reduces revelation to the confines of critical historical method and any philosophical or theological consequences which follow from that fact. See Vorgrimler [1967–1969], Vol. 3, p. 191. The sociology or psychology of religion are simply well-known variants of this widespread "positivistic" outlook.

13. Unless one suspends *all* the sciences in a phenomenologically consistent way, the only alternative is to fall into some form of scientific reductionism on the basis of psychology, sociology, history, politics, race, culture, etc. We have discussed the suspension of the sciences previously in Chapters Six, Eight, and Nine. How this is verbalized in theological language when the conceptual process is applied to the data of revelation may be found in Rigaux's remarks in Vorgrimler [1967–1969], Vol. 3, pp. 254–255.

14. See the few rather general remarks made in "Sacred Scripture in the Life of the Church," in Abbott [1966], pp. 125–128. As regards the postconciliar relationship between critical and Church exegesis, historical research and dogmatic tradition, see Ratzinger's observations in Vorgrimler [1967–1969], Vol. 3, p. 158.

15. This statement may stand equally well for an ("abstract," phenomenological) definition of *tradition*. See Ratzinger's important remarks on Vatican II's *abstract* notion of tradition in contrast to Trent's *concrete* notion in Vorgrimler [1967–1969], Vol. 3, p. 183. In the phenomenological matrix of Vatican II revelation and tradition are, in Husserlian terms, a manifold; hence, they are analysed and described simultaneously in a unified field of consciousness. Therefore, the *one* phenomenon *a parte objecti* is

revelation, but *a parte cogitantis* is living tradition. In such a context Ratzinger is quick to point out that tradition is "the many-layered yet one presence of the mystery of Christ throughout all the ages." See Vorgrimler [1967–1969], Vol. 3, p. 184. This type of tradition may then direct its reflection *ad extra* to the concrete, empirical "traditions" (in the Tridentine sense) in order to interpret them in a way consistent with the revealed noemata. However, any retrospective view of previous theologians or schools (e.g., German Romantic theology) as being a contributing influence on the formularies of Vatican II in all these matters would be, at most, a teleological-historical reflection in the style of Husserl, since phenomenological formulas or thematizations are transtemporal constructs.

16. See Ratzinger's commentary on article 4 in Vorgrimler [1967–1969], Vol. 3, esp. p. 175. In the ecclesial field of consciousness the Glorified Christ, as Logos-Shepherd, constitutes the universal concrete ontology. In chapter eight, as we previously remarked, the People of God is the correlated universal concrete ontology embodied in the Church itself. The Mystical Body, however, as standing outside of the Council's phenomenological analysis, constitutes the Church's universal abstract (i.e., conceptualized) ontology.

17. See Ratzinger's and Grillmeier's remarks in Vorgrimler [1967–1969], Vol. 3, pp. 196–198 and pp. 244–245, esp. nos. 3–4, respectively. From a phenomenological point of view the "analogy of faith" would be a theological way of speaking about the comprehensive isomorphism permeating the ecclesial consciousness.

18. What we have been describing here approximates the *academic discipline* known as the "phenomenology of religion." It is one of the four branches of the "History of Religions" (once popularly called "Comparative Religion"). In Germany this group of religious studies is known as *Allgemeine Religionswissenschaft*, i.e., "the general science of religions." See Allen [1978], pp. 4–5 and Baird [1971], pp. 28–30. As a working principle, we may accept the four branches to be those listed by Joachim Wach: history, phenomenology, psychology, and sociology of religion. For a concise introduction to how individual theologians tend to employ the phenomenology of religion for their academic purposes see Hebblethwaite [1980], pp. 23–43.

   Vatican II's use of the phenomenology of religion has differed in significant ways from the usual academic applications of this discipline. Some of the major differences would be: (1) the Council's analysis and description were done in a communitarian way; (2) by committed practitioners of the religion; (3) reflecting on their own (cross-cultural) religious experiences; (4) in quest of a common meaning-for-them (ontology); (5) for pastoral, not academic, purposes; (6) with a view to developing a new communication process and a global formation-apostolic program; (7) which would be adequate to the challenges of a uniquely critical moment in the history of mankind. Lastly, the Council has, of necessity, manifested its own unique phenomenology of religion since its focus is centered on the *living consciousness* of the Church. When contemplating objects (noemata) existing in the "eternal now," the Council's analytic process resembles that of M. Eliade. However, when the Church reflects on its *becoming* as incarnate body-subject (People of God) in eschatological time, the analytic process resembles that of A. Schutz on the natural life-world. We must remember, however, that only *one* religious life-world is being reflected upon in this bipolar way.

   If we may grant that Vatican II did produce a distinctive phenomenology of the Catholic religion, did it also produce a *theology*? Certainly the phenomenological method was employed at the Council for serious religious purposes and by ecclesiastical teachers with a special charism to carry out their office. Whether or not the bishops formulated a theology is really an *academic* question, properly speaking, and largely depends on the principles or assumptions on which one bases his definition of "theology." See "Is there such a subject?" in Hebblethwaite [1980], pp. 1–22. By reason of the pastoral (i.e., anthropological) purposes of Vatican II this academic question regarding a "theology" of Vatican II is quite secondary, and may profitably be relegated to the speculations of academicians. For myself, I prefer to think that the bishops formulated a "meta-theology" commensurate with the "meta-anthropology" on which they were intent.

19. See Ladner [1959], pp. 43–45 and in his Index under "Metamorphosis," "Transformation," and "Transfiguration."

20. See Frossard [1984], pp. 58–59.

21. As a case in point we cite Heidegger's philosophy. See Boelen [1975], Deely [1971], and Marx [1971].

22. I will cite only two instances. On Rahner see Hurd [1984]; on Schillebeeckx see Schreiter [1984], p. 21. My own opinions, however, on these theoretical mindsets in relation to Vatican II may be found in Excursus V on Anthropology under the subheading, "The radical nature of Vatican II's reflection."

23. The phenomenology of religion, as employed by Vatican II, poses a serious academic problem, particularly for historical studies. This problem is discussed in a basic way by Baird [1971], pp. 152–154, but in a more extensive way in "The Historical-Phenomenological 'Tension'" in Allen [1978], pp. 173–200. These academic concerns should be read in correlation with "The Project of Transcendental Philosophy," in Carr [1974], pp. 260–277. Although such academic concerns were not ignored by the Council, they were not an integral part of its pastoral goals. This will become more apparent later when we see how many important technical problems the Council chose *not* to deal with. (See note 26, *infra.*)

24. See Pope John's opening speech at the Council in Abbott [1966], p. 715. Ratzinger in Vorgrimler [1967–1969], Vol. 3, pp. 186–188 offers an interesting case study where he resolves by phenomenological means four utterly disparate objections to the dynamic concept of tradition developed by Vatican II: the objections had been posed by Ruffini and Leger (Catholic) and Cullmann and Reid (Protestant).

25. The origin and background of this document is narrated by Ratzinger in Vorgrimler [1967–1969], Vol. 3, pp. 155–166; the stages of the text are listed therein on pp. 165–166. Part One of Grillmeier's commentary on Chapter III of this constitution offers a working sample of the conciliar thought being synthesized through the various stages of the document. See Vorgrimler [1967–1969], Vol. 3, pp. 199–227.

26. A more comprehensive list of such topics as listed in Vorgrimler [1967–1969], Vol. 3, would be: inerrancy and historicity of the gospels (p. 163), the material completeness of scripture (pp. 157, 162), the controversy over the *sensus plenior* (pp. 219, 238), the question of the canon of scripture (p. 247), questions concerning the authenticity of various scriptural writings (p. 247), and the problem of criticizing tradition (p. 185).

27. For a sample of the optimism which reigned at the end of the Council, particularly as regards the scriptures, see Grillmeier's remarks in Vorgrimler [1967–1969], Vol. 3, p. 246.

28. Such efforts seem to have been originally inspired by Heidegger's call for "foundational thinking." See Landgrebe [1966], pp. 142–143, 173–175. Perhaps the earliest academic trend in this direction for North Americans was Dewart [1966].

29. The most blatant example of a historicist mindset calling for a new theological episte-
    mology on the basis of the Constitution on Revelation (*Dei verbum*) would be Baum
    [1967], pp. 62–63.

30. At the present time the most publicized incident of this trend would be Liberation
    Theology. On August 6, 1984, the Sacred Congregation for Doctrine and Faith issued
    "An Instruction on the Theology of Liberation." See *The Pope Speaks* 29:4 (Winter,
    1984) 289–310. This should be read in the context of the pope's address to the
    cardinals on December 21, 1984: "The charism of Peter: to serve universal unity
    by protecting and defending the Gospel's authenticity." See the English edition of
    L'Osservatore Romano 3:869 (Jan. 21, 1985) 6–8. In this talk the Holy Father dis-
    cusses the authentic sense of the Church's "option for the poor" (#9–10, pp. 7–8)
    and substantially formulates the issue in terms of the "dehumanization," which John
    XXIII discerned in *Humanae Salutis*. See Abbott [1966], pp. 703–704: "Painful
    considerations."

EPILOGUE: THE MORAL CHALLENGE OF THE NEW GLOBAL TASK

As I come to the end of my reflections on Vatican II and phenomenology, what impresses me is not so much the Council's sophisticated intellectual process, but the fact that its religious adaptation recapitulates and redirects human thought-patterns under development for well over a century. Vatican II and the "signs of the times" are telling us that the Age of the Enlightenment has come to an end: man can no longer live by reason alone.[1] Reason needs to be anchored in a primordial faith (or myth) larger than itself, a faith which confers self-respect, clarity of direction, and a hierarchy of fundamental values. At the Council the Church returned to its own religious life-world to reformulate a creative and contemporary expression of such a larger faith. This was necessary because the battleground of the foreseeable future will be a clash of faiths, myths, and life-worlds rather than a clash of scientific ideas. Vatican II has, accordingly, brought into historical comparative focus the three great faiths now contending to shape the man of the future: faith in Reason, faith in the Collectivity, and faith in God. This context provides us with a better perspective on the three foremost leaders of these trends in modern times: Hegel, Marx, and John XXIII.[2]

Myth in the service of ideas

When Husserl made the long journey back to the life-world in the *Crisis*, he was in search for the authentic foundation of reason and science. Considered in itself this quest was quite theoretical in purpose: Husserl desired to elaborate a unified field-theory of consciousness. In 1937, however, there was another overriding practical goal which set him on this theoretical quest: the renewal of European civilization. At the beginning of the nineteenth century Hegel had also conceived of a comparable return to man's life-world, particularly his religious life-world. In that self-assured period of the Enlightenment Hegel's purpose was not at all theoretical, but totally practical and quite revolutionary in its humanitarian intent. H.S. Harris provides us with the pertinent passage embodying Hegel's Grand Plan:

> Until we make the Ideas aesthetic, that is mythological, they have no interest for the people [Volk], and conversely until mythology is rational,

the philosopher must be ashamed of it. Thus in the end enlightened and unenlightened must clasp hands, mythology must become philosophical, and the people rational, and philosophy must become mythological, in order to make the philosophers sensible. Then reigns eternal unity among us. Never the scornful glance [of the philosopher despising the superstitious believer], never the blind trembling of the people before its wise men and priests. The first awaits *equal* development of *all* forces, of what is peculiar to each and of what is common to all [. . .]. No force shall any longer be oppressed, for then universal freedom and equality of spirit reigns! — A higher spirit sent from Heaven must found this religion, it will be the last, greatest work of mankind.[3]

Hegel's thought was, perhaps, the last great effort to domesticate religion and harness it to the chariot of the State as the bearer of enlightened progress. In modern Western democracies this optimistic view of the State has not significantly altered, but civil society, as essentially pluralist, must now view religious groups as purely volunteer organizations outside of the political process itself. Hegel's Grand Plan was that of a theorist, formulated at the end of an era when agriculture and the landed-nobility gave every impression of preserving the *status quo antea* into the future. His role in the Prussian educational system underwrote the trend toward nationalism which, in effect, became the people's civil religion.[4] In Denmark only Sören Kierkegaard raised an isolated and unloved voice against this type of coopted religion.[5]

By 1848, however, with the full arrival of the Industrial Revolution and social unrest throughout Europe Hegel's Idealism was in decline. What is far more significant, however, is that the Industrial Revolution introduced the age of the urbanized masses, and ever since that era there has been a growing sensitivity to the complexities of this problem and concern with managing it constructively. But in the middle of the nineteenth century men were only beginning to recognize the outlines of such problems. There arose, then, a need for a new type of theorist to guide men into a future becoming daily more turbulent. In these first pioneering efforts Hegel's vision of the unity of philosophers and the lower classes remained intact, but his conceptual Idealism had to go. By an adroit use of psychological projection Feuerbach transformed the substance of Hegelianism into absolute materialism. Like Hegel and many modern thinkers, Feuerbach was not desirous of getting rid of religion, only of reconstructing it according to his own preconceptions. His most significant achievement was to remove psychologism from the realm of academia and put it to work in the marketplace. In doing this Feuerbach established a linkage with a new brand of historicism intent on the total reorganization of society and thereby the eventual elimination of religion.

Myth in the service of the masses

Karl Marx is acknowledged today as the most important thinker of the nineteenth century to have recognized that the future belonged to the masses. He
identified these masses, however, with the proletariat of the industrialized
nations. His insights were based on a critical assessment of the political economy of that era, and his new "science" of history has since become known as
historical materialism.[6] From empiricism Marx took the general content of
history to be materialism, and from Hegel he saw its specific form or content
to be the dialectic. In this way he tried to resolve a problem which has been
a major focus of this book: the conflict between objectivity (Idealism) and
subjectivity (empiricism). To the extent Marx believed that all scientific knowledge was conditioned by history and necessarily a developmental process,
he was not really intent on producing a philosophy. That became the lot of
Friedrich Engels, Marx's intimate collaborator. Although Marx in *Das Kapital*
had formulated the economic theory of historical materialism, it was Engels
in *Anti-Dühring* who elaborated *dialectical materialism*, the mythology of
orthodox Marxism in the Soviet Union.

Roy Edgley provides us with a concise sense of what is involved in Engel's
new philosophy:

> On its own understanding dialectical materialism is cross-bred from the
> union of two bourgeois philosophies: the mechanistic materialism of the
> Scientific Revolution and Enlightenment, and Hegel's idealistic dialectics.
> The mechanicism of the former, which is incompatible with dialectics, and
> the idealism of the latter, which is incompatible with materialism, are
> rejected and opposed as "metaphysical" and "ideological." The result is a
> philosophy in the sense of a "world outlook," "the communist world
> outlook" as Engels calls it (*Anti-Dühring*, Preface to 2nd ed.): a body of
> theory taken to be true of concrete reality as a whole, and conceived as in
> a sense scientific, as a kind of "natural philosophy" generalizing and sup-
> ported by the findings of the special sciences as they advance to maturity,
> including the social science of historical materialism.[7]

A revolution succeeds only because there are practical men of action capable
of translating theory into practice. Two such men after the Russian revolution
were Lenin and Stalin. Among other noteworthy achievements Lenin recon-
ceptualized the notion and role of the Communist party.[8] Since Marxism, as
dialectical materialism, was not merely a political theory, but a science and a
world view, a new type of party was needed to educate the proletariat in the

class consciousness appropriate to this world view. With the help of its intellectuals the cadre party had to first cultivate this consciousness within itself. Then,
as the pedagogues of a new humanity, the cadre party had to transmit this class
consciousness to the working class. Hegel's Grand Plan had returned with a
vengence! Under Stalin all this became dogma and was used to ensure party
discipline. But a unique transformation had now taken place. In the leadership
role of the cadre party a new elite had arisen which combined the roles previously held by Enlightenment philosophers and the managerial class of capitalism. As the working classes of the industrialized nations proved resistant to
Communist propaganda, the new masses became the peasant populations of the
underdeveloped nations. In every instance, however, the people became sub-
servient to a tightly knit elite group of a totalitarian party.

Myth in the service of humanity

John XXIII differed in one important way from Hegel, Marx, and Engels: he was
no theorist. As *Humanae Salutis* made clear from the start, the pope called the
council because of complex world problems and solicitude for mankind. Since
he had no doubts about the Church's theoretical grasp of doctrine and morality,
he did not call for a council to deal with such matters.[9] Rather, in a critical
global situation he was looking for ways to make his religious truths work more
effectively at all levels so that men would be able to comprehend them in human,
everyday terms. Hence, he called a *pastoral* council. In such a pastoral council
the key-question is: "Granted we have the truth, how do we get it to work its
purposes in a seriously dislocated world very much in need of it?" The response
of the bishops and theologians at the council was: "As a first step we must
project the truth in such a way that it coincides with the authentic desires of
humanity and serves as a focal point for mankind in its collaborative efforts
toward progress and development. As a second step we must rethink our own
religious community, the Church, in these same terms so that our efforts at
renewal and adaptation will provide moral leadership for mankind and en-
courage Catholics to collaborate with any worthwhile program assisting people
to become better human beings. Lastly, we must give an example of peacemaking by healing, as far as possible, the divisions within Christianity itself."
As a result, the Council Fathers totally recast the dynamics of the Mystical
Body into that communion of minds and hearts now known as the People of
God.[10] This new symbolism embodies a mythic-communication process which
intends for Catholics what the Statue of Liberty does for Americans: one
glimpse, and you have the authentic idea and spirit of the whole enterprise!

Without compromising the traditional doctrines found in the conceptual formularies of the past, the bishops and theologians conceived a new *pastoral theology* commensurate with the global human concerns of Vatican II as a pastoral council. As derived from the corporate experience of the Church, this theology is quite sophisticated and complex; most of this book has been devoted simply to the methodology used to construct it. However, the cumulative purpose of the whole process has been to *reverse* the psycho-cultural impact of the Copernican Revolution on modern man.[11] As we recall, Copernicus transposed a system of the universe confirmed by everyday experience into a totally conceptual one. In so doing he unwittingly began that process whereby man became displaced as the center of creation.[12] Most of the advances in modern science have simply reinforced this awareness, until man today has no significance except as a member of some collectivity, whether it be political, economic, or racial. For serious reasons, then, the Church has turned aside from a merely conceptual grasp of reality to restore modern man's experiential appreciation of his authentic humanity. This shift is both profound and disturbing. The temptation, of course, is to make it the subject of academic study and a source of further speculation: everything, in short, which John XXIII did not want a pastoral council to be. To fall into this temptation is to miss one of the most obvious facts of contemporary social history. Vatican II's pastoral goals and theology constitute a *mirror-image* of modern Soviet Marxism: two global forces with *opposed* dynamics are in confrontation about what it means to be a human being. The confrontation here is moral, not political.

Dialectical materialism vs. dialectical Christianity

In suggesting this iconographic contrast between Soviet Economic Man and the People of God I am not implying that the Council consciously constructed this symmetry-by-way-of-opposition. In the abstract much of the same opposition exists in the direction of Capitalistic Economic Man. However, the total complex of concrete global problems which Vatican II set itself to confront made this comparison with Marxism somewhat inevitable. It was in the context of *global* human problems that John XXIII made the *temporal order* the crucible in which the efficacy of the supernatural order would be tested. Furthermore, when the Council opted for a *methodological Idealism*, this knitted Vatican II into the Post-Kantian intellectual heritage of Europe from which Marxist theory derives. Virtually all of the epistemologically related problems treated by this book (e.g., the relationship between subjectivity and objectivity, historicism, the historicity of consciousness, praxis, anthropology, and dialectics) are regular dietary fare of Hegelians, Marxists, phenomenologists, existentialists, and Transcendental Thomists.[13]

I am not so much intrigued here with the theoretical implications of the abovementioned, newly juxtaposed contrast in global strategic visions as I am with its challenge to pastoral leadership and management. Both viewpoints have their distinctive recipes for peace and human development. The first says human nature is determined by the mode of production; its theory of humanism is essentially a political economy. The second says human nature is a known constant brought to perfection by moral choices; its theory of humanism is essentially a religion or, to be more accurate, one specific religious man, Christ. In our turbulent age I am not inclined to think either party is much interested in further speculative arguments. Since both have a vested interest in any constructive dialogue or praxis oriented to peacemaking, economic progress, and human development, I assume that is where both factions will be concentrating their attention for the future. We know what kind of leadership and management direction Marxism has fostered over the last half-century. What the Church can offer is yet to be proved.

Pragmatism, science, and the new humanism

I realize my reflections have assumed a very pragmatic turn.[14] It is difficult to maintain a distanced and neutral attitude in the face of The Bomb, *Humanae Salutis*, and the either/or global choice between social engineering and creative charity. Recognition of the problem is far more important than the mode in which we transpose or interpret its meaning. However, as we must admit, Hegel's vision of the need for a practical unity of minds between theoreticians and the general populace is being forced upon us by world events. While we may not be ready for any new religion, we just might listen a bit more carefully to some talk about an ecumenical ethics and some needed reorganization of human affairs.

Am I also somehow suggesting that in this critical transition period of mankind the pursuit of theoretical knowledge for its own sake has been relegated to secondary importance? To offset this query let me recall an example from Joseph Weizenbaum which speaks for itself:

> In 1935, Michael Polanyi, then holder of the Chair of Physical Chemistry at the Victoria University of Manchester, England, was suddenly shocked into a confrontation with philosophical questions that have ever since dominated his life. The shock was administered by Nicolai Bukharin, one of the leading theoreticians of the Russian Communist Party, who told

Polanyi that "under socialism the conception of science pursued for its own sake would disappear, for the interests of scientists would spontaneously turn to the problems of the current Five Year Plan." Polanyi sensed then that "the scientific outlook appeared to have produced a mechanical conception of man and history in which there was no place for science itself." And further that "this conception denied altogether any intrinsic power of thought and thus denied any grounds for claiming freedom of thought."[15]

Now, one does not have to go to far-off Russia to be exposed to such a virus. I have encountered the same outlook in the Catholic Church among parochial-minded clergy and laity, but this overly pragmatic attitude is so endemic to American culture that I have usually written it off as a deviation from the larger Catholic heritage. However, we must begin to recognize that the situation of 1935 is not the situation of 1985! What I am suggesting is that the model of scholarship, sceptical rationalism, and individualistic humanism which has come down to us from the Enlightenment is no longer adequate to the complex challenges of the modern situation.[16] While I readily admit the necessity of demythologizing the bible, I see a far more pressing need today for demythologizing our academic preconceptions. This is a necessary precondition for the reform of our educational system, the quest for a new humanism, and the practical task of global civilization-building required by our times.[17] Such was the substance of Husserl in the *Crisis*, and such is the substance of Vatican II. If we have to wait another twenty years while Catholic theologians do their "foundational rethinking" and discover a "new ontology," it just may be too late to get started on this project.

The moral challenge

I, for one, happen to believe that mankind has the technological capacity and natural resources to solve its problems for the foreseeable future. Whether or not we have the time available to develop the political and economic structures to use this technology creatively and effectively is another matter entirely. Much of our challenge today is not so much cognitive but moral. E.F. Schumacher has, from a lifetime of experience, achieved a basic spiritual and human insight into the modern situation which coincides with much Vatican II had to say:

[. . .] There has never been a time, in any society in any part of the world, without its sages and teachers to challenge materialism and plead for a different order of priorities. The languages have differed, the symbols have varied, yet the message has always been the same: "Seek ye *first* the kingdom of God, and all these things [the material things which you also need] shall be *added* unto you." They shall be added, we are told, here on earth where we need them, not simply in an after-life beyond our imagination. Today, however, this message reaches us not solely from the sages and the saints but from the actual course of physical events. It speaks to us in the language of terrorism, genocide, breakdown, pollution, exhaustion. We live, it seems, in a unique period of convergence. It is becoming apparent that there is not only a promise but also a threat in these astonishing words about the kingdom of God — the threat that "unless you seek first the kingdom, these other things, which you also need, will cease to be available to you."[18]

This is the new realism at the heart of Vatican II, and it implies a return to some very elementary truths of Christianity. The problems of our dislocated world will take the moral and humanistic measure of every man and institution now in existence and constitute their Way of the Cross for the foreseeable future.[19] Pope John Paul II has a fundamentally correct insight into this issue. While addressing university students, he once said: "The cross is the cradle of the New Man." In this sense we are "in a unique period of convergence," discerned by John XXIII in *Pacem in Terris*, when traditional religious insights are coming into alignment with humanistic values. Such, too, was the insight Josiah Royce had into the humanistic implications of the doctrine of the atonement.[20] The Catholic renewal of Vatican II involves a uniquely new but humanly constructive *theologia crucis.*[21] The world crisis, which requires us "to reinvent politics, to reinvent the world," is a challenging moral choice with an echo of Hegel in it: ". . . it will be the last, greatest work of mankind."

Toward the end of his life Baron F. von Hügel had a profound insight into the heart of what really constitutes this great modern moral challenge. He wrote:

We need a prophetic and creative love which, by loving the repulsive, the hateful, ends by making it lovable; a love which sees what is not yet there; a love which by seeing it, wishing it, loving it, makes it come.[22]

NOTES

1. To appreciate this statement in an historical context see "The Eclipse of Thought," in Polanyi and Prosch [1975], pp. 3–21. The same topic from a more religious dimension would be found in Smith [1982].

2. My choice of these three figures displays my personal bias in favor of the Western cognitive (scientific) tradition. My assumption is that this tradition will be a major formative influence in any global civilization of the future. Among the world's major religions only Christianity has developed commensurately within this cognitive tradition. Consequently, I have no great confidence in trends suggestive of esoteric religious syncretism: e.g., Ferguson [1980] and Capra [1982].

3. See Harris [1981], p. 301. Any use of the term, "myth," relative to Hegel, Marx, or contemporary secular thinkers would also have to take into consideration the nineteenth century's outlook on this idea as developed in Comparative Religious Studies. See Allen [1978], esp. pp. 11–13. When we apply this concept to the Catholic religion and the work of Vatican II, we shall precise more clearly how we are using the term. (See note 10, *infra*.)

4. See Hayes [1960].

5. See Drucker [1971], pp. 50–65: "The Unfashionable Kierkegaard."

6. See William H. Shaw, "Historical Materialism," in Bottomore [1983], pp. 206–210.

7. See Roy Edgley, "Dialectical Materialism," in Bottomore [1983], p. 120.

8. See Iring Fetscher, "Marxism, development of," in Bottomore [1983], p. 311.

9. See Durant [1968], pp. 23–24: "In the United States the lower birth rate of the Anglo-Saxons has lessened their economic and political power; and the higher birth rate of Roman Catholic families suggests that by the year 2000 the Roman Catholic Church will be the dominant force in national as well as in municipal or state governments. A similar process is helping to restore Catholicism in France, Switzerland, and Germany; the lands of Voltaire, Calvin, and Luther may soon return to the papal fold. So the birth rate, like war, may determine the fate of theologies; just as the defeat of the Moslems at Tours (732) kept France and Spain from replacing the Bible with the Koran, so the superior organization, discipline, morality, fidelity, and fertility of Catholics may cancel the Protestant Reformation and the French Enlightenment. There is no humorist like history."

10. I understand "myth" here in the sense defined by M. Eliade:

Myth narrates a sacred history; it relates an event that took place in primordial Time, the fabled time of the 'beginnings.' In other words, myth tells how, through the deeds of Supernatural Beings, a reality came into existence .... In short, myths describe the various and sometimes dramatic breakthroughs of the sacred (or the 'supernatural') into the World ... the myth is regarded as a sacred story, and hence a 'true history,' because it always deals with *realities.*

Cited in Allen [1978], p. 13. Eliade expresses a "phenomenological understanding of myth." See Baird [1971], pp. 77–80. He further states that "the foremost function of myths is to reveal the exemplary models for all human rites and all significant human activities." Cited in Allen [1978], p. 13, footnote 29. For some contemporary anthropological implications of Vatican II's radical adaptation of the Church's core-myths see Allen [1978], pp. 244–246.

11. My assertion does not contravene the fact that there are significant theoretical implications for science in the Copernican "revolution." See Polanyi [1958], pp. 3–4.

12. See Lecture XVIII in Freud [1966], who was one of the first to reflect on the three "humiliations" of Post-Renaissance Man: i.e., the Copernican displacement of man and his earth as the center of the universe; biological evolution's dethronement of man as a

"special creation" of God; and the radical relativity of all human knowledge and values as revealed by the psychoanalytic revolution and historical scholarship.

13. The mere listing of these schools of thought is enough to indicate that they represent academic theorists. The first close contact between Catholics and Marxists came during the Second World War in the French Underground where, often enough, the works of Teilhard de Chardin provided a common ground for discussion. After the War this type of dialogical exchange continued with that group of intellectuals representing "Western Marxism." See Bottomore [1983], pp. 523–526. Although the methodological Idealism of Vatican II may be a product of this European mindstyle, the meaning and goals of the Council will have to be interpreted into other thought-categories if it expects to exercise influence beyond the narrow academic community mentioned above. For pastoral purposes, it seems, the Church has exchanged Latin for phenomenology as her new "international language" for intellectuals. As Latin once had to be interpreted into the vernacular, so the same prospect faces the phenomenological style of reflection.

14. No one has captured the "sense" of this pragmatic spirit in the Anglo-American tradition of ethical reflection better than Polanyi and Prosch [1975], esp. p. 10. Since the late 1960s, however, this spirit of restraint in ethical reasoning has been fast eroding. See Rieff [1966], pp. 8–9.

15. See Weizenbaum [1976], p. 1.

16. See "Beyond Nihilism" and "The Two Cultures," in Polanyi [1969], pp. 3–23 and pp. 40–46. For individualistic humanism American-style see Yankelovich [1981].

17. These are all themes found in Muller [1982]. The irony of Muller's book is that he sees more connection with these ideas to Teilhard de Chardin than to the work of Vatican II.

18. See Schumacher [1973], pp. 293–294.

19. This fact applies especially to the Church. See Wojtyla [1979b] and Nichols [1981], pp. 76–77.

20. See Royce [1968], esp. pp. 178–186.

21. The theme of the spiritual significance of human suffering is assuming great importance in the thought of the present Holy Father. See John Paul II [1984a].

22. Cited in Nédoncelle [1962]. See also Muller [1982], pp. 60–64.

EXCURSUS I: LIFE-WORLD (LEBENSWELT)

Introductory remarks

Spiegelberg [1982], p. 747 describes the life-world as "the encompassing world of our immediate experience which can be recovered from the world as given to scientific interpretation by a special type of reduction." This descriptive definition is just opaque enough to alert anyone with a theoretical mindset, whether scientist or theologian, that a return to such a prescientific social world of subjectivity, the world of the natural attitude and commonsense, may involve a serious psychological adjustment and be accomplished adequately only with some difficulty. This is the phenomenological version of "Unless you be converted and become as little children . . ." (Mt. 18:3)

Husserl's inspiration for the life-world

It is important to recall, as both Merleau-Ponty and Bidney do, that Husserl got his inspiration for the notion of the life-world from Levy-Bruhl's *Primitive Mythology*. See Natanson [1973b], Vol. 1, pp. 102, 129. In focusing on the primitive consciousness of these diverse intersubjective communities both Levy-Bruhl and Husserl are — at least initially — intent on studying the primordial (and functional) ontology structuring these historically manifest life-worlds which, as constituted by the prescientific consciousness to provide human meaning and to serve human concerns, are essentially anthropocentric. The life-world, consequently, and the world of science (wherein we must also include philosophical phenomenology and scholasticism) are two diverse worlds dealing with two different sets of "facts." "The facts of the life-world," as D. Bidney remarks, "are historic, practical, and relative to the experience of given subjects and their cultural worlds. The facts of objective science are universal, cross-cultural, and valid for all mankind." See Natanson [1973b], Vol. 1, p. 130.

The life-world in the context of the "Crisis"

It cannot be emphasized too strongly that the theme of the life-world received its fullest development and prominence from Husserl's book, the *Crisis*, written

on the verge of World War II. John XXIII penned *Humanae Salutis*, when mankind was on the verge of World War III. In essence both men were faced with
much the same problem. Both thinkers recognized that their *theoretical* principles should express their *efficiency* in the dislocated *temporal* (human) order:
i.e., the life-world. Both also realized that such life-worlds had established the
human priorities governing the lives of men. Therefore, both men appreciated
that they had to establish a linkage, empirically grounded in these *human*
priorities, which would provide a two-way bridge between the diverse worlds
of theory and praxis. Both were convinced that such a linkage (ontology or
isomorphism) could be established and that it would be compatible with and
discernible by human subjectivity. Husserl thought this could be achieved by
phenomenological method; John XXIII suggested, at least tentatively, the
traditional connatural knowledge. Vatican II chose to use both approaches and
fused them in a corporate display of transcendental intersubjectivity.

Source materials on the natural life-world

The notion of the life-world was introduced into France by Merleau-Ponty as
early as 1940. Consequently, his ideas too played an important role in popularizing
this motif among European intellectuals. A concise analysis of Husserl's treatment of the life-world may be found in Spiegelberg [1982], pp. 144–147. This
should, however, be compared with his treatment of Merleau-Ponty's conception
of the life-world which seems to approximate the type of bipolar phenomenology characteristic of Vatican II's use of the method. See Spiegelberg [1982],
pp. 549–556. For a more extended technical treatment grounded in Husserlian
theory see Schutz [1962–1976], Vol. 3, pp. 116–132 ("Some Structures of the
Life-World") and Vol. 1, esp. pp. 120–122, 130–136 ("Phenomenology and the
Social Sciences"). Also to be recommended is C.A. van Puersen, "Life-World and
Structures," in Edie, Parker, and Schrag [1970], pp. 139–153. A book-length
treatment of this theme is Schutz and Luckmann [1973].

From the natural to the religious life-world

All of the above discussions of the life-world deal only with the *natural* life-
world, a theme which did not surface in any significant way at Vatican II until
the Council Fathers reflected on *Gaudium et Spes*, "The Church in the Modern
World." Vatican II's doctrinal focus was primarily on the *religious* life-world
of the Church. Need it be emphasized that the religious life-world is not the
totality of reality? Just as human beings are composed of soul and body, so the
"split-level" type of pastoral theology suggested by John XXIII and implemented
by Vatican II sees both life-worlds as correlated and working in complementary
fashion. It should come as no surprise, then, that the consciousness of the

Church focuses primarily, and somewhat exclusively, on its own religious life-world, its own "soul."

From religious life-world to phenomenology of religion

Consequently, the Council displays religious intentionality in action, manifests the pervading structures, typifications, or "styles" of this religious life-world, and ultimately makes us aware of its (functional) ontology. Often enough it is the theorist who first introduces us to such a phenomenology of religion: e.g., Mircea Eliade or Henry Duméry. Such theorists, however, labor — from a Christian point of view — under a certain "handicap": they view the religious phenomena as disinterested, scientific observers. Vatican II, however, exemplifies active participants reflecting on their own religious life-world. Admittedly, the "scientific" expertise of theologians working on the various conciliar commissions assisted in the thematization of such reflections. However, the work of the commissions was only preparatory for the final and decisive vote of the bishops as the authentic teachers of doctrine and morals. (The complexity built into such a decision-process from a phenomenological point of view will be discussed briefly in Chapter 8, note 3, but from a scholastic point of view the very nature of the conciliar formularies, as non-formal statements, necessarily involves a use of connatural knowledge.) Instructed by the above observations, we begin to appreciate that the two doctrinal constitutions, *Dei verbum* and *Lumen Gentium*, represent a phenomenology of a religious life-world constructed from the *inside-out*, rather than in the manner of the outside-in typical of the scientific observer constructing a phenomenology of religion.

The life-world and the suspension of science

In this book the life-world is discussed in an important way in Chapter 6 in the section entitled: "Reductive phenomenology: two pertinent types." Spiegelberg [1982], p. 145 remarks: "As Husserl sees it, a peculiar type of first reduction, *a suspension of science*, is indispensable in order to get sight of the life-world and its structures." (Emphasis added.) This is a key-idea in the development of my essay, particularly when discussing the Council's prescientific and "ahistorical" view of its religious realities and when reflecting on the Council's use of phenomenology as a *via media* style of reflection.

The natural attitude toward the sciences in the
natural life-world

A somewhat imprudent, if not inaccurate, over-statement occurs in Abbott [1966], p. 190: "What the Constitution [*Gaudium et Spes*] accepts as its point of departure is the emergence of valid new intellectual disciplines, chiefly those of the psychological, social, and historical sciences, as well as the unfolding of world-wide trends such as urbanization and industrialization with their inevitable impact on man and his works." This is simply an uncritical expression of the natural attitude toward the sciences in the *natural* life-world, and it conveys the type of unnuanced euphoria which seemed to grip some minds toward the close of the Council. What the Constitution accepts as its point of departure is the pastoral theology of the *religious* life-world of the Church as formulated in *Lumen Gentium* and *Dei verbum*. In the pastoral constitution, *Gaudium et Spes*, the Council Fathers are — in a first, tentative way — trying to correlate the phenomenologically thematized theology of the above-mentioned two dogmatic constitutions with a phenomenology of a *global* natural life-world. They are hardly going to compromise or jeopardize their essentially theological enterprise (which technically involves the suspension of the sciences) by endorsing the unqualified validity of such contingently judgmental "sciences" as psychology, sociology, and history. Acknowledging their existence, utility, or sociocultural influence is not to be equated with any theoretical endorsement of their validity. See also J. Sittler's remarks in Miller [1966], pp. 424–427.

For a truly *nuanced* statement consider this response of Canon Moeller to a question posed about *Gaudium et Spes*'s position on a scientific point, as recorded in Miller [1966], p. 430:

> *Question*: *In the light of what we know about the history of life before man emerged, was created, can we any longer say that man would have been immune from bodily death except for'his sin?*
> *Moeller*: It is a difficult question, and I must say that I am unable to answer it alone. Article 18 speaks of "that bodily death from which man would have been immune had he not sinned." In this text we avoid taking a position on the biological, paleontological problem; it says only that without sin man would have been without ordination to death [i.e., Heidegger's "being-toward-death"?]. This does not affirm any theory about natural immortality or natural mortality.

The practical character of the religious life-world

Vatican II's religious life-world may reflect the primordial consciousness of the Church, but as a *pastoral* consciousness it is very much oriented to the twentieth-century and beyond. Although pretheoretical and intuitively given, this primordial consciousness has correlated itself with the authentic demands of a scientific and technological age. In no way must Vatican II be construed as a study in "historical primitivism" or in the operations of the "primitive mind" in some anthropological sense. See Lévi-Strauss [1966]. The religious life-world of Vatican II, however, is more encompassing than the scientific advances of any one generation and always remains the background against which such achievements play out their roles.

Important as the world of science may be for advances in human knowledge and achievement, the life-world — whether natural or religious — is the ultimate custodian of our very humanity. This is so because the life-world is:

> not theoretical at all, but rather practical. For consciousness at this level, the world is the domain of ends to be attained, projects to be carried out, materials to be used in carrying them out. It is not a mathematical manifold of entities to be known with theoretical exactness, but a pre-given horizon of the useful and the useless, the significant and the insignificant, the relevant and the irrelevant . . . . In much of what Husserl says about the perceived world here, one is reminded of Merleau-Ponty's warning that perception must not be analysed as if it were an "incipient science." The orientation of the perceived world around the lived body is a practical orientation of movement and accomplishment, not a theoretical orientation. Similarly, culture does not essentially present us with a "theory" of the world, but envelopes us in a domain, articulated according to spheres of action, providing norms and directives for getting around. The cultural world may contain a scientific theory among its elements, but it is not exhausted in the stock of objective truths the theory provides. Not that the concept of *truth* has no relevance here, for hand in hand with Husserl's new descriptions of consciousness and the world goes a new concept of truth. Here he refers to "situational" or "practical" truth, which is properly characterized as "merely relative" — i.e., relative to the subject or the community, relative to the project under consideration — only by contrast to the notion of "objective" truth, truth-in-itself about the world-in-itself.

See D. Carr in Elliston and McCormick [1977], p. 211.

"World" vs. life-world

When reading post-Husserlian phenomenologists, the reader should not think
they are necessarily talking about the life-world in their discussion of "world."
For quite serious *theoretical* reasons these scholars have chosen to depart from
Husserl. The train of their thought has been well summarized by Robert R.
Ehman:

> The radically new dimension in the recent phenomenological thought
> of Merleau-Ponty, Fink, Heidegger, and Dufrenne is the attempt to correct
> the idealist bias of the Husserlian approach without returning to the naive
> ontological realism of the tradition. These thinkers do not reduce being
> to meaning; nor on the other hand do they pass over meaning in favor of
> an exclusive concentration on being. They attempt to put them both in a
> *dialectical interrelation* in which each has an equal part in the constitution
> of a world in which we find our place. *While there remains a tension*
> *between the idealist and realist poles, there is a genuine endeavor to*
> *transcend the old dilemmas between idealism and realism in which Husserl*
> *is still enmeshed.* The endeavor to transcend these dilemmas focuses on the
> phenomena of the world: it is world that is to provide the perspective
> from which we can do equal justice to both poles without allowing either
> to suppress the other.

See Robert R. Ehman, "The Phenomena of the World," in Edie, Parker, and
Schrag [1970], pp. 85—86, emphasis added.

    The above development represents a very high level of philosophical *theorizing*
parallel to the type of philosophical phenomenology which Husserl engaged in
prior to the *Crisis.* In such theorizing the term, "world," can even become
synonymous with Being itself. The phenomenologists at Vatican II were certainly
alert to the *intent* of such theorizing, and it did influence their thinking. In one
place Ratzinger alludes approvingly to "the problem of understanding, the
emergence of which over the last decades has dissolved the clear antithesis of
object and subject, without leading to an identification of both." See Vorgrimler
[1967—1969], Vol. 3, p. 188. However, Vatican II was such a *pastoral* council, and
its membership came from so many different "schools" of phenomenology
employed at disparate levels for different purposes, that the *theoretical* positions
catalogued above had little direct impact on the Council's thinking. About the
only thing which the phenomenologists at the Council had in common was the
methodology itself. Since there are so many parallels between the "renewal"
concerns of Husserl and the anthropocentric concerns of Vatican II originating,

as these did, with John XXIII in *Humanae Salutis* this methodology and its results make best sense when interpreted within the purview set for it by Husserl himself.

Although the Council may have been sensitive to newer theoretical issues raised by post-Husserlian phenomenologists, it by-passed them all by focusing on a phenomenology of its own religious life-world. Here there is already vitally operative a *quasi-fusion* or *dialectical interrelation* of anthropocentrism, christo-centrism, and theocentrism orchestrated by the paradigm of the Glorified Christ as the Logos-Shepherd. "We know that God reveals Himself in Jesus Christ and that at the same time, according to the constitution *Gaudium et Spes* [#22], Jesus Christ reveals man to man: 'The mystery of man is truly illuminated only in the mystery of the Word incarnate.' " See Frossard [1984], p. 67.

The thematization of the life-world at Vatican II

The thematizing of the ecclesial life-world was the work of the theological commissions assigned to develop the documents into their finally accepted form. This complex task required that such bishops/theologians safeguard the pastoral nature of the Council while doing their phenomenological analysis in a professionally competent way. G. Funke in Natanson [1973b], Vol. 2, p. 29, captures some of the delicacy of this task:

> [. . .] The consciousness that uncovers the meaning of the relationships in the life-world is itself no longer a consciousness within the life-world. [. . .] we must emphasize that the comprehension of structures and the understanding of constitution is not just a simple knowing of intentional acts or experiences that runs along with such acts, but is something that can be disclosed only through a *post eventum* regressive reflective analysis and with the aid of the most diverse clues. The consciousness that is within the life-world cannot achieve what a later reflection, itself an eventful occurrence, can achieve.

The religious life-world and its modern "ecumene"

While Vonier [1937] never developed the notion explicitly, the appropriation of his theme, the People of God, by Vatican II did — in the context of modern global problems — occasion the need for some serious reflection about the nature and scope of a Christian *ecumene* in the modern world. Voegelin [1978], pp. 203—204, describes that concept in the following way:

To Herodotus we owe the concept of the ecumene, meaning the entire known world of culture that potentially might be organized. He mentions it in the context of the Persians. The concept of the ecumene then appears again in Polybius as a designation of the *telos* of Roman expansion. Finally it figures in Christianity and Manicheanism as the term for the *telos* of missionary expansion. The ecumene, meaning the respectively contemporaneous cultured humanity as a field of potential organization, seems to be a social field of consciousness that belongs to the structure of political reality. The problem deserves special attention because in our time the global ecumene has become just such a potential field of organization by ideological empires as the smaller ecumene of the Persians was in Herodotus' time.

Maritain [1973], pp. 127–255, as you may recall, grappled with a comparable idea under the rubric of a "New Christendom." Reflecting on "The Church in the Modern World" (see Abbott [1966], pp. 198–308) and the Council's extensive reflection on culture and acculturalization (see Abbott [1966], pp. 761–762 in the subject index under "Culture"), we appreciate that such Conciliar ideas are simply the expression of the *telos* inherent in its religious life-world. Tentative though Vatican II's reflection on world and culture may be, still such reflections give body and reality to its religious life-world formulated in the doctrinal constitutions, *Lumen Gentium* and *Dei verbum.* The Epilogue of this book presents some reflections on the two opposed ecumenes of the modern world.

Concluding remarks

For American readers perhaps the earliest intimation (*pace* W.R. Boyce Gibson) of the above "existentialist" trend in philosophical reflection appeared in Tillich [1944], pp. 44–70. Certainly this was much the case for most Catholic intellectuals, as may become more apparent when this book discusses the encyclical, *Humani Generis.* See Weigel [1951]. Only quite recently have I become aware of a process philosopher-theologian, Bernard Meland, who "suggests the skill of appreciative awareness as a corrective measure situated in the gap between subjectivism and objectivism." See Mueller [1984], p. 65. Although this may indicate some growing closeness between process thinking and phenomenology, there is no indication that process philosophy had any significant influence on Vatican II.

EXCURSUS II: SACRAMENTAL TIME-CONSCIOUSNESS, ANAMNESIS,
AND THE COMMUNION OF LIFE

The Judeo-Christian religious time-consciousness

As in all religions, both Judaism and Christianity possess an "eternal now," which is proper to their central religious mysteries. The basic sense of the "eternal now" is defined *a parte Dei* according to his transtemporality over any human sense of time and typically implies a primordial eternity grounding all the derivative mundane types of time. *A parte hominis*, however, the "eternal now" has a double aspect: punctive (punctuational) time and cyclical time. *Punctuational* time is achieved by philosophical or mystical contemplation (e.g., Plotinus). *Cyclical* time is expressed serially in the liturgy since its memorials of the central religious mysteries are structured on annual, seasonal or human life-cycles. This "eternal now," which is a totally *synchronic* view of events, expresses the *vertical*, ontological structuring of religious time-consciousness.

Distinctive to the Judeo-Christian tradition, however, is another co-ontological, *diachronic* structuring of religious time-consciousness in a *horizontal* way. This is the unfolding of God's Eternal Plan in profane chronological time. Within this time-consciousness function prophecy, messianism, eschatology, and the authentic mission of the Church. Since the rationale of such unfolding events depends on God's revelation, their teleological-historical sense often cannot be discerned except retrospectively. This would certainly be the case for the religious interpretation of the Old Testament as provided by the New Testament.

These two types of religious, ontological time-consciousness have been well-treated by Eliade [1954]. In his reflections on comparative religion Eliade uses an essentially *phenomenological* method, which makes his observations of special pertinence to the reflective process of Vatican II. See Eliade [1954], p. 73. While his analysis may be grounded on the critical historical method as a preliminary phase of research, the actual analysis requires a *methodological suspension* of contemporary physical and historical science in order for the student of comparative religion to be able to return to the primordial ontology or archetypal world at the heart of the primitive religious experience. See Eliade [1954], pp. 44–48. Inasmuch as Eliade's use of phenomenological hermeneutics plays an important role in our interpretation of Vatican II, we refer the reader to two important studies drawing out some of the implications of Eliade's methodology as impinging on historical studies: i.e., Allen [1978] and Baird [1971]. Recommended collateral reading for the professional scholar would be Lévi-Strauss [1966].

Anamnesis

Anamnesis is primarily a liturgical term referring to the prayer, *Unde et memores*, in the Latin Mass whereby the Church memorializes the redemptive acts of Christ. For a compact history of this liturgical usage see either Lallou [1945] or Smolarski [1982], pp. 67–70. See also Jungmann's comment on *memoriale* in Vorgrimler [1967–1969], Vol. 1, p. 33. Although this religious concept is not identical with phenomenological "recollection," the two concepts are worthy of comparison. See Carr [1974], pp. 94–95.

The religious reality involved in anamnesis is much larger than any liturgical prayer since we are dealing with the *vertical* dimension of religious ontological time in which the sacraments, particularly the Eucharist, operate. Anamnesis, then, is a term appropriate for that primordial process whereby the religious man *suspends* profane time to reestablish a faith-contact with the exemplary events at the heart of his *real* world. See Eliade [1954], pp. 73–92. We are, accordingly, dealing with a *punctuational* time-consciousness of the "eternal now" achieved in and through the celebration of liturgical mysteries. In the tradition of Christian mysticism the suspension of profane time is a process somewhat more comprehensive than any mere suspension of the sciences, and once a Christian thinker has embarked on this course, his only sure guide would be his connatural knowledge.

The communion of life

The type of theological reflection engaged in at the Council is comprehensible only as a "doctrinal penetration" of the exemplary events at the heart of the Church's religious life-world. The reality of such events occurs in "Sacramental Time," as discussed previously, and that is especially true of the Eucharist, whose unique effect is "the edification of the Church, the communion of life." See Tillard [1967], pp. 268–291, esp. p. 280. In the scholastic understanding of sacraments as signs and instrumental causes used by Christ, the sacraments not only signify what they cause, but *cause* what they signify. As mentioned in Chapter 3, note 7, when discussing "symbolic realism," such "non-objective" symbols "organize and regulate the flow of interaction between subjects and objects, or [. . .] attempt to sum up the whole subject-object complex or even point to the context or ground of that whole."

By contemplation of the exemplary events symbolized by the liturgy, the bishops quite naturally encountered the Glorified Christ in his Paschal Mystery. This faith-experience was constituted by several factors working together: the depth of the bishops' personal doctrinal penetration, the spiritual co-presence established among themselves by their religious dialogue, and each one's acquired connatural knowledge of spiritual realities. Thus in a *corporate* way, arising from an environment of shared faith, the bishops achieved a renewed sense of "communion of life" both with Christ and with one another.

This first faith-experience, acquired early in the Council from reflection on the liturgy, provided the germinal pattern later expanded in the doctrinal penetration displayed by the corporate ecclesial consciousness in *Lumen Gentium* and *Dei verbum.* The reflective style of the Council, having originated out of a faith-experience focused on the exemplary events symbolized in the liturgy, never became theological in an academic, "scientific" sense. Rather, it preserved a "eucharistic" tonality descriptive of a grateful Church at prayer and contemplating the mysteries shaping its religious life-world. Although this style of reflection may provide a good example of *mystical* theology, it needs a good deal of clarification to appreciate it as a *pastoral* theology. To do that, of course, has been the intended purpose of this book.

EXCURSUS III: CONCRETE HUMAN RELATIONSHIPS AND
CARDINAL SUENENS

Although the focus of the bishops throughout the Council was totally religious, in the first session of the Council two factors were at work shaping their deliberations: (a) a reaction against the objectivist, abstract approach of scholasticism and (b) the fact that the dominant bishops and theologians at the Council (i.e., the Northern European Alliance) had been influenced by a generation of phenomenological thinking in Europe. In such an environment seemingly pragmatic or otherwise insignificant suggestions could open "new horizons" or vistas not available to those unfamiliar with the phenomenological mindstyle.

For example, when Cardinal Suenens made his intervention on December 4, 1962, he later submitted its written form, accompanied by further extended suggestions, to the Central Commission. These suggestions contain a memorable line: "De necessitate Ecclesiae duo notare volo. Primo, necessarium est ut variae categoriae hominum relate ad pertinentiam ad Ecclesiam *concrete* indicentur, ita ut omnis controversia praecaveatur." See Latin Texts [1970–1980], Vol. I, pars IV, p. 225. (The emphasis in the text is that of Cardinal Suenens.) While the above suggestion is made in the context of seeming utilitarianism (i.e., to avoid unncessary technical controversy), in the larger European phenomenological context where *Erlebnisse* meant *concrete* mental states, this suggestion of Cardinal Suenens was about as subtle as sending up a signal flare. See Landgrebe [1966], pp. 20–21 and Carr [1974], p. 11 sq. Being a quite intellectual man, the Cardinal knew exactly what he was doing. For all practical purposes his outline on the proposed *De Ecclesia* document, as contained in his "adnotationes additae," became the substance of *Lumen Gentium* as we know it today. See Latin Texts [1970–1980], Vol. I, pars IV, pp. 225–227. Bouyer [1982], p. 166 ignores Suenens' contribution in the development of the Franco-Belgian text out of which *Lumen Gentium* developed and prefers to mention only Fr. Congar, Mgr. Charles Moeller, and Mgr. Philips.

Once we appreciate that there is a certain Franco-Belgian intellectual axis shaping the tonality of *Lumen Gentium*, if not its substance, then the association of phenomenological method with this constitution becomes more credible. Reflection on *concrete* human relationships has, as one of its several important purposes, *a deepening of the experience involved in intersubjective relations.*

One of the well-known pioneers in this style of thinking was the Catholic phil-
ospher, Gabriel Marcel, who experienced:

> the haunting sense of the *concrete* interpersonal relations which phil-
> osophy has to confront in the "mystery" of our inescapable involvement
> with others. To do this requires *an empiricism more concrete and more
> profound than what has traditionally gone under that name. It requires
> a new concept of experience.*
>
> It is therefore not only Being but beings in which we are involved, in
> whom we participate, and who are at the focus of Marcel's thought. *The
> idea of participation is fundamental for Marcel's conception of human
> existence. Existence is actually being-in-a-situation, and the fundamental
> situation is our participation in Being and in beings. In fact, being-with-
> others is the very nature of selfhood.* It is easy to see that such a con-
> ception of existence, once granted, has no difficulty in accounting for the
> connection of an isolated subject with its objects, with other subjects,
> and even with God.

See Spiegelberg [1982], pp. 452–453, emphasis added. The idea of the need
for a new concept of experience and a new empiricism traces, as you may recall,
as far back as Brentano. See Spiegelberg [1982], pp. 33–36. Marcel's notion
of a "participation in beings" suggests a certain "gravity shift" in philosophical
reflection congenial to Vatican II's preoccupation with its own religious life-
world, where participation in Being and beings can be pastorally fused in Christ
as the Word Incarnate and the authentic "self" of both the Church and the
faithful. The influence of Marcel, and more proximately that of Merleau-Ponty
(see Spiegelberg [1982], esp. pp. 549–571) lends such a theoretical aura to any
French reflection on the life-world that it always seems to come off as a speculative enterprise rather than a practical (or pastoral) one.

However, the pioneering thought of Marcel and Merleau-Ponty does lend
itself to the pastoral concept of the "enrichment of faith," so emphasized by
Wojtyla [1980], pp. 15–18. It does so, however, in a somewhat etherialized
and amorphous way.

> [Marcel's] conception of the primary function of his philosophy [. . .]
> is not to provide us with ready-made answers. Its real mission is *to awaken,
> to sensitize and to appeal*, rather than to teach and to give transferable
> information. The sense of "research" can only be conveyed by *making the
> reader participate in the search. A "concrete philosophy" such as Marcel
> envisages it can be changed only by concrete experiences and by promoting
> concrete experience in others.*

See Spiegelberg [1982], p. 453. This formulation of Marcel would probably be one valid philosophical interpretation of John XXIII's pastoral goal, expressed in *Humanae Salutis*, of revealing men to themselves. See Abbott [1966], p. 707. Just what its efficiency rating would be in today's turbulent world seems somewhat problematical. If the Church's being-in-a-situation is that described by "The Church in the Modern World," then perhaps the more viable approach would be had in A. Schutz's down-to-earth ideas.

EXCURSUS IV: "THE SIGNS OF THE TIMES"

Pope John XXIII's use of this terminology

The "signs of the times" is an important theme in the thought of John XXIII. The inspiration for this terminology is to be found in some remarks which Jesus directed to his Jewish critics: "You know how to read the face of the sky [i.e., the signs forecasting a change in the weather], but you cannot read the signs of the times." (Mt. 16:3) The text may be an interpolation, but its sense is reasonably clear. The "times" are the messianic age, and the "signs" are the miracles and teachings of Jesus portending the arrival of the messianic age. In this context Jesus declares that the definitive sign will be the "sign of Jonah" (i.e., his death and resurrection).

Inasmuch as the fullness of revelation has been given in Jesus to his apostles, Catholic theology does not allow for any substantially new revealed data from God — regardless what may be the "signs of the times" today. Consequently, Pope John's usage of this biblical terminology is metaphorical, just as he spoke of his hope that the Council would occasion a "New Pentecost." See Staff of the Pope Speaks Magazine [1964], pp. 444–445. However, as our study of Vatican II hopes to display, one can have a "New Pentecost" without implying any substantial change in the Catholic understanding of its religious truths. (See Chapter 8 under the subheading, "The new religio-social hierophany.")

The two most important locations where Pope John employed the expression, "signs of the times," were in *Humanae Salutis* and *Pacem in Terris*. See Abbott [1966], p. 704 and Carlen [1981], Vol. 5, #126–129, p. 121. In both cases he used this terminology to give an optimistic interpretation to essentially human developments which were tending toward moral values espoused by the Church. In other words Pope John was engaged in a process of spiritual discernment in order to alert the Church to the unique spiritual opportunities of this age. Spiritual discernment, as I employ the term, always implies the theory of connatural knowledge.

A post-conciliar controversy

Gremillion [1976], p. 135 allueds to a post-conciliar development in some Catholic writers when he asks: "Does the 'signs of the times' approach to

God-world relations introduce another source of 'revelation' differing from or adding to the revelation of Scripture and Christian tradition? . . . Do the 'signs of the times' offer true *loci theologici* for theological reflection?" Essentially the same questions were asked in the days of Joachim of Fiore (c. 1135–1202) and the Spiritual Franciscans; the answer then and now is *no*. The global human events, which Pope John grouped under the "signs of the times," are merely natural events which may be subjected to any legitimate analysis deriving from science, ethics, or religion. In many respects the Holy Father's resume of the situation tells us more about the religious paradigm guiding his reflections than about the turbulent events which he is contemplating. Such "signs of the times," then, are not a new source of revelation on a par with Christ, scripture, tradition, etc. The question really implies a serious misconception about the Council's *pastoral* use of phenomenology, and if this issue is not clarified, Vatican II will gradually metamorphose from a pastoral council into a *doctrinal* one. (This technical issue is discussed in notes 38 and 39 of Chapter Nine.)

Gremillion further asks: "Does the Church therefore learn from Galileo, Darwin, Marx, Freud, Einstein, Gandhi?" I should hope so, and in the course of this book I have purposely focused on Galileo in order to illustrate this point. Possibly this case-study, so central to Husserl's theorizing in the *Crisis*, will prove illuminating to all parties. There is another question, however, which in all fairness needs to be voiced: "In a dislocated world with awesome atomic weaponry can the descendent of Galileo, Darwin, Marx, etc., learn from the Church?" If the substance of this book is appreciated, possibly the message of Vatican II will be appreciated in its true grandeur and the men of this age will be more disposed to reflect more profoundly on what the Church is saying.

In summary, then, the "signs of the times" refer only to empirical human data illumined by a wholesome (and I would add, consciously optimistic) spiritual discernment, in order to foster hope and constructive collaboration in a dislocated world. Another type of wholesome discernment could equally point out that such pastoral optimism occasionally needs to be nuanced. See Ratzinger's remarks in Vorgrimler [1967–1969], Vol. 3, pp. 173–174. For the postconciliar development of the "signs of the times" in papal teachings see Gremillion [1976], #147–150, pp. 561–562.

EXCURSUS V: ANTHROPOLOGY, ANTHROPOGONY, AND PHENOMENOLOGICAL METHOD

Anthropology

There are at least six modern definitions of hermeneutics today. See Palmer [1969], pp. 33–45. For each type of hermeneutics it is possible to construct a *speculative* science of man (i.e., an "anthropology"). This intellectual problem was pioneered by I. Kant as early as 1800 when in his *Introduction to Logic* he asked, "What is man?" and simultaneously raised the whole question of philosophical anthropology. See Schrag [1980], pp. 30–31. A book-length treatment of "Kant as Philosophical Anthropologist" may be found in Pitte [1971]. H.O. Pappé has a good introductory article on the more contemporary aspects of "Philosophical Anthropology," in Edwards [1967], Vol. 6, pp. 159–166. However, the term, "anthropology," is used so loosely by some writers today that any "science" (e.g., history, sociology, etc.) may be used as a foundation for developing a science of man.

Catholic reflection on this topic may be found in Rahner [1968–1970], Vol. 3: philosophical anthropology (pp. 358–361); biblical anthropology (pp. 361–365); theological anthropology (pp. 365–370); for metaphysical anthropology see Rahner [1968–1970], Vol. 2, p. 294a.

It should be emphasized that in *Pacem in Terris* Pope John has formulated the rudiments of a pastoral (i.e., practical) anthropology which is not to be equated with any of the theoretical types listed above. His "theological hermeneutics" is grounded in his Catholic consciousness which, as we know, was both integralist and quite traditionalistic when it comes to matters of faith and morals. The object of his spiritual discernment in this encyclical is trends in the modern global human consciousness which under pressures generated by modern global problems are gradually coming into alignment with goals and values espoused by Christianity. The paradigm of human values outlined in *Pacem in Terris* may be somewhat conveniently catalogued as a Christian anthropology, provided it is not immediately preempted by one of the speculative types listed above. The anthropology, which Pope John XXIII outlined in a rudimentary way, Vatican II took up and brought to perfection in a highly sophisticated way.

Anthropogony

The new humanistic anthropology, which both Marx and John XXIII — in their different ways — discerned as under development in their respective eras, has some of the awesome characteristics of a new *anthropogony*. This latter term is used in the comparative study of religions to refer to the mythological origins of man. See Eliade [1954], p. 22. Possibly, a more familiar term, drawn from modern empirical anthropology, would be *anthropogenesis*, but this term is really limited to the scientific origin and development of man. There is, of course, a compromise way of constructively using both terms in a correlated way in order to express the split-level type of pastoral theology intended by Pope John XXIII. At the *religious* level we may use "anthropogony" to express the new religio-social hierophany or mythic projection of the New Humanity, formulated in *Lumen Gentium*, Vatican II's document on the Church. (See Chapter 8 of this book.) At the *empirical* level its counterpart-to-be-developed would involve a socio-cultural "anthropogenesis" since human evolution would now be seen dependent, not so much on the older biological causes, but rather on the socio-cultural influences shaping the progress and development of corporate mankind. In such a context, perhaps, the thought of Teilhard de Chardin and John XXIII may find a working compatibility, if not total reconciliation.

The anthropogony, which I am talking about here, may not only be seen in correlation with the various life-worlds existent today (as Vatican II intended), but also in some relationship with the various *social archetypes*, which have had a role in sociological theorizing for the last half-century. In Western intellectual history Max Scheler was the first to call attention to these social types, but in America they have best been explained by Drucker [1939], p. 45:

> Every organized society is built upon a concept of the nature of man and of his function and place in society. Whatever its truth as a picture of human nature, this concept always gives a true picture of the nature of the society which recognizes and identifies itself with it. It symbolizes the fundamental tenets and beliefs of society by showing the spheres of human activity which it regards as socially decisive and supreme.

In 1939 Drucker felt that since the fall of Rome three ideal types had successively dominated social change in Western civilization: the Spiritual Man (Christendom), the Intellectual Man (Reanaissance), and Economic Man (Industrial Revolution). With the advent of Fascism in Europe a new type seemed to be developing: Heroic Man. In an article, today largely forgotten, Tolman [1941] developed a new social model which has since gained a great deal of currency in America: Psychological Man. On how this conceptualization of man factually operates today in secular America see Yankelovich [1981] and Ferguson [1980].

During the Industrial Revolution Marx discerned the genesis and development of a new humanistic type of Man. Within the general social paradigm of Economic Man his intuition or insight into human economic relationships underwent a certain "gravity shift" from the minority group of the capitalistic managerial class to the majority group of the workers. The resulting "shift in the visual Gestalt" regarding Economic Man constituted a new social archetype which today may possibly be called Socialist (or Proletarian) Man. A century later, however, Pope John XXIII discerned that critical global problems were shaping the birth of a new *moral* humanism, the social archetype of which would be the Peacemaker or, if you will, the Peace-builder. See Gremillion [1976], #137–138, p. 559; also J.T. Noonan, Jr., "From Social Engineering to Creative Charity," in Ong [1969], pp. 179–180. At the Second Vatican Council, however, when the bishops returned to the depths of the primordial ecclesial consciousness by way of an essentially phenomenological method, out of these same depths they educed a new religious anthropogony synthesizing the humanistic, social, and anthropological vision which John XXII — somewhat like Moses viewing the Promised Land — perceived on the horizon, but with an old man's eyes. A discussion of these matters may be found in Chapter 8: The New Ecclesial Hermeneutics.

Vatican II's consequent openness to phenomenological method

The use of an essentially descriptive-analytic style of reflection at the Council becomes more understandable if we recall a few of the circumstances shaping Vatican II itself. First, in a quite real sense the Council was simply a necessary theological stop-over on the way to creating an anthropology adequate to the needs of modern times. As Pelikan has remarked, ". . . if the problem of history and of historicity has created difficulties for traditional christology, it has proved disastrous for traditional anthropology." See Pelikan [1969–1970], Vol. 2, p. 20. This merely means that while religion may be confronted with important theoretical problems, none of these are anywhere as serious as the *practical* problem of what constitutes an authentic human being in the world today. Both Max Scheler and John XXIII recognized the primacy of this practical problem, and *Humanae Salutis* formulated the pastoral goal of Vatican II in the light of this problem.

Secondly, Ratzinger is quite faithful to the pastoral nature of Vatican II when he remarks, ". . . it is in accordance with the best conciliar tradition that the Church's teaching office should not decide academic controversies at a council." In the past such academic disputes were viewed quite narrowly as confined to schools of *scholasticism* within the Church: e.g., Thomism, Scotism, Molinism, etc. In today's world, however, theoretical controversies have broadened to include all scientific ideas and methodologies on collision-course: e.g., natural science, history, psychology, scholastic theology, biblical theology, etc. In the first session of Vatican II there was a strong reaction against Roman school theology favored by the Curia. As a result, the majority of bishops tried to avoid the scholastic intellectualism of the past which had come to be identified with a defensive spirit, attachment to verbalistic formulas, static views of historical change, and a legalistic spirit. This is a journalistic over-simplification of things, but there was enough wooden practice of scholasticism and canon law to lend a justified credence to the accusation. Intent as they were on positive and prac- tical community-building, the bishops did not want to get involved in refereeing academic disputes among theological technicians, but they were on the lookout for fresh ideas which would promote pastoral flexibility and creativity in a world that lived and breathed. See Ratzinger's comments in Vorgrimler [1967–1969], Vol. 3, pp. 159–161, 172, *et passim.*

Thirdly, by turning to Northern European theologians for their fresh new ideas the majority of bishops also accepted their descriptive-analytical style of reflection, but only the more educated ones with some academic exposure to this European style of reflection recognized the full implications of this trans- ition. In this category we would certainly have to place Pope Paul VI. This new style of reflection allowed the bishops to put scholasticism "on hold" for the duration of the Council. That handful of highly educated bishops and theologians trained in phenomenology knew that a Council was no place to bring up the theoretical problems inherent in the fact of the existing "schools" of phenom- enology or academic problems associated with the use of this methodology. Those points could be argued out after the Council by the theological and philosophical technicians. Rather, the Council's common project to develop a new Christian anthropology for practical, renewal purposes and the Council's common focus on the role of the Glorified Christ welded their methodology into a working unity and into an instrument of consensus-building regarding the religious life-world of the Church.

The radical nature of Vatican II's reflection

When the bishops at the Council "bracketed" scholasticism, they did not intend to reject it. Nonetheless, this procedure meant that — in phenomenological terms — they had performed their first *suspension of a "science,"* i.e., of scholastic philosophy as the sole epistemological theory with which the vast majority of bishops were acquainted. As a *religious* move, this was quite legitimate since they were now putting their reliance, not in an ontology deriving from a philosophy, but in one deriving from a *Person*, i.e., the Glorified Christ. Let us not decieve ourselves: the bishops always remained scholastics. If they bracketed scholastic theory, they also bracketed *Husserlian* theory and that of the later phenomenologists. They exemplified the same outlook as the members of the Société Thomiste in 1932: they recognized "the possibility of an assimilation of the phenomenological approach by Catholic philosophers *without commitment to Husserl's or Heidegger's conclusions."* See Spiegelberg [1982], p. 433. Anyone, therefore, who tries to impose a rigidly philosophical or scientific grid of interpretation on Vatican II, as a *pastoral* council, is doomed to failure. Having learned its lesson in the Galileo Case, the Church — in this instance at least — has relinquished *all* scientific expertise and returned to its own religious life-world.

The reduction of the sciences, operative in an imperfect and controverted way in the first session, prepared the way initially for the bishops to enter their religious life-world in their reflections on the liturgy. However, it is the contemporary seriousness of the *anthropological* problem which justifies this "bracketing" of the Church's first line of defense in epistemological controversies. In philosophical matters this would be the equivalent of either Russia or the United States developing their future war strategies in total abstraction from their nuclear weaponry.

Once such a radical path into the life-world had been taken, it had to be followed to its logical conclusion if a new Christian anthropology were to be formulated. In the conciliar documents there soon appeared a further *suspension of historical "science,"* as noted by Cullmann in Chapter Three of this essay. Ultimately, of course, the Council's discussion of the religious significance of creation, as applicable to both cosmos and man, involved a final suspension of *all* the sciences, i.e., the natural sciences, especially paleontology. For an example of this see Canon Moeller's remarks in Miller [1966], p. 430. As this process gradually evolved at the Council, the only academically responsible way of interpreting such radical procedures was to see it as a phenomenological inquiry into the religious life-world of the Church. In this regard we have a religious process now paralleling the philosophical reflections of a growing number of philosophers inquiring into our natural life-world for serious humanistic reasons. Two quite recent examples of this would be Schrag [1980] and Bernstein [1983].

The shift of the visual Gestalt and its dialectical resolution

Toward the end of Chapter Eight in this book I referred to the radical shift in the visual gestalt of Christianity, as orchestrated by the reflections of the Second Vatican Council. By the new ecclesial hermeneutics the christocentric focus of the Church has been involved in a serious anthropocentric gravity-shift. Such a radical shift in religious dynamics can be psychologically very damaging to religiously sensitive people. The experiments of Bruner and Postman [1949], pp. 206–223 illustrate that when a shift of the visual gestalt cannot be assimilated in one's ordinary functionings, there is the possibility of complete disorientation, if not breakdown.

Often enough, clarification of this religious gravity-shift has been sought by way of scientific reductionism. In America this usually means psychology or sociology. Since the Vision of the New Humanity implies some reordering of our socio-political priorities, many religious thinkers have been quick to "politicize" the teachings of the Council. In more academic circles clarification has been sought by way of philosophical reductionism, which transmutes Vatican II from being a purely pastoral council into one with great epistemological implications comparable to Kant's "Copernican Revolution" in philosophy. The immediate consequence of this most serious misinterpretation is the need to reconceptualize and reconstruct all of theology. See Dewart [1966].

The most intelligent resolution of all the above difficulties has been given by Pope John Paul II in his encyclical, *Dives in Misericordia* (see Carlen [1981], Vol. 5, #4, p. 276). There on the basis of a bipolar phenomenology, which calls for christocentrism and anthropocentrism to be held in a dialectical interrelationship, he says:

> The more the Church's mission is centered upon man – the more it is, so to speak, anthropocentric – the more it must be confirmed and actualized theocentrically, that is to say, be directed in Jesus Christ to the Father. While the various currents of human thought both in the past and at the present have tended and still tend to separate theocentrism and anthropocentrism, and even set them in opposition to each other, the church, following Christ, seeks to link them up in human history in a deep and organic way. And this is also one of the basic principles, perhaps the most important one, of the teaching of the last council.

See also Paul VI [1966], p. 62, where substantially the same idea is emphasized. See also Frossard [1984], pp. 185–186.

EXCURSUS VI: DIALOGUE, MARTIN BUBER, AND THE COUNCIL

Paul VI on dialogue

Paul VI's extended reflections on dialogue in *Ecclesiam Suam* (#58–118) make good pastoral sense *ad extra* (i.e., outside the Church), particularly in an age of intellectual pluralism and religious ecumenism. This type of converse, as typically understood today, intends "to bring about greater understanding and better human relations in an atmosphere of sincerity, integrity, respect for persons, and mutual confidence." See "Dialogue," in Meagher, O'Brien, and Aherne [1979], Vol. 1, p. 1050. Such dialogue typically aims at doing away with antiquated or artificial barriers, promoting cooperation in commonly agreed upon projects, or cultivating an honest search for truth. Paul VI also recognized the pastoral value *ad intra* (i.e., within the Church) since he established the Synod of Bishops on September 15, 1965. See Abbott [1966], pp. 720–724. Being a quite educated man, however, Paul VI realized that the very concept of dialogue was fraught with serious dangers for the magisterium of the Church.

Martin Buber

Although dialogue has a rich and diversified history in philosophy, literature, and even science (e.g., Galileo) dating back to the era of Plato, the *twentieth-century* notion of dialogue developed within a quite specific intellectual environment, quite different from anything ever known in the past. This newer approach was first popularized by Martin Buber, the Jewish philosopher. His writings seem to have had more impact on Christian intellectuals than Jewish ones. Buber addressed himself to the two major philosophical problems of the early twentieth century: first, the impasse between subjectivity and objectivity; and, secondly, the relationship between life's spontaneous immediacy and the detached, deliberative character of spirit (mind). See Wood [1969], p. xi. Like Husserl and with a descriptive method approximating phenomenology, Buber formulated an ontological *a priori* termed "Presence," which eliminated the dichotomy between the subjective and objective. Here in the region called the "Between" the subject and object were bound together in an identity-in-difference.

It is in this context of experiential and unsystematic Post-Kantian speculation
that Buber formulated his reflections on dialogue and I-Thou relationships.

The religious hazards of dialogue

Paul VI, accordingly, was quite sensitive to this intellectual background and the
hazards which it posed for the axiom of doctrinal integralism and the role of the
magisterium. Intellectual pluralism and proliferating academic specializations
have had their impact on changing methodologies in theology. In the light of
such speculative and technical issues as posing a potential danger for Catholic
theology itself, Paul VI's pastoral endorsement of dialogue is prudently guarded
in *Ecclesium Suam.* The Holy Father was quite aware that some Catholic theologians were insisting that such speculative problems could only be solved on a
dialogical basis. See Roberts [1967], pp. 272–275. However, there is no indication that any modern popes have entertained so expansive a notion of the
magisterium, at least when it comes to faith and morals.

From cautious endorsement to real sensitivity

It is easy enough to endorse dialogue as an abstract issue, but what its practical
implications are can only be discerned in its actual practice. The essential purpose of dialogue is to be a tool of community-building. "One-on-one" dialogue
does not present too much difficulty, but the process becomes quite complicated when a whole group proceeds to dialogue with another group, or simply
among themselves. Genuine dialogue promotes growth in sensitivity, and there
was evidence of this at the Council particularly as regards the audience *ad extra*
(i.e., outside the Church). While speaking on a preliminary draft ("Clause 13")
of the Church in the Modern World, Bishop K. Wojtyla remarked:

> In the text that we see here, the Church is doing nothing but instructing
> the world, since she speaks from the treasures of truth that are hers
> alone. . .
>
> Clause 13, on the contrary, must so express itself that the world will
> recognize that we . . . are working *together* with the world to seek a true
> and just solution to the difficult problems of human life. The question is
> not whether the truth is manifest to us, but rather how the world can find
> and appropriate the truth to itself. Every teacher knows from experience

about what is called the "heuristic method:" the student is enabled, so to speak, to find the truth within himself. The method excludes anything that betrays a "clerical" approach: for example, the hue and cry over the alas! lamentable state of the world today . . . or the all-too-thoughtless appropriation by the Church of all the good that exists in the world . . . such attitudes place obstacles in the path of dialogue with the world, from the outset; and so this dialogue remains a monologue, a soliloquy. Let us take care that our Clause 13 not become a monologue.

See Hebblethwaite and Kaufmann [1979], p. 70.

The popes as monitors of group dynamics

The growing sensitivity which the Council Fathers displayed toward groups outside the Church did not always function toward the minority group of bishops within the Council. Anyone who has ever engaged in dialogue within a fairly large group knows that the trouble starts once the group dynamics sort out the majority group. From that point on the minority group is in real difficulty: first, it is patronized, then it is ignored, and finally it is resented. Such developments, intensified by the tight time-schedule under which the group is operating, work against the very process of dialogue which is intended to build community, consensus, and solidarity. When this pattern of majority insensitivity developed at the Council, it was typically the popes who moderated it by showing concern for the sensibilities of the minority.

A sensitive, comprehensive study should be made of John XXIII's and Paul VI's interventions at the Council. In general, such interventions were motivated by three broad reasons: (1) to safeguard some point of religious ontology; (2) to assist in the consensus-building process by showing adequate concern for the minority's anxieties; and (3) to display an empathy toward a serious devotional concern (e.g., the inclusion of St. Joseph's name in the Canon of the Mass). Commenting on Paul VI's opening speech at the third session, September 14, 1964, Gérard Philips, remarks:

> This speech [which emphasized the forthcoming document, *Lumen Gentium*] was clearly aimed at winning over a certain number of Fathers, who were still hesitant about the draft put before them for their vote. A council does not in fact try to establish the view of a majority against that of a minority; by its very nature it must strive to bring about practical

unanimity. Paul VI was tireless in his efforts to achieve this end, so persistent in fact that he evoked a psychologically understandable reaction among the large number who were favourably disposed to the draft. He could congratulate himself finally on having brought the opposition to consent, without their being oppressed by a sense of defeat.

See Vorgrimler [1967–1969], Vol. 1, p. 127.

Post-conciliar dialogue and the problem of insensitivity

The solicitous concern of Paul VI for the difficulties raised by the minority of bishops is not to be interpreted in a patronizing way. Among such bishops were some very learned and capable men who recognized, perhaps only dimly, some of the complex implications of the Council's deliberations. Not too long after the Council their anxiety was shared even by outstanding Catholic lay intellectuals. Two of these are worthy of special mention: Eppstien [1971], an authority on international law, and Maritain [1968], the well-known philosopher. As early as 1966, however, Leslie Dewart of St. Michael's College in Toronto alerted the English-speaking world that the minority of bishops at the Council had focused on some very serious problems connected with the work of Vatican II. Dewart [1966], p. 14 writes:

> [. . .] it follows that the differences between "conservative" and "liberal" Catholic opinion today [. . .] run considerably deeper than *liberals* have ordinarily admitted. The conservatives may have been closer to the mark when they have "alerted" the Church to a profound division within the Catholic faith. For these two ways of thinking manifest fundamental differences in one's most basic orientation towards the problem of the relation of the Catholic faith to the contemporary (and, indeed, to any given) stage of human development. We have to do here with divergent orientations towards the meaning of the Christian faith, towards the meaning of religion itself — and therefore towards the Catholic's very understanding of his self-disposition towards God. Ultimately, we may have to do with divergent conceptualizations of the God of Christian belief.

Dialogue in the context of eschatology

The above type of highly intellectual difficulties are not the only ones to have surfaced in the postconciliar era. The eschatology which permeates Christianity

constitutes something of a "ticking time-bomb" under its normally placid surface. Whenever the Catholic Church notices an eschatological movement developing anywhere, she tries to channel its essentially charismatic energies into
some ecclesiastical structure: e.g., the religious life, secular institutes, or some
form of Catholic Action. In his essay, "Von Ranke," written about 1840, Lord
Macaulay remarked: "She [the Catholic Church] thoroughly understands what
no other Church has ever understood, how to deal with enthusiasts." As a
result — until the era of post-Vatican II — the last serious threat to institutional
stability from such an internal source was the Spiritual Franciscans in the Middle
Ages, inspired by the millennarianism of Joachim of Fiore (c. 1135–1202).

Modern millennarianism is largely of Protestant inspiration deriving from
Thomas Munzer and the radical Anabaptists. This type of religiously inspired social
revolution later percolated through the Diggers and Levellers of Cromwell's rebel-
lion, and flamed anew in Gracchus Babeuf's "conspiracy of equals" during the
French Revolution. Thereafter, it "passed into the common currency of the revolutionary movements of the nineteenth century." See Bell [1962], esp. footnote
on p. 281. In the postconciliar era where there has been such a confusing prolifer-
ation of liberation-type movements, supposedly of religious inspiration, it is becoming more and more difficult to distinguish these movements from the revolutionary movements described above. In a dislocated and destabilized world,
armed with nuclear weapons, such religious movements cannot be allowed to
develop in isolation but must be drawn into a larger dialogical relationship with
the Church.

The above situation is complicated by a further factor. In the Catholic
Church there is a sense of *realized* eschatology by reason of her tradition of
contemplative mysticism and the traditional view that sanctifying grace here
on earth is an inchoative participation in the state of the redeemed in heaven.
It should come as no surprise, then, that the documents of Vatican II project
a certain *realized messianism.* Some of this comes from John XXIII's call to
religious efficiency or efficaciousness, as voiced in *Humanae Salutis.* A charismatic sense of eschatology wedded to an urgent drive toward a realized messianism is a powder keg of trouble, unless constructively channelled. The theme
of realized messianism is not a popular one as yet; the only Catholic writer I am
aware of who has discussed it is Henry Duméry. See Farley [1975], esp. footnote 45, p. 255. Unless this concept and others like it are dialogued in the spirit
and manner of Vatican II, they can easily be appropriated by the tradition of
millennarianism deriving from Thomas Munzer.

Concluding remarks

Given the complex nature of Vatican II, it seems that the postconciliar dialogue
is very much in need of some sort of "monitor," as the popes exemplified at

the Council. Here I do not wish to be misunderstood: I am simply suggesting the need for some regulatory agency to promote dialogue in a truly constructive and productive way on a regular basis. Whether one calls such persons or groups "facilitators," "arbitrators," or "courts of final appeal," such agencies must be institutionalized according to circumstances and in a productive way.

EXCURSUS VII: OBEDIENTIAL POTENCY

The scholastic notion

In his *Summa Theologiae* (III, q. 11, a. 1) St. Thomas writes:

> In anima humana, sicut in qualibet creatura, consideratur *duplex potentia passiva*, una quidem per comparationem ad *agens naturale*; alia vero per comparationem ad *agens primum*, quod potest quamlibet creaturam reducere in actum aliquem altiorem actu, in quem reducitur per agens naturale: et haec consuevit vocari *potentia obedientialis* in creatura. [Emphasis added.]

In scholastic theology obediential potency is used to "explain" in a *post factum* way the *revealed* truth that there can be genuine commerce between the absolutely transcendent divine order and the natural order. The outstanding example of this would, of course, be the Incarnation of Christ. In this mystery the human nature of Christ *must* have at least an "obediential potency" to be united with the divine nature through the Person of the *Logos*. Obediential potency, however, has a broader application to *all* men since the call to salvation is also a call to every individual to be ultimately united with God in the supernatural order. In this latter case obediential potency is grounded on two biblical truths: God's infinite power and man's nature as somehow created in God's image. Man, as such, has no natural capacity to be united immediately with the transcendent God, but God's "image" in him constitutes a *potential* (i.e., an ontological principle) subject to or obedient to God's infinite power.

A phenomenological interpretation

As customarily used in scholastic theology obediential potency is generally expressed in a context of *efficient causality*: e.g., the log has an obediential potency to be made into a table, the woman has an obediential potency to conceive a child. However, the same concept can easily be transposed into Husserlian phenomenology by recognizing that the natural world has an obediential potency to be *understood* by consciousness. This provides a new modality for conceptualizing the relationships implied in obediential potency. What was previously viewed in terms of active agent/passive recipient may now be viewed in a new set of intentional relationships: i.e., in terms of consciousness (noesis) and any *objects* (*noemata*) *in potency to be understood or have meaning*. In such a relationship it is the egological consciousness which provides the intentional entelechy whereby such objects take on meaning.

An application to the ecclesial consciousness

Since the intentional ground of the ecclesial consciousness is totally christocentric (i.e., theocentrism as brought to focus in Christ as the perfect *imago Dei* and as Mystical Body), in a *religious* sense the Church can "see" *only* human beings and *only* to the extent they have an obediential potency to be conformed to Christ. Only *indirectly*, or on the "fringes" of the Church's religious horizon, does non-human or infra-human nature enter into this religious paradigm of reality. The *direct* focus is always God, man, and the relationships consequent upon this spiritual order. Certain objects and relationships, which we customarily interpret as falling outside this spiritual order, are transmuted once they are incorporated into it. For example, the ecological awareness typical of modern educated people would go through a certain christocentric reorientation when it is integrated into the above religious paradigm of reality. Such a *noetic* "gravity-shift" is an *intentional* transmutation of objects (noemata) derived from the natural order, and is not merely the work of the imagination. It is greatly facilitated by an awareness of the cosmotheandric role which Christ plays in the Catholic religion or by the moral consciousness-raising which an ecological sensitivity tends to foster in people. In the Christian order of things there can be no morality apart from Christ. A striking example on the American scene of such a religious transmutation would be the christocentric reorientation being given to management by the concept of Servant Leadership. See Greenleaf [1977].

The implications of obediential potency at the Council

Once we have a basic understanding of obediential potency, we can begin to appreciate the totally "hominized" paradigm of religious reality which Vatican II presents for our reflection and how this paradigm naturally lends itself to the challenge of Christian Anthropology.

We may start out by asking: "If we may assume that the interventions of the bishops at Vatican II are based on the empirical *a priori* of their concrete religious experiences, just *what* are the bishops describing?" Each bishop is intent on voicing the *ordered religious meaning for him* of these experiences (phenomena) as constituted in his individual consciousness. While these experiences may have originated from historical or other natural human influences, their total religious ordering, or intentional character, derives from the christocentric paradigm shaping each bishop's "natural attitude" as a believing Christian.

The originary historical experiences grounding the Catholic consciousness derive from the New Testament, and may be summed up by the phrase, "the word received and believed." The teleological-historical sense of these events — both in the past and at the present — is exemplified by the living Christ, the *Logos*, as the fullness of God's revelation. Consequently, unless a person, thing, or event has at least an "obediential potency" to be related to Christ, understood as the primordial paradigm of intelligibility and meaning, it can have no *religious* sense. Hence, the principle both of ordered meaning and of religious intersubjectivity is radicated in an interpersonal faith-relationship with the transcendent Christ, who grounds any *noesis/noemata* relationship found at the Council. We need not be dismayed by the comprehensive role faith plays at the Council. Such a "faith-relationship" is always involved with any use of the phenomenological method, even when it confronts the realities of the natural life-world: "... believing-in-the-world is the paradigm of normality." See Natanson [1973a], p. 15. In this sense, then, we can say that Vatican II's reflection on its own religious life-world also presents us with a paradigm of normality.

Critiquing such ideas

If the documents of Vatican II deal with such a primordial religious life-world and use scholastic notions adapted to the needs of phenomenology, how can we possibly critique their contents? The Council did not presume to answer that as an *academic* question. As Ratzinger remarks: "Vatican II ... has more or less ignored the whole question of the criticism of tradition." (See Vorgrimler [1967–1969], Vol. 3, p. 185, but also pp. 186–198 for the full context.) If such is the case, the Council said even less about the *modality* in which such traditional truths were expressed.

Once one understands the phenomenological methodology employed at the Council, even the *refusal* to be critiqued by scientific methodologies of any type becomes quite legitimate; to allow the contrary would be a concession to scientific reductionism in one form or another. Such academic questions,

however, fell beyond the original *pastoral* goals for the Council as formulated
by John XXIII in *Humanae Salutis*. There he evidenced a far greater concern
for the judgment which a seriously dislocated world could exercise on both the
Church and mankind unless they changed their ways of thinking and acting.
The *efficiency* of these transcendent truths in the temporal order was the
canon of criticism formulated by John XXIII.

EXCURSUS VIII: THE MYSTICAL BODY AS GROUND OF VATICAN II

The Mystical Body in *Lumen Gentium*

If paragraph eight of *Lumen Gentium* is read in conjunction with the sources in footnotes 17–21 (see Abbott [1966], pp. 22–23), then we appreciate that Vatican II is not simply presenting a biblical image of the Church as understood by early Christianity but the developed doctrine, *as then-understood* at the time of the Council. In such a context the technical observations of O'Connor [1984] make eminent good sense. What the above paragraph eight does is establish the Mystical Body as the doctrinal or "epistemological" ground of the Christocentric focus of the ecclesial consciousness. (In a quite true sense this chapter of *Lumen Gentium*, especially as it culminates in paragraph eight, stands *outside the pastoral focus* of Vatican II: it provides the "objectivistic," conceptual source of light for that focus.) In the anticipated correlation of the Mystical Body and the People of God at the Council there is a hierarchy of "form" to "matter" in the juxtaposition of these two ideas.

This interpretation of the conceptual and structural role of the Mystical Body in its developed doctrinal state is important since there are two dangers latent in the Council's phenomenological style of theologizing: (1) a tendency for theological theorists to employ the methodology in such a way that they drift off into the type of solipsism sometimes attributed to Husserl; or (2) for the theologically uninformed to fall victim to scientific reductionism in interpreting the anthropocentric aims of the Council. In such a context the *theoretical* concerns of Paul VI centering on this doctrine become clear, both in his December 5, 1962 speech (see Latin Texts [1970–1980], Vol. I, pars IV, esp. p. 292) and in his encyclical, *Ecclesium Suam* (see Carlen [1981], Vol. 5, #35–38, pp. 141–143). Inasmuch as the Council is about to present its *new* pastoral directions for the Church, Paul VI prudently abstracts from any concrete pastoral applications historically associated with the doctrine of the Mystical Body, except those which flow from its very nature. See Carlen [1981], Vol. 5, #37–38, pp. 142–143.

The fact that the Council assigned this epistemological importance to the Mystical Body does *not* mean that this doctrinal data-base is the only one which could carry such a load. By reason of the isomorphism which permeates the doctrinal deposit of Catholicism any of the New Testament images of the

Church listed in the first chapter of *Lumen Gentium* could, in theory at least, have been used in the same pastoral way as the Mystical Body in the Council's phenomenological style of reflection. The biblical image in this regard which comes most readily to mind is the Church as the Spouse of Christ. See Abbott [1966], #5–6, pp. 17–20. However, in view of their pastoral objectives, which included a serious *anthropocentric* emphasis, the bishops chose the Mystical Body as their epistemological anchor since its doctrinal clarity had been extensively developed in this century and correlated well with the pastoral and human aims of the Council. The Mystical Body, accordingly, provided the basic score which the bishops were about to transpose into a "new key."

Lastly, while I have insisted on the epistemological (i.e., doctrinal) importance of the first chapter, paragraph eight, of *Lumen Gentium*, it also serves other purposes. When Vonier was on the verge of formulating his views on the People of God, he first voiced the common sentiments of Catholics toward that image of the Church projected in *Lumen Gentium*, #7–8:

> that particular sentiment awakened in us by what we read concerning the Church in the New Testament. It stands there as an unsurpassable power of sanctification, as a pillar and column of truth, as a continuation of Christ's Person, as an organism vivified by the Paraclete. These aspects are directly *the sources of light* for Catholic theology which is chiefly concerned with the ways of man's salvation.

See Vonier [1937], p. xvi, emphasis added.

The Mystical Body as integrating the pastoral sense of Vatican II

The key-role which the doctrine of the Mystical Body plays in integrating the "pastoral sense" of the major constitutions of Vatican II may be found in Chapter Ten under the subheading, "Towards a solution of this larger pastoral problem."

EXCURSUS IX: THE INTERPRETATION AND CLASSIFICATION OF THE
COUNCIL'S DOCUMENTS

The interpretation of Council documents

To the extent the intentional core of Vatican II's major documents is the product
of phenomenological method as explained by this book, this fact should have
some impact on the principles of interpretation brought to bear both on the
Council's promulgated documents and even on the various theological commissions' reports recorded in Latin Texts [1970–1980]. The use of a technical
scholastic term, such as "subsists" in *Lumen Genium* (#8), may simply mean it
is employed *consistently* with its previous scholastic usage, not identically.
Luijpen [1967] also recognizes that a similar sensitivity must be shown in even
larger scholastic clusters of ideas, such as natural law. This type of careful and
nuanced approach to the interpretation of Vatican II's promulgated documents,
their resource materials, and themes is required not merely by the phenomenological method employed at the Council but also by the global scope of the
religio-cultural renewal formulated at Vatican II. At a minimum, this program
is comparable to early Christianity's adjustment to the larger hellenized world,
but as you may recall from our discussion in Chapter Seven (note 11), Vatican II
in all likelihood surpasses the Deuteronomic reform in the Old Testament.

Let us recall again the well-meaning attempt in O'Connor [1984] to interpret
the technical sense of some scholastic terminology in *Lumen Gentium*. Necessary
as such efforts may be, a rigidly scholastic and defensive mindset has to be
avoided lest such narrow technical analyses unwittingly distract us from the
larger issues which the Council was trying to grapple with. Much the same can
be said of a similar case where Cardinal Cicognani sent a technically correct
(and even biblically based) response to Karl Barth on November 11, 1968,
when the Lutheran theologian wrote to Paul VI regarding the papal teaching
found in *Humanae Vitae*. See Barth [1981], pp. 314, 487–488. The technical,
theological answer was given, but the larger human and religio-cultural issues
in the modern world went unnoticed.

It should be recalled that at the Council the *religious issues as pastorally
focused*, not their related technical questions, were the center of discussion.
However, if an enquiry (*modus*) is presented to a conciliar commission in a
technical way, generally the formal response (*relatio*) will answer the problem

raised within the technical confines of the enquiry (e.g., history, philosophy, etc.). This does *not* necessarily mean that the statement found in the promulgated document and regarding which the enquiry was made must be understood in terms of the technical strictures of the formal response, but only in a way *consistent* with it. The Council, having suspended the sciences as part of its methodology, would hardly contradict itself and endorse scientific reductionism as the path to its authentic interpretation. Accordingly, a postconciliar work such as Charles and Maclaren [1982], while quite orthodox and conservative in its use of Vatican II's documents, stands in need of important nuancing due to its heavy reliance on historical method. A more mature postconciliar work, Walgrave [1972], makes no reference whatsoever to Vatican II as somehow underwriting its technical research.

Situating the constitution on the liturgy

It is no easy task to situate the important constitution on the liturgy within the phenomenological pattern of reflection which I have discerned in the two dogmatic constitutions (*Lumen Gentium* and *Dei verbum*) and more imperfectly in the pastoral constitution (*Gaudium et Spes*). This is to be expected since the liturgy document was formulated prior to the mature methodology of *Lumen Gentium* and served as something of a consensus-building vehicle for the bishops in the early stages of the Council. The Council Fathers recognized the somewhat ambivalent character of this constitution and did not categorize it either as doctrinal or pastoral.

Since the constitution's Chapter One, Part I, "The Nature of the Sacred Liturgy and Its Importance in the Life of the Church" (see Abbott [1966], pp. 139–143) deals with the substantive issue of liturgy itself, it can be correlated with theological topics in the dogmatic constitutions which we discussed in the book within a phenomenological framework. The portion which deals with the *nature* of the liturgy must be related to matters in Sacramental Time (see Excursus II) since the liturgy deals with such things in a cyclical timeframe. Hence, this portion is most closely associated with the matters dealt with in *Dei verbum* (Revelation), which also functions in Sacramental Time but in a punctuational time-frame. The portion which deals with the *importance* of the liturgy seems to be directed to the People of God, their essentially religious mission, and appropriate roles; these are all topics of *Lumen Gentium* which functions in an eschatological time-frame.

Chapter One, Part II, "The Promotion of Liturgical Instruction and Active Participation" (see Abbott [1966], pp. 144–145), seems to be a "declaration" of intent (i.e., a policy statement) meant for Church members, whereas the appendix on calendar reform (see Abbott [1966], pp. 177–178) is a declaration meant for all men. The rest of the document (see Abbott [1966], pp. 146–178) seems to consist of generic "decrees," i.e., the establishment of normative guidelines.

As a document elaborated outside of the genetic development of the Council's mature intellectual process, the document on the liturgy seems to be a mixture of all the types of documents eventually developed as proper to the Council. Since it is a *constitution*, the bishops meant it to be one of the major documents of the Council. At the same time its early positioning in the work of the Council seems to have attenuated its content as pastoral theology. For that, one should read this document within the more mature reflections of *Dei verbum* and *Lumen Gentium*, but something more is also required. As our book has indicated, liturgy in abstraction from the global pastoral concerns formulated by John XXIII in *Humanae Salutis* is not a pastoral liturgy in the sense intended by Vatican II. Consequently, the pastoral constitution on "The Church in the Modern World" (*Gaudium et Spes*) is an integral background document for any authentic interpretation of the liturgical constitution.

The classification of the Council's documents

At this time I would like to reflect on the generally-accepted classification of Vatican II's documents, but from a phenomenological perspective. This is not an easy task, since the canonical classification is freighted with such long-standing associations that it is somewhat difficult to maintain a phenomenological focus when reflecting on these matters. We may, however, start out with the canonical nomenclature and classifications as presented by an American canonist, Morrisey [c. 1975], p. 7:

> Four different types of documents were prepared by the Council Fathers: *Constitutions*, *Decrees*, *Declarations*, and *Messages*. It is quite difficult to state precisely why one document is given a specific qualification rather than another. It would seem that the Constitutions are addressed to the universal Church, while the Decrees are directed more specifically to a given category of the faithful or to a special form of apostolate, v.g., to members of the Eastern Churches, to Bishops, religious, and so forth. The Declarations are policy statements giving the ordinary teaching of the Church, while the Messages are exhortations addressed to various categories of people at the conclusion of the first session of the Council.

It is probably the matter itself which determined whether a particular document was to be given a certain title. The declarations presented teaching that, for the time being, was evolving and had not yet reached a definitive stage.

The pheonomenology of the religious life-world, which this book has advanced, allows us to accept the canonical classification, given above, but re-see the Council documents in their vital coherence (*"communio"*) as expressions of the consciousness, attitudes, and prioritized values of the Church in the modern world. The phenomenological focus of this book has centered on the two dogmatic constitutions (*Dei verbum* and *Lumen Gentium*) as correlated with the practical, pastoral challenge of *Humanae Salutis* and *Gaudium et Spes*. It would, consequently, nuance the classification of the conciliar documents on the basis of two important themes of Vatican II: i.e., (Christian) anthropology and "service of the world."

The notion of *Christian anthropology* is by now, I hope, the easier to understand. We have spoken of it extensively, particularly in Chapters 8—10 and in the Epilogue. Fundamentally it is the (*ad intra*) ecclesial expression of religious humanism, and as a pastoral goal of the Council it embodies the elements of a formation-program for all the faithful in today's world. The notion of the *"service of the world"* simply expresses the *ad extra* dimension (praxis) of the *same* pastoral concept as Christian anthropology. Hence, as I am using the phrase here, the "service of the world" means the "service of human beings" by providing them with whatever is necessary to achieve their authentic humanity. The religious values shaping Christian anthropology and the "service of the world," which are both *pastoral* notions, derive from the Logos-Shepherd ontology structuring the contemporary ecclesial consciousness. As viewed in the abstract, this ontology is simply traditional Catholic belief or theology. It is, however, the "new moment" of human history, "the crisis in human beings," as described by this book, which provides this abstract ontology with its *pastoral* specificity. It is the turning point in world history which provides the rationale for such a serious shift in the Catholic consciousness to human and social concerns. If at some future date these grave problems were solved, then a new gravity shift could occur to meet other needs.

When we reflect on the canonical classification of the conciliar documents, we can do so more productively if we keep a background question in mind: "What does this classification tell me about Christian anthropology and 'service of the world'?" As ecclesiastical documents, all these writings directly address members of the Church. In a sense, people outside the Church are being given an opportunity to eavesdrop, so to speak, as the corporate ecclesial consciousness reflects on its own presentday attitudes, values, and concerns both for its own members and mankind made in God's image.

The *Constitutions*, by traditional definition, are the most important documents of the Council. Two of these constitutions (*Lumen Gentium* and *Dei verbum*) deal with doctrinal matters, and in an experiential, pastoral way provide the horizontal and vertical dimensions of the religious consciousness which should inform any Christian anthropology. *Gaudium et Spes*, the pastoral constitution, is a first, tentative effort on the part of the Church to apply the new Christian anthropology to the "service of the world." All three constitutions, however, should be viewed as a comprehensive *pastoral unit*, which might easily have been given the title, "The Church in the Modern World." This correlation of Christian anthropology and the "service of the world" (praxis) exemplifies the split-level type of pastoral theology conceived by John XXIII. (The fourth constitution on the Sacred Liturgy has already been discussed in the earlier portion of this Excursus; by simply recalling that discussion the constitution on the liturgy can be integrated into the pastoral paradigm, outlined above.)

The declarations and decrees, as the beginnings of a pastoral formation-program for the faithful or as tentative steps toward "service of the world" (praxis), should be read against the background of pastoral theology, discussed above. An appreciation of their pastoral sense may be found in Wojtyla's remarks recorded earlier. (See Preface, note 9.) An *exception* to the above general principle would be the "Decree on the Instruments of Social Communication," which is the Ishmael of the Council. (See Chapter 5, note 16.) The *Declarations* combine broad policy statements and teachings (not to mention attitudinal stances) under development, as Morrisey pointed out above. The two declarations on Education and Religious Freedom offer additional aspects to *Gaudium et Spes*. The *Decrees* may be viewed as having some generic directive force for various groups in the Church. But such decrees (and the Declaration on Non-Christian Religions) should be seen in relationship to the "horizons" of humanity found in the second chapter of *Lumen Gentium*. In this panorama of mankind the need for revitalized human relationships, the formation of attitudes, and "service of the world" assume their authentic religious and global importance.

Final canonical observations

From a purely canonical point of view only the constitutions, declarations, and decrees are officially part of the documentation of Vatican II. You may find the *Messages* of the Council in the documents listed in the back of Latin

Texts [1966], pp. 839–1102. Here you will find many documents connected with the Council (e.g., *Humanae Salutis*) but really not a part of it, if matters are viewed in a very technical sense. These documents contain a rich mine of religious source material for interpreting the pastoral theology and sense of Vatican II.

BIBLIOGRAPHY

All works are listed alphabetically by author, and where more than one work by an author is included, they have been arranged in chronological order.

Abbott, Walter M., SJ, ed. (1966). *The Documents of Vatican II.* Trans. editor V. Rev. Joseph Gallagher. New York: America Press.

Alexander, Franz, MD. (1942). *Our Age of Unreason: A Study of the Irrational Forces in Social Life.* Philadelphia: J.B. Lippincott Co.

Allen, Douglas. (1978). *Structure and Creativity in Religion: Hermeneutics in Mircea Eliade's Phenomenology and new directions.* The Hague: Mouton.

Anderson, Bernhard W. (1966). *Understanding the Old Testament.* Second edition. Englewood Cliffs, NJ: Prentice-Hall, Inc.

Anderson, Floyd ed. (1965–1966). *Council Daybook: Vatican II.* 3 vols. Washington, DC: National Catholic Conference.

Anthony, Dick and Robbins, Thomas. (1982). "Spiritual Innovation and the Crisis of American Civil Religion." *Daedalus* 111:1 (Winter, 1982) 215–234.

Arrupe, Pedro, SJ. (1981). "Marxist Analysis by Christians." *Catholic Mind* 79:1355 (Sept., 1981) 58–64.

Bachelard, Suzanne. (1968). *A Study of Husserl's Formal and Transcendental Logic.* Trans. by Lester E. Embree. Evanston: Northwestern University Press.

Baird, Robert D. (1971). *Category Formation and The History of Religions.* The Hague: Mouton.

Balthasar, Hans Urs von. (1963). *A Theology of History.* New York: Sheed and Ward.

Balthasar, Hans Urs von. (1967). *A Theological Anthropology.* New York: Sheed and Ward.

Balthasar, Hans Urs von. (1982). *The Glory of the Lord: A Theological Aesthetics.* Vol. I: Seeing the Form. Trans. by Erasmo Leiva-Merikakis. Edited by J. Fessio, SJ, and John Riches. San Francisco: Ignatius Press.

Barrett, William. (1962). *Irrational Man.* Garden City, NY: Doubleday & Co.

Barrett, William and Aiken, Henry D., eds. (1962). *Philosophy in the Twentieth Century: An Anthology.* 4 vols. New York: Random House.

Barth, Karl. (1981). *Letters 1961–1968*. Edited by Jürgen Fangmeir and Hinrich Stoevesandt. Trans. and edited by G.W. Bromiley. Grand Rapids, MI: William B. Eerdmans Pub. Co.

Bauer, Johannes B., ed. (1970). *Sacramentum Verbi: An Encyclopedia of Biblical Theology*. 3 vols. New York: Herder and Herder.

Baum, Gregory. (1967). "Vatican II's Constitution on Revelation: History and Interpretation." *Theological Studies* 28 (1967) 51–75.

Bea, Augustin Cardinal. (1963). *The Unity of Christians*. Edited by Bernard Leeming, SJ. New York: Herder and Herder.

Bea, Augustin Cardinal. (1967). *The Church and Mankind*. Chicago: Franciscan Herald Press.

Beauduin, Lambert, OSB. (1926). *Liturgy, the Life of the Church*. Trans. by Virgil Michel, OSB. Collegeville, MN: Liturgical Press.

Bell, Daniel. (1962). *The End of Ideology: On the Exhaustion of Political Ideas in the Fifties*. New York: Collier Books.

Bell, Daniel. (1967). "The Year 2000 – The Trajectory of an Idea." *Daedalus* 96:3 (Summer, 1967) 639–651.

Benda, Julien. (1928). *The Treason of the Intellectuals*. Trans. by Richard Aldington. New York: W.W. Norton & Co.

Berdyaev, Nicholas. (1933). *The End of Our Time*. Trans. by Donald Atwater. New York: Sheed and Ward.

Berger, Peter L. (1977). "Secular Theology and the Rejection of the Supernatural: Reflections on Recent Trends." *Theological Studies* 38:1 (Mar., 1977) 39–56.

Berger, Peter L. and Luckmann, Thomas. (1966). *The Social Construction of Reality: A Treatise in the Sociology of Knowledge*. Garden City, NY: Doubleday & Co.

Berkouwer, G.C. (1965). *The Second Vatican Council and the New Catholicism*. Trans. by Lewis B. Smedes. Grand Rapids, MI: William B. Eerdmans Co.

Bernstein, Richard J. (1983). *Beyond Objectivism and Relativism: Science, Hermeneutics and Praxis*. Philadelphia: University of Pennsylvania Press.

Besancon, Alain. (1979). "The Confusion of Tongues." *Daedalus* 108:2 (Spring, 1979) 21–42.

Bettelheim, Bruno. (1983). *Freud and Man's Soul*. New York: Alfred A. Knopf.

Bidney, David. (1953). *Theoretical Anthropology*. New York: Columbia University Press.

Boelen, Bernard J. (1971). *Existential Thinking: A Philosophical Orientation*. New York: Herder and Herder.

Boelen, Bernard J. (1975). "Martin Heidegger as a Phenomenologist," in Philip J. Bossert, ed., *Phenomenological Perspectives: Historical and Systematic*

Essays in Honor of Herbert Spiegelberg. The Hague: Martinus Nijhoff. p. 93–114.

Boelen, Bernard J. (1978). *Personal Maturity: The Existential Dimension.* New York: Seabury Press.

Bottomore, Tom, ed. (1983). *A Dictionary of Marxist Thought.* Cambridge, MA: Harvard University Press.

Bottomore, Tom and Nisbet, Robert, eds. (1978). *A History of Sociological Analysis.* New York: Basic Books.

Bourdeau, F. and Danet, A. (1966). *Introduction to the Law of Christ.* Preface by Bernard Häring, CSsR. Trans. by Edward Gallagher. Staten Is., NY: Society of St. Paul.

Bouyer, Louis. (1982). *The Church of God: Body of Christ and Temple of the Spirit.* Chicago: Franciscan Herald Press.

Brand, P., Schillebeeckx, E. and Weiler, A., eds. (1983). *Twenty Years of "Concilium" – Retrospect and Prospect.* New York: Seabury Press.

Brown, Lester R. (1981). *Building a Sustainable Society.* New York: W.W. Norton & Co.

Bruner, Jerome S. and Postman, Leo. (1949). "On the Perception of Incongruity: A Paradigm." *Journal of Personality* 18 (1949) 206–223.

Brunner, F.A. (1967). "Anamnesis." *New Catholic Encyclopedia* 1 (1967) 475–476.

Byrne, E.F. and Marziarz, E.A. (1967). "Faith and Reason." *New Catholic Encyclopedia* 5 (1967) 807–811.

Callahan, Daniel. (1967). "The Quest for Social Relevance." *Daedalus* 96:1 (Winter, 1967) 151–179.

Camus, Albert. (1960). *The Rebel: An Essay on Man in Revolt.* New York: Vintage Books.

Cannon, Walter B., MD. (1932). *The Wisdom of the Body.* New York: W.W. Norton & Co.

Canon Law Society of America. (1983). *Code of Canon Law: Latin-English Edition.* Washington, DC: Canon Law Society of America.

Cantore, Enrico, SJ. (1971). "Humanistic Significance of Science: Some Methodological Considerations." *Philosophy of Science* 38:3 (Sept., 1971) 395–412.

Cantore, Enrico, SJ. (1977). *Scientific Man: The Humanistic Significance of Science.* New York: ISH Publications.

Caporale, Rock, SJ. (1964). *Vatican II: Last of the Councils.* Baltimore: Helicon.

Caporale, Rocco and Grumelli, Antonio, eds. (1971). *The Culture of Unbelief: Studies and Proceedings from the First International Symposium on Belief Held at Rome, Mar. 22–27, 1969.* Berkeley: University of California Press.

Capovilla, Loris. (1964). *The Heart and Mind of John XXIII: His Secretary's Intimate Recollections*. Trans. by Patrick Riley. New York: Hawthorne Books.

Capra, Fritjof. (1982). *The Turning Point: Science, Society and the Rising Culture*. New York: Bantam Books.

Carlen, Claudia, IHM. (1981). *The Papal Encyclicals*. 5 vols. Wilmington, NC: McGrath Pub. Co.

Carlo, William E. (1962). "The Role of Essence in Existential Metaphysics: A Reappraisal." *International Philosophical Quarterly* 2:4 (Dec., 1962) 557–590.

Carr, David. (1974). *Phenomenology and the Problem of History*. Evanston: Northwestern University Press.

Charles, Rodger, SJ, and Maclaren, Drostan, OP. (1982). *The Social Teaching of Vatican II: Its Origin and Development. Catholic Social Ethics: an historical and comparative study*. San Francisco: Ignatius Press.

Cogley, John. (1968). "The Search for Final Meaning." Preface by A. Toynbee. H. Ashmore, ed., *Britannica Perspectives*. Vol. 3, pp. 441–597. Chicago: Encyclopaedia Britannica, Inc.

Collingwood, R.G. (1946). *The Idea of History*. Oxford: University Press.

Congar, Yves M.-J., OP. (1968). *A History of Theology*. Trans. and edit. by H. Guthrie, SJ. Garden City, NY: Doubleday & Co.

Conley, Kieran, OSB. (1963). *A Theology of Wisdom: A Study in St. Thomas*. Dubuque, IA: Priory Press.

Connolly, James M. (1961). *The Voices of France: A Survey of Contemporary Theology in France*. New York: Macmillan & Co.

Connolly, James M. (1965). *Human History and the Word of God: The Christian Meaning of History in Contemporary Thought*. New York: Macmillan & Co.

Cousins, Norman. (1972). *The Improbable Triumvirate: John F. Kennedy, Pope John, Nikita Khrushchev*. New York: Norton & Co.

Cox, Harvey. (1984). *Religion in the Secular City: Toward a Postmodern Theology*. New York: Simon and Schuster.

Crowe, Frederick, SJ. (1980). *The Lonergan Enterprise*. Cambridge, MA: Cowley Publications.

Cullmann, Oscar. (1964). "The Place of the Bible at the Council." *Journal of Biblical Literature* 83 (1964) 247–252.

Daly, Gabriel, OSA. (1980). *Transcendence and Immanence: A Study of Catholic Modernism and Integralism*. Oxford: Clarendon Press.

Dansette, Adrien. (1961). *Religious History of Modern France*. 2 vols. New York: Herder and Herder.

Deely, John N. (1971). *The Tradition via Heidegger: An Essay on the Meaning of Being in the Philosophy of Martin Heidegger*. The Hague: Martinus Nijhoff.

Deferrari, R.J., Barry, M.I. and McGuiness, I., OP, eds. (1948). *A Lexicon of St. Thomas Aquinas based on The Summa Theologica and selected passages of his other works*. Washington, DC: Catholic University of America.

De Waelhens, Alphonse. (1962). "The Outlook for Existential Phenomenology." *International Philosophical Quarterly* 2:3 (Sept., 1962) 458–473.

Dewart, Leslie. (1966). *The Future of Belief: Theism in a World Come of Age*. New York: Herder and Herder.

Dondeyne, Albert. (1962). *Contemporary European Thought and Christian Faith*. Trans. by Ernan McMullin and John Burnheim. Pittsburgh: Duquesne University Press.

Douglas, Mary. (1982). "The Effects of Modernization on Religious Change." *Daedalus* 111:1 (Winter, 1982) 1–19.

Dru, Alexander. (1963). *The Contribution of German Catholicism*. New York: Hawthorne Books.

Drucker, Peter F. (1939). *The End of Economic Man*. New York: Day. (A good summary may be found in P.F. Drucker, "The End of Economic Man in Europe." *Harper's Monthly* 178 (1939) 561–570.)

Drucker, Peter F. (1969). *The Age of Discontinuity: Guidelines to Our Changing Society*. New York: Harper & Row.

Drucker, Peter F. (1971). *Men, Ideas & Politics*. New York: Harper & Row.

Dufrenne, Mikel. (1973). *The Phenomenology of Aesthetic Experience*. Trans. by Edward S. Casey, Albert A. Anderson, Willis Domingo, and Leon Jacobson. Evanston: Northwestern University Press.

Duméry, Henry. (1975). *Phenomenology and Religion: Structures of the Christian Institution*. Berkeley: University of California Press.

Durant, Will and Ariel. (1968). *The Lessons of History*. New York: Simon and Schuster.

Edie, J.M., Parker, F.H. and Schrag, C.O., eds. (1970). *Patterns of the Life-World: Essays in Honor of John Wild*. Evanston: Northwestern University Press.

Editors of Herder Correspondence. (1965). *John XXIII: Pope Paul on His Predecessor and a Documentation*. New York: Herder and Herder.

Edwards, Paul, ed. (1967). *The Encyclopedia of Philosophy*. 8 vols. New York: Macmillan Pub. Co., Inc., & The Free Press.

Eigo, Francis A., OSA, ed. (1981). *Whither Creativity, Freedom, Suffering?: Humanity, Cosmos, God*. Villanova, PA: Villanova University Press.

Eliade, Mircea. (1954). *Cosmos and History: The Myth of the Eternal Return*. Trans. by W.R. Trask. New York: Harper & Row.

Eliade, Mircea. (1959). *The Sacred and the Profane: The Nature of Religion.* Trans. by W.R. Trask. New York: Harcourt Brace Jovanovich.

Eliade, Mircea. (1963). *Myth and Reality.* Trans. by W.R. Trask. New York: Harper & Row.

Eliade, Mircea. (1969). *From Primitives to Zen: A Thematic Sourcebook of the History of Religions.* New York: Harper & Row.

Elliston, Frederick A. and McCormick, Peter, eds. (1977). *Husserl: Expositions and Appraisals.* Notre Dame: University of Notre Dame Press.

Ellul, Jacques. (1978). *The Betrayal of the West.* Trans. by M.J. O'Connell. New York: Seabury Press.

Eppstein, John. (1971). *Has the Catholic Church Gone Mad?* London: Tom Stacey, Ltd.

Fackenheim, Emil L. (1961). *Metaphysics and Historicity.* Aquinas Lecture, 1961. Milwaukee: Marquette University Press.

Faricy, Robert L., SJ. (1964). "Connatural Knowledge." *Sciences Ecclesiastiques* 16 (1964) 155–163.

Farley, Edward. (1975). *Ecclesial Man: A Social Phenomenology of Faith and Reality.* Philadelphia: Fortress Press.

Ferguson, Marilyn. (1980). *The Aquarian Conspiracy: Personal and Social Transformation in the 1980s.* Los Angeles: J.P. Tarcher.

Ferré, Frederick. (1976). *Shaping the Future: Resources for the Post-Modern World.* New York: Harper & Row.

Feuerbach, Ludwig. (1957). *The Essence of Christianity.* Trans. by George Eliot. Introd. by Karl Barth. New York: Harper Torchbooks.

Flannery, Austin, OP, ed. (1975). *Vatican Council II: The Conciliar and Postconciliar Documents.* Vol. 1. Northport, NY: Costello Pub. Co.

Flannery, Austin, OP, ed. (1982). *Vatican Council II: More Postconciliar Documents.* Vol. 2. Northport, NY: Costello Pub. Co.

Frankl, Viktor, E. (1967). *Psychotherapy and Existentialism: Selected Papers on Logotherapy.* With contributions by J.C. Crumbaugh, H.O. Gerz, and L.T. Maholick. New York: Simon and Schuster.

Franklin, R.W. (1975). "Guéranger: A View on the Centenary of His Death." *Worship* 49 (1975) 318–328.

Franklin, R.W. (1976). "Guéranger and Pastoral Liturgy: A Nineteenth Century Context." *Worship* 50 (1976) 146–162.

Franklin, R.W. (1977). "Guéranger and Variety in Unity." *Worship* 51 (1977) 378–399.

Franklin, R.W. (1979). "The Nineteenth Century Liturgical Movement." *Worship* 53 (1979) 12–39.

Freud, Sigmund. (1966). *The Complete Introductory Lectures on Psychoanalysis.* Trans. by James Strachey. New York: W.W. Norton.

Friedman, Maurice. (1964). *The Worlds of Existentialism: A Critical Reader.* New York: Random House.

Frings, Manfred S. (1965). *Max Scheler: A Concise Introduction into the World of a Great Thinker.* Pittsburgh, PA: Duquesne University Press.

Frossard, André. (1984). *"Be Not Afraid": Pope John Paul II Speaks Out on his Life, his Beliefs, and his Inspiring Vision for Humanity.* New York: St. Martin's Press.

Fullam, Raymond B., SJ. (1969). *Exploring Vatican 2: Christian Living Today and Tomorrow.* Staten Is., NY: Alba House.

Fuller, R. Buckminster. (1981). *Critical Path.* Adjuvant: Kiyoshi Kuromiya. New York: St. Martin's Press.

Gay, Peter. (1954). *The Party of Humanity: Essays in the French Enlightenment.* New York: W.W. Norton.

Gay, Peter. (1976). *The Enlightenment: An Interpretation. The Rise of Modern Paganism.* New York: Alfred A. Knopf.

Geffré, C., Gutiérrez, G., and Elizondo, V., eds. (1984). *Different Theologies, Common Responsibility: Babel or Pentecost?* Edinburgh: T. & T. Clark, Ltd.

Gilby, Thomas, OP, ed. (1963). *St. Thomas Aquinas: Summa Theologiae.* Vol. 1 (1a, 1). New York: McGraw-Hill Book Co.

Gleason, Philip. (1979). "In Search of Unity: American Catholic Thought (1920–1960)." *The Catholic Historical Review* 65:2 (April, 1979) 185–205.

Gonzalez, J.L., SSP, ed. (1966). *The Sixteen Documents of Vatican II and the Introduction on the Liturgy.* N.C.W.C. Translation. Boston, MA: Daughters of St. Paul.

Gorresio, Vittorio. (1970). *The New Mission of Pope John XXIII.* Trans. by C.L. Markmann. New York: Funk & Wagnalls.

Greeley, Andrew M. (1982). "The Failures of Vatican II After Twenty Years." *America* 146:5 (Feb. 6, 1982) 86–89.

Greenleaf, Robert K. (1977). *Servant Leadership: A Journey into the Nature of Legitimate Power and Greatness.* New York: Paulist Press.

Gremillion, Joseph. (1976). *The Gospel of Peace and Justice: Catholic Social Teachings since Pope John.* Maryknoll, NY: Orbis Books.

Gurwitsch, Aron. (1966). *Studies in Phenomenology and Psychology.* Evanston: Northwestern University Press.

Hales, E.E.Y. (1965). *Pope John and His Revolution.* Garden City, NY: Doubleday & Co.

Hall, David L. (1973). *The Civilization of Experience: A Whiteheadian Theory of Culture.* New York: Fordham University Press.

Hamer, Jerome, OP. (1964). *The Church is a Communion*. Trans. by R. Matthews. New York: Sheed and Ward.

Häring, Bernard, CSSR. (1961–1966). *The Law of Christ*. 3 vols. Trans. by E.G. Kaiser, CPPS. Westminster, MD: Newman Press.

Harris, H.S. (1981). "Religion as the Mythology of Reason." *Thought* 56:222 (Sept., 1981) 301–315.

Harvey, Van Austin. (1966). *The Historian and the Believer: The Morality of Historical Knowledge and Christian Belief*. New York: Macmillan & Co.

Hayes, Carlton J.H. (1960). *Nationalism: A Religion*. New York: Macmillan & Co.

Hebblethwaite, Brian L. (1980). *The Problems of Theology*. Cambridge: Cambridge University Press.

Hebblethwaite, Peter. (1985). *Pope John XXIII: Sheperd of the Modern World*. Garden City, NY: Doubleday & Co.

Hebblethwaite, Peter and Kaufmann, Ludwig. (1979). *John Paul II: A Pictorial Biography*. New York: McGraw-Hill Book Co.

Heidegger, Martin. (1961). *An Introduction to Metaphysics*. Trans. by R. Manheim. Garden City, NY: Doubleday & Co.

Heidegger, Martin. (1962). *Being and Time*. Trans. by J. Macquarrie and E. Robinson. New York: Harper & Row.

Heidegger, Martin. (1976). "Only a God Can Save Us." *Philosophy Today* 20 (Winter, 1976) 267–284.

Heisenberg, Werner. (1971). *Physics and Beyond: Encounters and Conversations*. Trans. by A.J. Pomerans. New York: Harper & Row.

Hellman, John. (1980–1981). "John Paul II and the Personalist Movement." *Cross Currents* 30:4 (Winter, 1980–1981) 409–419.

Henry, Patrick. (1979). *New Directions in New Testament Study*. Philadelphia: Westminster Press.

Herr, Dan. (1982). "Aggiornamento at 20: An Agenda for Vatican III." *Notre Dame Magazine* 11:4 (Oct., 1982) 23–25.

Hitchcock, James. (1980). "Postmortem on a Rebirth: The Catholic Intellectual Renaissance." *The American Scholar* (Spring, 1980) 211–225.

Hollis, Christopher. (1967). *The Achievement of Vatican II*. New York: Hawthorne Books.

Hoyt, Robert G., ed. (1968). *The Birth Control Debate*. Kansas City, MO: National Catholic Reporter.

Hughes, Philip. (1961). *The Church in Crisis: A History of the General Councils, 325–1870*. Garden City, NY: Hanover House.

Hurd, Robert L. (1984). "Heidegger and Aquinas: A Rahnerian Bridge." *Philosophy Today* 28:2/4 (Summer, 1984) 105–137.

Husserl, Edmund. (1964). *The Idea of Phenomenology.* Trans. by W.P. Alston and G. Nakhnikian. The Hague: Martinus Nijhoff.

Husserl, Edmund. (1970). *The Crisis of European Sciences and Transcendental Phenomenology: An Introduction to Phenomenological Philosophy.* Trans. with an Introd. by David Carr. Evanston: Northwestern University Press.

Husserl, Edmund. (1973). *Experience and Judgment: Investigations in a Genealogy of Logic.* Revised and edited by Ludwig Landgrebe. Evanston: Northwestern University Press.

Husserl, Edmund. (1975a). *Introduction to the Logical Investigations.* Trans. by Philip J. Bossert and Curtis H. Peters. The Hague: Martinus Nijhoff.

Husserl, Edmund. (1975b). *The Paris Lectures.* Trans. and Introductory Essay by Peter Koestenbaum. The Hague: Martinus Nijhoff.

Husserl, Edmund. (1976). *Ideas: General Introduction to Pure Phenomenology.* Trans. by W.R. Boyce Gibson. New York: Humanities Press.

Husserl, Edmund. (1977). *Phenomenological Psychology.* Trans. by John Scanlon. The Hague: Martinus Nijhoff.

Husserl, Edmund. (1978). *Formal and Transcendental Logic.* Trans. by Dorion Cairns. The Hague: Martinus Nijhoff.

Husserl, Edmund. (1980). *Phenomenology and the Foundations of the Sciences.* Third Book: Ideas pertaining to a pure phenomenology and to a phenomenological philosophy. Trans. by Ted E. Klein and William E. Pohl. The Hague: Martinus Nijhoff.

Husserl, Edmund. (1982). *Cartesian Meditations: An Introduction to Phenomenology.* Trans. by Dorion Cairns. The Hague: Martinus Nijhoff.

Hutchins, Robert M. (1952). *The Great Conversation: The Substance of a Liberal Education.* Chicago: Encyclopaedia Britannica, Inc.

Ihde, Don. (1971). *Hermeneutic Phenomenology: The Philosophy of Paul Ricoeur.* Evanston: Northwestern University Press.

Ingarden, Roman. (1973a). *The Cognition of the Literary Work of Art.* Trans. by Ruth Ann Crowley and Kenneth R. Olson. Evanston: Northwestern University Press.

Ingarden, Roman. (1973b). *The Literary Work of Art: An Investigation on the Borderlines of Ontology, Logic and Theory of Literature.* With an Appendix on the Functions of Language in the Theater. Trans. by George G. Grabowicz. Evanston: Northwestern University Press.

Jaspers, Karl. (1961). *The Future of Mankind.* Trans. by E.B. Ashton. Chicago: University of Chicago Press.

John, Helen James, SND. (1962). "The Emergence of the Act of Existing in Recent Thomism." *International Philosophical Quarterly* 2:4 (Dec., 1962) 595–620.

John, Helen James, SND. (1966). *The Thomist Spectrum*. New York: Fordham University Press.

John XXIII, Pope. (1965). *Journal of a Soul*. Edited by Loris Capovilla. Trans. by Dorothy White. New York: McGraw-Hill Book Co.

John XXIII, Pope. (1966). *Mission to France, 1944–1953*. Edited by Loris Capovilla. Trans. by Dorothy White. New York: McGraw-Hill Book Co.

John XXIII, Pope. (1969). *Letters to his Family*. Trans. by Dorothy White. New York: McGraw-Hill Book Co.

John Paul II, Pope (see also Wojtyla, Karol). (1981). *Original Unity of Man and Woman: Catechesis on the Book of Genesis*. Preface by Donald W. Wuerl. Boston: St. Paul Editions.

John Paul II, Pope (see also Wojtyla, Karol). (1984a). "On Human Suffering." Apostolic Letter of Pope John Paul II on the Christian meaning of human suffering (Feb. 11, 1984). *The Pope Speaks* 29:2 (Summer, 1984) 105–139.

John Paul II, Pope (see also Wojtyla, Karol). (1984b). "The Norm of 'Humanae Vitae' Arises From the Natural Law and Revealed Moral Order." General Audience of July 18, 1984. *L'Osservatore Romano* 30:844 (July 23, 1984) 1. (English edition)

Johnson, Paul. (1981). *Pope John Paul II and the Catholic Restoration*. New York: St. Martin's Press.

Kahn, Herman and Wiener, Anthony J. (1967). "The Next Thirty-Three Years: A Framework for Speculation." *Daedalus* 96:3 (Summer, 1967) 705–732.

Kaiser, Robert Blair. (1963). *Pope, Council and World: The Story of Vatican II*. New York: Macmillan Co.

Kobler, John F. (1983a). "The Church Which *Civilizes* by Evangelizing." *Review For Religious* 42:6 (Nov./Dec., 1983) 893–902.

Kobler, John F. (1983b). "Vatican II and the Fate of the Earth." *Notre Dame Magazine* 12:2 (May, 1983) 80.

Kobler, John F. (1983c). "Vatican II Revisited." *Cara Forum For Religious* 4:2 (1983) 3.

Kockelmans, Joseph J. (1965). *Martin Heidegger: A First Introduction to his Philosophy*. Pittsburgh, PA: Duquesne University Press.

Kockelmans, Joseph J. and Kisiel, Theodore J. (1970). *Phenomenology and the Natural Sciences: Essays and Translations*. Evanston: Northwestern University Press.

Kuhn, Thomas S. (1957). *The Copernican Revolution: Planetary Astronomy in the Development of Western Thought*. Cambridge, MA: Harvard University Press.

Kuhn, Thomas S. (1962). *The Structure of Scientific Revolutions*. 2nd edition, enlarged. Chicago: University of Chicago Press.

Kuhn, Thomas S. (1977). *The Essential Tension: Selected Studies in Scientific Tradition and Change.* Chicago: University of Chicago Press.

Kress, Robert. (1967). "Church and Communio." *New Catholic Encyclopedia* 17 (1967) 121–124.

Kwant, Remy C., OSA. (1963). *The Phenomenological Philosophy of Merleau-Ponty.* Pittsburgh, PA: Duquesne University Press.

Kwant, Remy C., OSA. (1965). *Phenomenology of Social Existence.* Pittsburgh, PA: Duquesne University Press.

Ladner, Gerhart B. (1959). *The Idea of Reform: Its Impact on Christian Thought and Action in the Age of the Fathers.* Revised edition. New York: Harper & Row.

Lallou, William J. (1945). "Unde et Memores." *The American Ecclesiastical Review* 113 (1945) 81–93.

Landgrebe, Ludwig. (1966). *Major Problems in Contemporary European Philosophy: From Dilthey to Heidegger.* Trans. by Kurt F. Reinhardt. New York: Frederick Unger Pub. Co.

Laszlo, Ervin. (1972). *Introduction to Systems Philosophy: Toward a New Paradigm of Contemporary Thought.* Forword by Ludwig von Bertalanffy. New York: Gordon and Breach, Science Publishers.

Latin Texts. (1960–1961). *Acta et Documenta Concilio Vaticano II apparando – Series I: Antepraeparatoria.* 16 vols. Vatican City: Typis Polyglottis Vaticanis.

Latin Texts. (1962–1963). *Concilium Vaticanum Secundum Schemata Constitutionum et Decretorum.* 4 vols. Vatican City: Typis Polyglottis Vaticanis.

Latin Texts. (1964–1969). *Acta et Documenta Concilio Vaticano II apparando – Series II: Praeparatoria.* 7 vols. Vatican City: Typis Polyglottis Vaticanis.

Latin Texts. (1966). *Sacrosanctum Oecumenicum Concilium Vaticanum II: Constitutiones, Decreta, Declarationes.* Vatican City: Typis Polyglottis Vaticanis.

Latin Texts. (1970–1980). *Acta Synodalia Sacrosancti Concilii Oecumenici Vaticani II.* 26 vols. Vatican City: Typis Polyglottis Vaticanis.

Lauer, Quentin, SJ. (1978). *The Triumph of Subjectivity: An Introduction to Transcendental Phenomenology.* New York: Fordham University Press.

Leahy, D.G. (1980). *Novitas Mundi: Perception of the History of Being.* New York: New York University Press.

Leeuw, Gerardus van der. (1963). *Religion in Essence and Manifestation.* 2 vols. Trans. by J.E. Turner. New York: Harper & Row.

Léon-Dufour, Xavier, ed. (1973). *Dictionary of Biblical Theology.* 2nd edition. Trans. by P. Joseph Cahill, SJ. Revision and new articles trans. by E.M. Stewart. New York: Seabury Press.

Lercaro, Giacomo and De Rosa, Gabriel. (1966). *John XXIII: Simpleton or Saint?* Trans. by Dorothy White. Chicago: Franciscan Herald Press.

Lévi-Strauss, Claude. (1966). *The Savage Mind.* Chicago: University of Chicago Press.

Levin, David Michael. (1970). *Reason and Evidence in Husserl's Phenomenology.* Evanston: Northwestern University Press.

Lindbeck, George A. (1970). *The Future of Roman Catholic Theology: Vatican II – Catalyst for Change.* Philadelphia: Fortress Press.

Lombardi, Riccardo. (1958). *Towards a New World.* New York: Philosophical Library.

Lorenz, Konrad Z. (1952). *King Solomon's Ring: New Light on Animal Ways.* New York: Time, Inc.

Luijpen, William A., OSA. (1964). *Phenomenology and Atheism.* Pittsburgh, PA: Duquesne University Press.

Luijpen, William A., OSA. (1965a). *Existential Phenomenology.* Pittsburgh, PA: Duquesne University Press.

Luijpen, William A., OSA. (1965b). *Phenomenology and Metaphysics.* Pittsburgh, PA: Duquesne University Press.

Luijpen, William A., OSA. (1967). *Phenomenology of Natural Law.* Trans. by Henry J. Koren. Pittsburgh, PA: Duquesne University Press.

Lukas, Mary and Lukas, Ellen. (1977). *Teilhard: The Man, The Priest, The Scientist.* Garden City, NY: Doubleday & Co.

Lunn, Arnold. (1931). *The Flight From Reason.* New York: Dial Press.

McCool, Gerald A. (1977). *Catholic Theology in the Nineteenth Century: The Quest for a Unitary Method.* New York: Seabury Press.

McCormick, Peter and Elliston, Frederick, eds. (1981). *Husserl: Shorter Works.* Forword by Walter Biemel. Notre Dame: University of Notre Dame and Harvester Press.

MacEoin, Gary. (1966). *What Happened at Rome? The Council and its Implications for the Modern World.* Introd. by John Cogley. New York: Holt, Rinehart and Winston.

McNamara, Kevin, ed. (1968). *Vatican II: The Constitution on the Church: A Theological and Pastoral Commentary.* Chicago: Franciscan Herald Press.

Mann, Peter, OSB. (1969). "Masters in Israel: IV. The Later Theology of Karl Rahner." *Clergy Review* 12 (1969) 936–948.

Marcel, Gabriel. (1951). *Homo Viator: Introduction to a Metaphysic of Hope.* Trans. by Emma Craufurd. Chicago: Henry Regnery Co.

Marcel, Gabriel. (1952). *Metaphysical Journal.* Trans. by Bernard Wall. Chicago: Henry Regnery Co.

Marcel, Gabriel. (1962). *Man Against Mass Society.* Trans. by G.S. Fraser. Forword by D. Mackinnon. Chicago: Henry Regnery Co.

Marcel, Gabriel. (1967). *Problematic Man.* Trans. by Brian Thompson. New York: Herder and Herder.

Marcel, Gabriel. (1973). *Tragic Wisdom and Beyond: including conversations between Paul Ricoeur and Gabriel Marcel.* Evanston: Northwestern University Press.

Marcus, John T. (1971). "East and West: Phenomenologies of the Self and the Existential Bases of Knowledge." *International Philosophical Quarterly* 11:1 (Mar., 1971) 5–48.

Maritain, Jacques. (1953). *Creative Intuition in Art and Poetry.* The A.W. Mellon Lectures in the Fine Arts. New York: Pantheon Books.

Maritain, Jacques. (1959). *Distinguish to Unite or The Degrees of Knowledge.* Newly translated from the fourth French edition under the supervision of Gerald B. Phelan. New York: Charles Scribner's Sons.

Maritain, Jacques. (1968). *The Peasant of the Garonne: An Old Layman Questions Himself About the Present Time.* Trans. by Michael Cuddihy and Elizabeth Hughes. New York: Holt, Rinehart and Winston.

Maritain, Jacques. (1973). *Integral Humanism: Temporal and Spiritual Problems of a New Christendom.* Trans. by Joseph W. Evans. Notre Dame: University of Notre Dame Press.

Martin, Malachi. (1972). *Three Popes and the Cardinal.* New York: Farrar, Straus and Giroux.

Martin, Malachi. (1981). *The Decline and Fall of the Roman Church.* New York: G.P. Putnam's Sons.

Marx, Werner. (1971). *Heidegger and the Tradition.* Trans. by Theodore Kisiel and Murray Greene. Evanston: Northwestern University Press.

Mascall, E.L. (1968). *The Secularization of Christianity: An Analysis and a Critique.* New York: Holt, Rinehart and Winston.

May, Rollo, Angel, E., and Ellenberger, H.F., eds. (1958). *Existence: A New Dimension in Psychiatry and Psychology.* New York: Basic Books.

May, W.E. (1967). "Knowledge, Connatural." *New Catholic Encyclopedia* 8 (1967) 228–229.

Meagher, P.K., O'Brien, T., and Aherne, C.M., eds. (1979). *Encyclopedic Dictionary of Religion.* 3 vols. Washington, DC: Corpus Publications.

Menninger, Karl, MD, Mayman, M. and Pruyser, P. (1963). *The Vital Balance: The Life Process in Mental Health and Illness.* New York: Viking Press.

Merleau-Ponty, Maurice. (1963a). *In Praise of Philosophy.* Trans., with a Preface by John Wild and James M. Edie. Evanston: Northwestern University Press.

Merleau-Ponty, Maurice. (1963b). *The Structure of Behavior.* Trans. by Alden L. Fisher. Boston: Beacon Press.

Merleau-Ponty, Maurice. (1964a). *The Primacy of Perception: And Other Essays on Phenomenological Psychology, the Philosophy of Art, History, and*

Politics. Edited, with an Introd. by James M. Edie. Evanston: Northwestern University Press.

Merleau-Ponty, Maurice. (1964b). *Sense and Non-Sense.* Trans. by Hubert L. Dreyfus and Patricia Allen Dreyfus. Evanston: Northwestern University Press.

Merleau-Ponty, Maurice. (1964c). *Signs.* Trans., with an Introd. by Richard C. McCleary. Evanston: Northwestern University Press.

Mersch, Emile, SJ. (1938). *The Whole Christ: The Historical Development of the Doctrine of the Mystical Body in Scripture and Tradition.* Trans. by John R. Kelly, SJ. Milwaukee: Bruce Pub. Co.

Mersch, Emile, SJ. (1951). *The Theology of the Mystical Body.* Trans. by Cyril Vollert, SJ. St. Louis: B. Herder Book Co.

Miller, John H., CSC, ed. (1966). *Vatican II: An Interfaith Appraisal.* International Theological Conference, University of Notre Dame, March 20–26, 1966. Notre Dame: University of Notre Dame Press.

Miller, Jonathan. (1983). *States of Mind.* New York: Pantheon Books.

Mische, Gerald and Patricia. (1977). *Toward a Human World Order: Beyond the National Security Straitjacket.* New York: Paulist Press.

Modras, Ronald. (1980). "The Moral Philosophy of Pope John Paul II." *Theological Studies* 41:4 (Dec., 1980) 683–697.

Molnar, Thomas. (1968). *Sartre: Ideologue of our Time.* New York: Funk & Wagnalls.

Moraczewski, Albert S., OP *et al.*, eds. (1983). *Technological Powers and the Person: Nuclear Energy and Reproductive Technologies.* St. Louis, MO: The Pope John Center.

Moreno, A., OP. (1970). "The Nature of St. Thomas' Knowledge 'Per Connaturalitatem.'" *Angelicum* 47 (1970) 44–62.

Morrisey, Francis, OMI. (c. 1975). *The Canonical Significance of Papal and Curial Pronouncements.* Toledo, OH: Canon Law Society of America.

Mounier, Emmanuel. (1938). *A Personalist Manifesto.* Trans. by monks of St. John's Abbey. London: Longmans, Green and Co.

Mounier, Emmanuel. (1948). *Existentialist Philosophies: An Introduction.* Trans. by Eric Blow. London: Rockliff.

Muck, Otto, SJ. (1968). *The Transcendental Method.* Trans. by William D. Seidensticker. New York: Herder and Herder.

Mueller, J.J., SJ. (1984). "Appreciative Awareness: The Feeling Dimension in Religious Experience." *Theological Studies* 45:1 (1984) 57–79.

Muggeridge, Malcolm. (1975). "Living Through an Apocalypse." J.D. Douglas, (ed.), *Let the Earth Hear his Voice.* International Congress on World Evangelization, Lausanne, Switzerland. Minneapolis: World Wide Publications. Pp. 449–456.

Muggeridge, Malcolm. (1980). *The End of Christendom*. Introd. by John North. Grand Rapids, MI: William B. Eerdmans Pub. Co.

Muller, Robert. (1982). *New Genesis: Shaping a Global Spirituality*. Garden City, NY: Doubleday & Co.

Muralt, André de. (1974). *The Idea of Phenomenology: Husserlian Exemplarism*. Trans. by Garry L. Breckon. Evanston: Northwestern University Press.

Murnion, Philip. (1984). "Catholic Church Offers Blueprint for Social Change." *National Catholic Reporter* 20:36 (Aug. 3, 1984) 1, 20–24.

Naisbitt, John. (1982). *Megatrends: Ten New Directions Transforming Our Lives*. New York: Warner Books.

Natanson, Maurice. (1973a). *Edmund Husserl: Philosopher of Infinite Tasks*. Evanston: Northwestern University Press.

Natanson, Maurice. (1973b). *Phenomenology and the Social Sciences*. 2 vols. Edited by Maurice Natanson. Evanston: Northwestern University Press.

Nédoncelle, Maurice. (1962). "A Recently Discovered Study of von Hügel on God." *International Philosophical Quarterly* 2:1 (Feb., 1962) 5–24.

Nichols, Peter. (1968). *The Politics of the Vatican*. London: Pall Mall Press.

Nichols, Peter. (1981). *The Pope's Divisions: The Roman Catholic Church Today*. New York: Holt, Rinehart and Winston.

Nisbet, Robert. (1980). *History of the Idea of Progress*. New York: Basic Books.

Nota, John H., SJ. (1967). *Phenomenology and History*. Trans. by Louis Grooten and the author. Chicago: Loyola University Press.

Novak, Michael. (1964–1965). *The Men Who Make The Council*. 24 vols. Edited by Michael Novak. Notre Dame: University of Notre Dame Press.

Novak, Michael. (1967). "Christianity: Renewed or Slowly Abandoned?" *Daedalus* 96:1 (Winter, 1967) 237–266.

Novak, Michael. (1982). "Aggiornamento at 20: The Disaster of Vatican II." *Notre Dame Magazine* 11:4 (Oct., 1982) 19–22.

O'Brien, Elmer, SJ. (1965). *Theology in Transition: A Bibliographical Evaluation of the "Decisive Decade," 1954–1964*. New York: Herder and Herder.

O'Connor, James T. (1984). "The Church of Christ and the Catholic Church." *Homiletic & Pastoral Review* 84:4 (Jan., 1984) 10–21.

O'Dea, Thomas F. (1958). *American Catholic Dilemma: An Inquiry into the Intellectual Life*. New York: Sheed and Ward.

O'Dea, Thomas F. (1967). "The Crisis of the Contemporary Religious Consciousness." *Daedalus* 96:1 (Winter, 1967) 116–134.

O'Dea, Thomas F. (1968). *The Catholic Crisis*. Boston: Beacon Press.

O'Malley, John W., SJ. (1971). "Reform, Historical Consciousness, and Vatican II's Aggiornamento." *Theological Studies* 32 (1971) 573–601.

O'Malley, John W., SJ. (1983). "Developments, Reforms, and Two Great

Reformations: Towards a Historical Assessment of Vatican II." *Theological Studies* 44:3 (Sept., 1983) 373–406.

O'Meara, Thomas F., OP. (1981). "Of Art and Theology: Hans Urs von Balthasar's Systems." *Theological Studies* 42:2 (June, 1981) 272–276.

O'Meara, Thomas F., OP. (1982). *Romantic Idealism and Roman Catholicism: Schelling and the Theologians.* Notre Dame: University of Notre Dame Press.

Ong, Walter, SJ, ed. (1968). *Knowledge and the Future of Man: An International Symposium.* New York: Holt, Rinehart and Winston.

Otto, Rudolf. (1923). *The Idea of the Holy: An Inquiry into the non-rational factor in the idea of the divine and its relation to the rational.* Trans. by John W. Harvey. London: Oxford University Press.

Palmer, Richard E. (1969). *Hermeneutics: Interpretation Theory in Schleiermacher, Dilthey, Heidegger, and Gadamer.* Evanston: Northwestern University Press.

Panikkar, Raimundo. (1982). *Blessed Simplicity: The Monk as Universal Archetype.* New York: Seabury Press.

Paul VI, Pope. (1966). "The Last General Meeting." (Dec. 7, 1965) *Catholic Mind* 64:1202 (April, 1966) 57–64.

Paul VI, Pope. (1971–1975). *The Teachings of Pope Paul VI* (1970–1973). 4 vols. Washington, DC: United States Catholic Conference.

Paul VI, Pope. (1975). "Evangelization in the Modern World." (Dec. 8, 1975) *The Pope Speaks* 21:1 (Spring, 1976) 4–51.

Pelikan, Jaroslav, ed. (1969–1970). *Twentieth Century Theology in the Making.* 3 vols. Trans. by R.A. Wilson. New York: Harper & Row.

Pfänder, Alexander. (1967). *Phenomenology of Willing and Motivation and Other Phaenomenologica.* Trans. by H. Spiegelberg. Evanston: Northwestern University Press.

Pitte, Frederick P. Van De. (1971). *Kant as Philosophical Anthropologist.* The Hague: Martinus Nijhoff.

Polanyi, Michael. (1958). *Personal Knowledge: Towards a Post-Critical Philosophy.* Chicago: University of Chicago Press.

Polanyi, Michael. (1969). *Knowing and Being.* Edited by M. Grene. Chicago: University of Chicago Press.

Polanyi, Michael and Prosch, Harry. (1975). *Meaning.* Chicago: University of Chicago Press.

Pribram, Karl. (1969). "The Neurophysiology of Remembering." *Scientific American* 220:1 (1969) 73–86.

Pribram, Karl and Goleman, Daniel. (1979). "Holographic Memory." *Psychology Today* 12:9 (Feb., 1979) 71–84.

Quade, Quentin L., ed. (1982). *The Pope and Revolution: John Paul II Confronts Liberation Theology.* Washington, DC: Ethics and Public Policy Center.

Quitslund, Sonya A. (1973). *Beauduin: A Prophet Vindicated.* New York: Newman Press.

Rahner, Karl, SJ. (1968–1970). *Sacramentum Mundi: An Encyclopedia of Theology.* 6 vols. Edited by Karl Rahner, SJ, *et al.* New York: Herder and Herder.

Rahner, Karl, SJ. (1979). "Toward a Fundamental Theological Interpretation of Vatican II." *Theological Studies* 40:4 (Dec., 1979) 716–727.

Ratzinger, Joseph. (1969). *Introduction to Christianity.* Trans. by J.R. Foster. London: Burns & Oates.

Ratzinger, Joseph. (1983). "Sources and Transmission of the Faith." *Communio* 10:1 (Spring, 1983) 17–34.

Rauschning, Hermann. (1939). *The Revolution of Nihilism: Warning to the West.* Trans. by E.W. Dickes. New York: Alliance Book Corp.

Ricoeur, Paul. (1967). *Husserl: An Analysis of His Phenomenology.* Trans. by Edward G. Ballard and Lester E. Embree. Evanston: Northwestern University Press.

Rieff, Philip. (1966). *The Triumph of the Therapeutic: Uses of Faith After Freud.* New York: Harper & Row.

Roberts, Louis. (1967). *The Achievement of Karl Rahner.* New York: Herder and Herder.

Roche, Douglas J. (1968). *The Catholic Revolution.* New York: David McKay Co.

Roncalli, Angelo Giuseppe (see John XXIII, Pope).

Roth, John K., ed. (1971). *The Philosophy of Josiah Royce.* New York: Thomas Y. Crowell.

Royce, Josiah. (1968). *The Problem of Christianity.* With a new introduction by John E. Smith. Chicago: University of Chicago Press.

Rynne, Xavier. (1963). *Letters from Vatican City: Vatican Council II (First Session): Background and Debates.* New York: Farrar, Straus & Co.

Sacred Congregation For Religious. (1978). "Relations between Bishops and Religious (*Mutuae Relationes*): A Document Issued by the Sacred Congregation for Religious and Secular Institutes and the Sacred Congregation for Bishops (May 14, 1978)." *The Pope Speaks* 23:4 (Winter, 1978) 344–380.

Sacred Congregation For Religious. (1980). "Religious Profession and Human Development: A Document of the Sacred Congregation for Religious and Secular Institutes (August 12, 1980)." *The Pope Speaks* 26:2 (Summer, 1981) 97–122.

Salm, Luke, FSC, ed. (1975). *The Catholic Theological Society of America: Proceedings of the Thirtieth Annual Convention.* June 9–12, 1975. Bronx, NY: Manhattan College.

Sartre, Jean-Paul. (1953). *Being and Nothingness: An Essay on Phenomenological Ontology.* Trans. by Hazel E. Barnes. New York: Washington Square Press, Inc.

Schall, James V., SJ, ed. (1984). *Sacred in All Its Forms.* Boston: Daughters of St. Paul.

Scheler, Max. (1973a). *Formalism in Ethics and Non-Formal Ethics of Values: A New Attempt toward the Foundation of an Ethical Personalism.* Trans. by Manfred S. Frings and Roger L. Funk. Evanston: Northwestern University Press.

Scheler, Max. (1973b). *Selected Philosophical Essays.* Trans. by David R. Lachterman. Evanston: Northwestern University Press.

Schell, Jonathan. (1982). *The Fate of the Earth.* New York: Avon Books.

Schillebeeckx, Edward, OP. (1965). *The Church and Mankind.* Concilium: Theology in the Age of Renewal. Vol. I. Edited by E. Schillebeeckx, OP. Glen Rock, NJ: Paulist Press.

Schillebeeckx, Edward, OP. (1967). *The Real Achievement of Vatican II.* Trans. by H.J.J. Vaughan. New York: Herder and Herder.

Schoof, Mark, OP. (1970). *A Survey of Catholic Theology, 1800–1970.* Trans. by N.D. Smith. Glenrock, NJ: Paulist Newman Press.

Schrag, Calvin O. (1980). *Radical Reflection and the Origin of the Human Sciences.* West Lafayette, IN: Purdue University Press.

Schreiter, Robert J., ed. (1984). *The Schillebeeckx Reader.* New York: Crossroads.

Schumacher, E.F. (1973). *Small is Beautiful: Economics as if People Mattered.* New York: Harper & Row.

Schutz, Alfred. (1962–1976). *Collected Papers.* 3 vols. Vol. I: "The Problem of Social Reality." Edited by Maurice Natanson. Vol. II: "Studies in Social Theory." Edited by Arvid Brodersen. Vol. III: "Studies in Phenomenological Philosophy." Edited by I. Schutz. The Hague: Martinus Nijhoff.

Schutz, Alfred. (1967). *The Phenomenology of the Social World.* Trans. by George Walsh and Frederick Lehnert. Evanston: Northwestern University Press.

Schutz, Alfred and Luckmann, Thomas. (1973). *The Structures of the Life-World.* Trans. by Richard M. Zaner and H. Tristram Engelhardt, Jr. Evanston: Northwestern University Press.

Sheed, F.J., trans. (1943). *The Confessions of St. Augustine.* New York: Sheed and Ward.

Shook, L.K., CSB, ed. (1968). *Theology of Renewal: Proceedings of the Congress on the Theology of the Renewal of the Church, Centenary of Canada, 1867–1967.* 2 vols. New York: Herder and Herder.

Smart, James D. (1979). *The Past, Present, and Future of Biblical Theology.* Philadelphia: Westminster Press.

Smith, Houston. (1982). *Beyond the Post-Modern Mind.* New York: Crossroad.

Smith, John E. (1967). *Religion and Empiricism.* Aquinas Lecture. Milwaukee: Marquette University Press.

Smolarski, Dennis C., SJ. (1982). *Eucharistia: A Study of the Eucharistic Prayer.* New York: Paulist Press.

Sokolowski, Robert. (1974). *Husserlian Meditations: How Words Present Things.* Evanston: Northwestern University Press.

Spiegelberg, Herbert. (1972). *Phenomenology in Psychology and Psychiatry: A Historical Introduction.* Evanston: Northwestern University Press.

Spiegelberg, Herbert. (1975). *Doing Phenomenology: Essays on and in Phenomenology.* The Hague: Martinus Nijhoff.

Spiegelberg, Herbert. (1981). *The Context of the Phenomenological Movement.* The Hague: Martinus Nijhoff.

Spiegelberg, Herbert. (1982). *The Phenomenological Movement: A Historical Introduction.* Third Revised and Enlarged Edition. The Hague: Martinus Nijhoff.

Staff of the Pope Speaks Magazine. (1964). *The Encyclicals and Other Messages of John XXIII.* With commentaries by John F. Cronin, SS, Francis X. Murphy, CSSR, and Ferrer Smith, OP. Washington, DC: TPS Press.

Stevenson, W. Taylor. (1969). *History as Myth: The Import for Contemporary Theology.* New York: Seabury Press.

Stewart, David and Mickunas, Algis. (1974). *Exploring Phenomenology: A Guide to the Field and its Literature.* Chicago: American Library Association.

Suppe, Frederick, ed. (1977). *The Structure of Scientific Theories.* Second Edition. Urbana, IL: University of Illinois Press.

Szacki, Jerzy. (1979). *History of Sociological Thought.* Westport, CT: Greenwood Press.

Teilhard de Chardin, Pierre. (1966). *The Vision of the Past.* Trans. by J.M. Cohen. New York: Harper & Row.

Teller, Edward. (1980). *The Pursuit of Simplicity.* Malibu, CA: Pepperdine University.

Tillard, J.M.R., OP. (1967). *The Eucharist: Pasch of God's People.* Staten, Is., NY: Alba House.

Tillich, Paul. (1944). "Existential Philosophy." *Journal of the History of Ideas* 5:1 (1944) 44–70.

Tinder, Glen. (1980). *Community: Reflections on a Tragic Ideal.* Baton Rouge, LA: Louisiana State University Press.

Tolman, Edward Chace. (1941). "Psychological Man." Reprinted from *The Journal of Social Psychology* (Feb., 1941) in E.C. Tolman, *Behavior and Psychological Man.* Berkeley: University of California Press, 1958. Pp. 207–218.

Townes, Charles H. (1966). "The Convergence of Science and Religion." *Think* 32 (Mar.–Apr., 1966) 2–7.

Toynbee, Arnold J. (1958). *Civilization on Trial and The World of the West.* New York: Meridian Books.

Tracy, David, Kung, H., and Metz, J.B., eds. (1978). *Towards Vatican III: The Work That Needs To Be Done.* New York: Seabury Press.

Tymieniecka, Anna-Teresa. (1962). *Phenomenology and Science in Contemporary European Thought.* New York: Farrar, Straus, and Giroux.

Tymieniecka, Anna-Teresa. (1971–1983). *Analecta Husserliana: The Yearbook of Phenomenological Research.* 16 vols. Dordrecht: D. Reidel Pub. Co.

Tymieniecka, Anna-Teresa. (1979). "The Origins of the Philosophy of John Paul Second." *Proceedings of the Catholic Philosophical Association* 53 (1979) 16–27.

Van Ackeren, G.P. (1967). "Theology." *New Catholic Encyclopedia* 14 (1967) 39–49.

Voegelin, Eric. (1978). *Anamnesis.* Trans. by Gerhart Niemeyer. Notre Dame: University of Notre Dame Press.

Vollert, Cyril, SJ. (1951). "*Humani Generis* and the Limits of Theology." *Theological Studies* 12 (1951) 3–23.

Vonier, Anscar, OSB. (1937). *The People of God.* London: Burns Oates and Washbourne.

Vorgrimler, Herbert, ed. (1967–1969). *Commentary on the Documents of Vatican II.* 5 vols. New York: Herder and Herder.

Walgrave, Jan Hendrick. (1972). *Unfolding Revelation: The Nature of Doctrinal Development.* Philadelphia: Westminster Press.

Wallace, William A., OP. (1977). *Galileo's Early Notebooks: The Physical Questions. A Translation from the Latin with Historical and Paleographical Commentary.* Notre Dame: University of Notre Dame Press.

Wallace, William A., OP. (1983a). "Aquinas, Galileo, and Aristotle." Aquinas Medalist Address, American Catholic Philosophical Association, New York, April 9, 1983. MS copy.

Wallace, William A., OP. (1983b). "Galileo and Aristotle in the *Dialogo.*" *Angelicum* 60:3 (1983) 311–332.

Ward, Barbara. (1976). *The Home of Man.* New York: W.W. Norton & Co.

Weigel, Gustave, SJ. (1951). "The Historical Background of the Encyclical *Humani Generis." Theological Studies* 12 (1951) 208–230.

Weizenbaum, Joseph. (1976). *Computer Power and Human Reason: From Judgment to Calculation.* San Francisco: W.H. Freeman & Co.

Wiener, Philip P., ed. (1968). *Dictionary of the History of Ideas.* 4 vols. New York: Charles Scribner's Sons.

Wigginton, F. Peter. (1983). *The Popes of Vatican Council II.* Chicago: Franciscan Herald Press.

Williams, George Huntson. (1981). *The Mind of John Paul II: Origins of His Thought and Action.* New York: Seabury Press.

Williams, Robert. (1975). "Ecclesial Man: A Radical Approach to Theology through Husserl's Phenomenology." *Philosophy Today* 19 (Winter, 1975) 369–376.

Wiltgen, Ralph M., SVD. (1978). *The Rhine Flows into the Tiber: A History of Vatican II.* Devon: Augustine Pub. Co.

Winters, Francis X., SJ. (1984). "After Tension, Detente: A Continuing Chronicle of European Episcopal Views on Nuclear Deterrence." *Theological Studies* 45:2 (June, 1984) 343–351.

Wojtyla, Karol (see also John Paul II, Pope). (1979a). *The Acting Person.* Edited by A-T. Tymieniecka. Trans. by A. Potocki. Dordrecht, Holland: D. Reidel Pub. Co.

Wojtyla, Karol (see also John Paul II, Pope). (1979b). *Sign of Contradiction.* New York: Seabury Press.

Wojtyla, Karol (see also John Paul II, Pope). (1980). *Sources of Renewal: The Implementation of the Second Vatican Council.* Trans. by P.S. Falla. San Francisco: Harper & Row.

Wood, Barbara. (1984). *E.F. Schumacher: His Life and Thought.* New York: Harper & Row.

Wood, Robert E. (1969). *Martin Buber's Ontology: An Analysis of I AND THOU.* Evanston: Northwestern University Press.

Woznicki, Andrew N. (1980). *A Christian Humanism: Karol Wojtyla's Existential Personalism.* New Britain, CT: Mariel Publications.

Yankelovich, Daniel. (1981). *New Rules: Searching for Self-Fulfillment in a World Turned Upside Down.* New York: Random House.

Zizola, Giancarlo. (1978). *The Utopia of Pope John XXIII.* Trans. by Helen Barolini. Maryknoll, NY: Orbis Books.

THEMATIC INDEX

Pedagogical utility has shaped the design of this index. It intends to assist the reader in three ways:

(1) To see the topics indexed, not so much as subjects (or "concepts"), but as *themes* typifying the human consciousness in its natural or religious functioning.

(2) To see a spectrum of isomorphic relationships, ranging from the speculative to the practical order, between the more overtly related themes. After most entries, therefore, a list of related topics, introduced by the italicized word *See*, is presented in a "sense order," rather than alphabetically.

(3) To see the internal cohesion pulling together a whole "region" of consciousness or reality such as – for example – Phenomenology, Vatican II, etc. Such larger clusters of themes are a small index unto themselves.

Humanity, message to: 25, 29, 60, 141.
   See: Radio broadcast (Sept. 11, 1962);
   Peace, problem of; Integralism.

I-Thou relationships: 200. *See*: "We-phenomenon;" Dialogue; Participation; Consensus-formation; Communio.
Idealism: (a) *Post-Kantian*: 3, 5, 74, 83,
   128, 149, 166–167, 169, 180, 200. (b)
   methodological (of Vatican II): 16,
   73–74, 135, 140, 144, 158, 169, 174.
   See: Hegelianism; Materialism; Via
   Media; Methodology; Theology, Pastoral.
Imagination, Free variation in: 71, 78, 81,
   93, 206. *See*: Phenomenology of appearances; Esthetics; Artistic enterprise
   (of Vatican II).
Induction (in phenomenology): 16, 61.
   See: A priori (empirical); Appresen-
   tation(s).
Industrial revolution: *See* Economic Man;
   Masses, Rise of the; Capitalism; Marxism; Social Catholicism; Psychological
   man; Crisis; Mater et Magistra; Humanae
   Salutis; Populorum Progressio.
Integralism: (a) *as a historical movement*:
   27–28, 38, 193. (b) *from a doctrinal
   viewpoint*: 9, 28–29, 31, 33, 38, 44–46,
   59–60, 64, 67–69, 72–73, 78, 105–
   106, 112, 153, 159, 169, 193, 200–
   202, 209. *See*: Modernism (theological);
   Humani Generis; Humanae Salutis;
   Humanae Vitae.
Intention(ality): (a) *philosophical*: 3, 11–
   12, 32, 46, 80, 93–94, 99, 102, 107,
   144, 147, 206. (b) *religious*: 45, 73,
   92, 98–99, 101–103, 120, 136, 147,
   153, 177, 206–207, 211. *See*: Meaning;
   Hominization; Discernment; Connatural
   knowledge; Phenomenology.
Interpretation: 11, 25, 27, 32, 37, 41, 43,
   70, 75–76, 85, 87, 102, 107, 113,
   115, 121, 123–124, 126, 142, 144,
   147, 156, 170, 183, 189, 191, 209,
   211–213. *See*: Discernment; Hermeneutics.
Intersubjectivity: 23, 27, 44, 48, 71, 74,
   76, 78, 89, 100, 102, 107–108, 112–

113, 123, 126, 136, 153, 162, 175–
   176, 187, 207. *See*: Subjectivity; Alter
   ego; Communio; Phenomenology of the
   natural attitude.
Intuition: (a) *in general*: 9, 85, 92. (b)
   eidetic: 61, 76, 80, 83, 92, 95, 103,
   185. (c) *affective*: 10, 23, 26–27, 53,
   80, 91, 120, 182, 185. (d) *individual*:
   26, 45, 51, 68, 74, 78–79, 89, 108. (e)
   corporate: 29–30, 45, 50–52, 68, 74,
   76, 78–79, 81, 86, 95, 101, 108, 169,
   185. *See:* Meaning; Intentionality; Apperception; Connanural knowledge;
   Phenomenology.
Isomorphism: 52, 62, 86, 89, 101, 103–
   104, 113–116, 124, 129, 133–134,
   140, 144–145, 150–151, 153, 162,
   176, 198, 209. *See*: Teleology (telos);
   Homeostasis; Analogy (of proportionality); Complementarity, Principle of;
   Order, concept of; Ontology.

Jesus Christ: 21–23, 42, 45, 86, 155, 181,
   191, 205. *See*: Christocentrism; Word
   (Logos); Glorified Christ; New Adam.
Journal of a Soul: 10, 15, 44, 98–99, 106.
   See: Architectonic theme (of Vatican
   II); "Church, what do you say of your-
   self?"; Retreat (Vatican II as a spiritual).

Kantianism: 6, 13, 83, 101, 193, 198.
   See: Idealism; Anthropology; Hegelianism.
Kerygma: 12, 16, 34–35, 54, 93, 96, 121,
   149, 157. *See*: Evangelization; Catechesis; Communication; Integralism.

Laicism: 119. *See*: Secularism; Enlighten-
   ment.
Leader(ship), Pastoral: 21, 39, 167–168,
   170–171. *See*: Servant leader(ship);
   Service; Management theory (Pastoral);
   Logos-Shepherd; Good Samaritan.
Lebenswelt: *See* Life-world.
Leib: *See* Body-subject, incarnate (*Leib*).
Liberation theology: 34, 138, 164, 203.
   See: Goal(s) of Vatican II; Populorum
   Progressio; Poverty (worldwide); Poor,

250

logy of religion; Hegelianism; Marxism; Social Archetypes.

Natural law: 35, 55, 64, 90, 144, 211. *See*: Order, concept of; Ontology; Teleology (telos); Isomorphism.

New Adam: 35, 56, 119, 153. *See*: Creation theology; Unity of mankind; Logos-Shepherd; Transfiguration; Vision of the New Humanity.

"New theology" (Nouvelle Theologie): (a) *prior to Vatican II*: 6, 14. (b) *of Vatican II*: 29, 102. (c) *post-Vatican II*: 34, 71, 76, 134, 138, 140, 158, 163, 198, 202. *See*: Integralism; Humani Generis; Modernism (theological).

Noema(ta): 33, 52, 75, 81–82, 86, 93, 96, 101, 103, 123–124, 128, 136, 139–141, 143–145, 147–148, 150, 154, 160, 162, 206–207. *See*: Essence(s); Universal(s); A priori, empirical; Phenomenology of essences; Noesis.

Noesis: 52, 82, 93, 96, 101, 150, 206–207. *See*: Consciousness; Belief (phenomenological sense); Noema(ta).

Nuclear war: 10, 19, 30, 39, 58, 62, 131, 170, 176, 192, 203. *See*: Hiroshima; Humanae Salutis; Cuban missile crisis; Pacem in Terris.

Obediential potency: 45, 63, 74, 85, 91, 99, 106, 119, 126, 129, 141, 205–207. *See*: Creation theology; Teleology (telos); Isomorphism.

Objectivism: 4, 11–12, 33–35, 38, 53, 56, 61, 68, 72–73, 77, 83, 88, 90, 94, 101, 104, 106, 112, 114, 116, 127–128, 130, 135, 148, 155, 159, 161, 167, 169, 179–180, 182, 187, 199, 209. *See*: Mathematization of nature; Subjectivism; Via media; Two cultures, Facets of the problem of the.

Ontology: (a) *theoretical/philosophical*: 4, 12, 45, 58, 64, 90, 95, 111, 113–115, 124, 145, 176, 197. (b) *functional*: 52, 92, 104, 113, 116, 122, 124, 125, 177. (c) *religious*: 20, 28, 38, 43–46, 48, 53–57, 62, 72, 78–80, 87, 92, 94–95, 98, 102–103, 106, 113, 115, 117, 123, 126, 129, 138, 140, 143–144, 149, 153, 156, 161–162, 183, 206–207, 214. (d) *of the life-world*: 52, 95, 108, 115, 124, 133–134, 151, 158, 181. (e) *"new" ontology*: 95, 171, 198, 202. *See*: Being; Existence, Act of; Hominization; Horizon; Analogy; Teleology (telos); Mystical Body; Glorified Christ; New Adam.

Operationalism: 3, 12. *See*: Empiricism; Pragmatism; Positivism; Evidence.

Order, concept of: (a) *in scholasticism*: 33, 35, 115. (b) *in Catholic belief*: 25, 39, 55–56, 157, 206–207. *See*: Ontology; Analogy; Isomorphism; Complementarity, principle of; Creeds (religious).

Pacem in Terris: 10, 28, 33, 36–37, 39, 46, 49, 53, 55, 59–60, 62, 69, 73, 75–77, 79, 82, 88–89, 118, 121, 135, 137, 172, 191, 193. *See*: Hiroshima; Cuban missile crisis; Nuclear war; Crisis; Peace, Problem of; Peacemaker; Anthropology; Unity of mankind.

Parousia: 86.

Participation: 83, 102, 105, 128, 162, 177, 188, 203, 212. *See*: Hominization; Communio; Alter ego; Socialization; Self(hood); Motivation; Attitude; Praxis; Cross, Theology of; Liturgy, Sacred.

Paschal Mystery: 43, 50, 57–58, 116, 185. *See*: Reification; Glorified Christ; Logos-Shepherd; New Adam; Liturgy, Sacred.

Pastoral, concept of: 14–15, 20, 24, 28, 30–31, 34, 36, 38, 43–45, 50–54, 59–60, 67–69, 71, 75–82, 85–87, 93, 95, 100, 106, 111, 115–116, 125, 130–131, 135, 139, 148–150, 152–153, 156–159, 161–162, 168–169, 174, 179–181, 188, 192, 195, 197–200, 208–211, 213–215. *See*: Speculative vs. practical (order); Goal(s) of Vatican II; Efficiency in the temporal order; Communication; Strategic vision; Hominization; Participation; Unity of mankind; Renewal.